Language and Globalization

Series Editors: **Sue Wright**, Universit
Holmes, University of Limerick, Irelar

In the context of current political anc
group is not so clearly defined and de
dominant in every domain, and cro:
than a small elite, new patterns of lan
provide a framework for reporting on and analysing the linguistic outcomes or globalization and localization.

Titles include:

David Block
MULTILINGUAL IDENTITIES IN A GLOBAL CITY
London Stories

Jenny Carl and Patrick Stevenson (*editors*)
LANGUAGE, DISCOURSE AND IDENTITY IN CENTRAL EUROPE
The German Language in a Multilingual Space

Diarmait Mac Giolla Chriόst
LANGUAGE AND THE CITY

Julian Edge (*editor*)
(RE)LOCATING TESOL IN AN AGE OF EMPIRE

Aleksandra Galasińska and Michał Krzyżanowski (*editors*)
DISCOURSE AND TRANSFORMATION IN CENTRAL AND EASTERN EUROPE

Roxy Harris
NEW ETHNICITIES AND LANGUAGE USE

Clare Mar-Molinero and Patrick Stevenson (*editors*)
LANGUAGE IDEOLOGIES, POLICIES AND PRACTICES
Language and the Future of Europe

Clare Mar-Molinero and Miranda Stewart (*editors*)
GLOBALIZATION AND LANGUAGE IN THE SPANISH-SPEAKING WORLD
Macro and Micro Perspectives

Ulrike Hanna Meinhof and Dariusz Galasinski
THE LANGUAGE OF BELONGING

Leigh Oakes and Jane Warren
LANGUAGE, CITIZENSHIP AND IDENTITY IN QUEBEC

Colin Williams
LINGUISTIC MINORITIES IN DEMOCRATIC CONTEXT

Forthcoming titles:

John Edwards
LANGUAGE AND SOCIAL LIFE

Jane Jackson
THE LANGUAGE OF INTERCULTURALITY

Language and Globalization
Series Standing Order ISBN 978–1–4039–9731–9 Hardback
Series Standing Order ISBN 978–1–4039–9732–6 Paperback
(outside North America only)

You can receive future titles in this series as they are published by placing a standing order. Please contact your bookseller or, in case of difficulty, write to us at the address below with your name and address, the title of the series and the ISBN quoted above.

Customer Services Department, Macmillan Distribution Ltd, Houndmills, Basingstoke, Hampshire RG21 6XS, England

Also by Michał Krzyżanowski

(UN) DOING EUROPE: Discourses and Practices of Negotiating the EU Constitution (*with F. Oberhuber*)

QUALITATIVE DISCOURSE ANALYSIS IN THE SOCIAL SCIENCES (*with R. Wodak*)

THE POLITICS OF EXCLUSION: Debating Migration in Austria (*with R. Wodak*)

THE EUROPEAN PUBLIC SPHERE AND THE MEDIA: Europe in Crisis (*with A. Triandafyllidou and R. Wodak*)

Discourse and Transformation in Central and Eastern Europe

Edited by

Aleksandra Galasińska

and

Michał Krzyżanowski

palgrave
macmillan

Softcover reprint of the hardcover 1st edition 2009 978-0-230-52102-5

First published 2009 by
PALGRAVE MACMILLAN

Palgrave Macmillan in the UK is an imprint of Macmillan Publishers Limited, registered in England, company number 785998, of Houndmills, Basingstoke, Hampshire RG21 6XS.

Palgrave Macmillan in the US is a division of St Martin's Press LLC, 175 Fifth Avenue, New York, NY 10010.

Palgrave Macmillan is the global academic imprint of the above companies and has companies and representatives throughout the world.

Palgrave® and Macmillan® are registered trademarks in the United States, the United Kingdom, Europe and other countries.

ISBN 978-1-349-35600-3 ISBN 978-0-230-59429-6 (eBook)
DOI 10.1057/9780230594266

This book is printed on paper suitable for recycling and made from fully managed and sustained forest sources. Logging, pulping and manufacturing processes are expected to conform to the environmental regulations of the country of origin.

A catalogue record for this book is available from the British Library.

Library of Congress Cataloging-in-Publication Data

Discourse and transformation in Central and Eastern Europe / [edited by] Aleksandra Galasińska, Michał Krzyżanowski.
p. cm.—(Language and globalization)
Includes bibliographical references and index.

1. Discourse analysis – Europe Eastern. 2. Mass media – Europe, Eastern. 3. Europe, Eastern – History – 1989– I. Galasińska, Aleksandra. II. Krzyżanowski, Michał, 1977–

P302.15.E852D57 2009
401′.410943—dc22 2008034843

10 9 8 7 6 5 4 3 2 1
18 17 16 15 14 13 12 11 10 09

Transferred to Digital Printing in 2014

Contents

Illustrations

Figures

Table

Contributors

Brian P. Bennett is Associate Professor of Religious Studies at Niagara University (USA). His research focuses on religious languages and discourses in Russia. His articles have appeared in *Slavonic and East European Review, Numen: International Review for the History of Religions,* and *Method & Theory in the Study of Religion.* He is currently writing a book on Church Slavonic.

Brigitta Busch is Senior Research Fellow at the Department of Applied Linguistics, University of Vienna. Between 1999 and 2003 she was the head of the Centre for Intercultural Studies at the University of Klagenfurt. During her work as an expert for the Council of Europe's Confidence-Building Measures Programme, she was involved in a number of intercultural projects in Eastern and South-Eastern Europe. Her main research interests focus on: sociolinguistics (multilingualism), discourse analysis, media policies and intercultural communication. Her recent publications include: *Sprachen im Disput. Medien und Öffentlichkeit in multilingualen Gesellschaften.* (Drava, 2004); *Bewegte Identitäten. Medien in transkulturellen Kontexten.* (with B. Hipfl and K. Robins; Drava, 2001); *Language, Discourse and Borders in the Yugoslav Successor States* (with H. Kelly-Holmes; Multilingual Matters, 2004).

Aleksandra Galasińska is Senior Research Fellow in European Studies in the History and Governance Research Institute, University of Wolverhampton. Her main research interests focus on ethnographic and discursive aspects of lived experience of post-communism as well as post-enlargement migration. She has published on these topics in *Narrative Inquiry, Multilingua, Journal of Ethnic and Migration Studies, Ethnicities, Discourse & Society,* and *Journal of Multicultural Discourses.*

Dariusz Galasiński is Professor of Discourse and Cultural Studies at the University of Wolverhampton. His published work concerns strategic and deceptive communication and, more recently, national and gender identities. He is currently working on projects on masculinity and mental health. His recent books include: *The Language of Deception* (Sage, 2000); *Cultural Studies and Discourse Analysis* (with Chris Barker; Sage, 2001); *Men and the Language of Emotions* (Palgrave Macmillan, 2004); *Metalanguage* (with Adam Jaworski and Nikolas Coupland;

Mouton De Gruyter, 2004); *The Language of Belonging* (with U. H. Meinhof; Palgrave Macmillan, 2005), and *Men's Discourses of Depression* (Palgrave Macmillan, 2008).

Gabrielle Hogan-Brun is Senior Research Fellow at the University of Bristol. Her research fields are migration and multiculturalism, language ideologies, language attitudes, and language-in-education policy, with a particular focus on Central/Eastern Europe. Among her publications are *Language Policies and Practices in the Baltic States* (Current Issues in Language Planning, 2007), *Language and Social Processes in the Baltic Republics Surrounding EU Accession* (guest editor of *Journal of Multilingual and Multicultural Development*, 2005), and *Minority Languages in Europe: Frameworks – Status – Prospects* (Palgrave Macmillan, 2003). She is an editor of the journal *Current Issues in Language Planning*, and of the book series *Palgrave Studies in Minority Languages and Communities*. She has also directed the British Academy-funded *Baltic Language and Integration Network* (BLaIN; www.blain-online.org).

Helen Kelly-Holmes is Lecturer in Sociolinguistics with New Media at the University of Limerick, Ireland. Her research interests focus on the interrelationship between media, markets and languages, in particular the language of market-driven media texts, economic aspects of multilingualism, new media, globalisation and multilingualism, and texts and consumerisation in the transition economies of Central and Eastern Europe. Her publications include: *Advertising as Multilingual Communication* (Palgrave Macmillan, 2005); *Language, Discourse and Borders in the Yugoslav Successor States* (with Brigitta Busch; Multilingual Matters, 2004); *European Television Discourse in Transition* (Multilingual Matters, 1999); and *The European Business Environment: Germany* (with Nigel Reeves; International Thompson Business Press, 1997).

Michał Krzyżanowski is Senior Research Fellow in the Department of Linguistics and English Language at Lancaster University and Assistant Professor at the School of English, Adam Mickiewicz University, Poznań, Poland. His main research interests are in Critical Discourse Analysis (CDA) and the development of CDA's 'Discourse-Historical' approach to the synchronic and diachronic study of social, political and institutional change in Europe and the EU. His recent and forthcoming book publications are: *(Un) Doing Europe. Discourses and Practices of Negotiating the EU Constitution* (with F. Oberhuber; P.I.E.-Peter Lang, 2007); *Qualitative Discourse Analysis in the Social Sciences* (with R. Wodak; Palgrave Macmillan, 2008); *The Politics of Exclusion: Debating Migration* *in Austria* (with R. Wodak; Transaction Publishers, 2008); *Becoming European: Discourses of Identity and Social Change in Polish Politics after 1989* (John Benjamins, 2009); *The European Public Sphere and the Media: Europe in Crisis* (with A. Triandafyllidou and R. Wodak; Palgrave Macmillan, 2009).

Igor Nosál is Assistant Professor of Sociology in the Faculty of Social Studies, Masaryk University, Brno, Czech Republic. His main research interests focus on post-communist political culture and discursive aspects of contemporary childhood. He is the co-editor of the book *Mozaika vre-konstrukci: Formování sociálních identit v současné Střední Evropě* (Mosaic in Reconstruction: Formation of Social Identities in Contemporary Central Europe) (with Csaba Szaló; Mezinárodní politologický ústav Masarykovy univerzity, 2003) and the editor of the book *Obrazy dětstvív dnešní české společnosti* (Images of Childhood in Contemporary Czech Society) (Barrister & Principal, 2004).

Cristian Tileagă is Lecturer in the School of Psychology at the University of East London. He completed a PhD in social psychology in the Department of Social Sciences at Loughborough University with a thesis on racism and nationalism in Romania. His main research interests are in critical social psychology of racism and political discourse analysis. He has written on extreme prejudice, representation of ethnic minorities and inequality in such journals as *Discourse & Society, Journal of Community and Applied Social Psychology, Ethnicities,* and the *British Journal of Social Psychology.* His current research explores how official and, in most instances, controversial political imaginary and histories of the Romanian communist/post-communist past are produced and accomplished in talk and text.

Ruth Wodak is Distinguished Professor and Chair of Discourse Studies at the Department of Linguistics and English Language, Lancaster University. Until September 2004, she was a Chair of Applied Linguistics at the Department of Linguistics, University of Vienna, where she remains the Director of the Research Centre 'Discourse, Politics, Identity'. Besides various other prizes, she was awarded the Wittgenstein Price for Elite Researchers in 1996. She is a member of the editorial board of a range of linguistics journals, and co-editor of the journals *Discourse and Society, Critical Discourse Studies* and *Journal of Language and Politics.* Together with Greg Myers (Lancaster University), she also edits the book series Discourse Approaches to Politics, Society and Culture (DAPSAC, John Benjamins). She is also section editor of 'Language and Politics' for the second edition of the *Elsevier Encyclopedia* *of Language and Linguistics* (2006). Recent book publications: *Methods of Critical Discourse Analysis* (with M. Meyer; Sage, 2001 and 2009); *Discourse and Discrimination: Rhetorics of Racism and Antisemitism* (with Martin Reisigl; Routledge, 2001); *Critical Discourse Analysis. Theory and Interdisciplinarity* (with Gilbert Weiss; Palgrave Macmillan, 2003, revised edition 2007); *A New Research Agenda in Critical Discourse Analysis* (with Paul Chilton; John Benjamins, 2005, revised edition 2007).

Igor Ž. Žagar studied philosophy, sociology and linguistics in Ljubljana, Paris and Antwerp. He received his doctoral degree in Sociology of Culture from the University of Ljubljana. He is a Senior Research Fellow and the Head of the Centre for Discourse Studies at the Educational Research Institute, and Professor of Rhetoric and Argumentation at the Faculty of the Humanities, University of Primorska (where he holds the position of the Head of the Department for Slovenian Studies). He has lectured in the United States, China and the United Kingdom. His interests lie in pragmatics (speech act theory, discourse analysis), argumentation, and rhetoric. He is (co)author and editor of ten books, and about 100 articles. Recent books include *Čas in dejanje v jeziku: oblikovanje performativne teorije na Slovenskem* (Time and Act in Language, The Formation of Performative Theory in Slovenian), with Matejka Grgič (Založba, 2004) and *Argumentiranost kot model (uspešne) komunikacije*, (Argumentation as a Model of Successful Communication), with Barbara Domajnko and Igor Saksida (Izolit, 2006).

Introduction: Discourses of Social and Political Transformation in the 'New Europe'[1]

Michał Krzyżanowski and Aleksandra Galasińska

1 The 'New Europe'?

When in January 2003 European politics became divided over the (forthcoming) US-led invasion of Iraq, the US Secretary of Defence Donald Rumsfeld controversially spoke about 'old Europe' to refer to the (Western) European countries which did not want to join the US in their anti-Iraq actions. Though initially treated as just a diplomatic mistake or a slip of the tongue, Rumsfeld's label was quickly picked up by the media in several European countries: debates started on who actually belongs to the 'old Europe' (in addition to France, Germany and other Western European opponents of the US), while even more intensified efforts were made to define who, in fact, could thus belong to the counter-category of the 'new Europe'. Members of the latter were soon identified among several Central and Eastern European countries (CEECs), an astonishing majority of which supported the US invasion. And, although many Western European countries (such as, for example, the UK, Denmark, the Netherlands and Italy) supported the US in the 2003 invasion on an equal footing with their Central and Eastern European allies, it was only the latter who were defined as the 'new Europe'. That label has persisted until today, contrary to that of the 'old Europe' which disappeared from the public debates once the intra-European divisions over the Iraq crisis calmed down.

The vividness of the labels such 'new Europe' applied to the Central and Eastern European countries proves that there still exists an extremely strong tendency in public discourse to group or collate CEE countries into one, more or less uniform entity. That tendency is in accordance with the same logic which once – that is, during the Cold War – defined the CEECs as 'the Soviet bloc' or simply as 'Eastern Europe'. The tendency is also, we claim, very ideological: while 'richness in diversity' (an actual slogan widely used in the politics of the European Union) is usually fully recognised with regard to diverse Western European countries (as well as their politics, economies, societies, and the like), both the media and European politicians still tend to to treat Central and Eastern Europe as a homogeneous bloc. Thus, there exists a difficulty in establishing a public-wide recognition of the diversity of forms of social and political change taking place throughout the CEEC since the late 1980s. And perhaps the aforementioned 2003 debates on the Iraq-related positions are the best example of these tendencies: while the CEECs (that is the 'new Europe') were commonly defined in those debates as, in effect, 'US supporters', we have very rarely heard about the diverse historical, geopolitical, social and economic motivations and intra-national public debates which preceded the (however mistaken) pro-US actions in each of the CEECs. Hence, despite several key congruencies (such as, for example, an orchestrated move to free-market economies or a tendency to vividly support and possibly join the processes of European integration, see below) which have amounted to a large-scale 'transformation' of the CEECs after 1989, that geographical region does in fact consist of a set of politically, socially, economically, linguistically and religiously very diverse countries. In each of them, sometimes very radically diverse forms of context-specific intra-national changes and transformations have taken place.

2 Transformation in CEECs: the common ground

Since this volume focuses on the diversity rather than the uniformity of social and political changes in CEECs after 1989 (see below), one cannot sketch a general list of post-1989 occurrences that comprise all the focal transformations in all of the studied contexts. Therefore, while each of the contributions provides a deeper contextualisation of the events which are then approached empirically from a discourse-analytic perspective (see below), we only outline here a general background of the post-1989 transformations. By presenting pivotal aspects of the post-1989 transformations in CEECs in general – with reference to the countries studied below – we aim to provide a broad socio-historical context for the detailed nationally specific case studies presented later on.

Although it is widely assumed that 'everything happened in 1989', it must be borne in mind that social and political change in the CEECs should be viewed as a gradual and prolonged process which in many cases started already in the mid to late 1980s. In the period before 1989, we could see, *inter alia*, the development of the 'Perestroika' and 'Glasnost' politics of Mikhail Gorbachev in the Soviet Union, as well as a development of a gradual dialogue between democratic opposition and communist rulers in such countries as Poland (with the 'Round Table' in 1988), Czechoslovakia (the run up to the the 'Velvet Revolution'), Hungary and many others. The year 1989 brings, however, the final culmination, or rather a cascade, of revolutionary changes throughout the CEEC. The events of 1989 include, *inter alia*, the process leading to the introduction of the multi-party system in Hungary in early spring, the first free Polish post-war elections in June, the opening of the Hungarian-Austrian border in August, the events leading to the resignation of communist rulers in the GDR and the actual fall of the Berlin Wall in October and November, and finally the installation of the first largely non-communist government in Czechoslovakia in December and the subsequent riots and violent fall of communist rule in Romania.

While in most cases the changes of 1989 resulted in the introduction (albeit at a very diversified pace) of new, multiparty and parliamentary liberal-democratic systems and free-market capitalist economies within the countries whose geographical terrains matched exactly their pre-1989 antecedents (as was the case in, for example, Bulgaria, Poland, Hungary or Romania), it must be borne in mind that the post-1989 period also saw many shifting borders of the CEE nation states. And while the latter shifted only once towards a unification of territories divided during the communist times – as was the case with the former-GDR provinces joining the Federal Republic of Germany in October 1990 – if it took place, the shift of borders in CEECs resulted mainly in the dissolution of many state-conglomerates. The most symbolic of such 'breaking into pieces' was the largely peaceful dismantling of the former Soviet Union when many former Soviet republics (including, among others, Latvia, Lithuania and Estonia) gained their independence in 1990 and 1991. In a similar way, after two years of continuing their walk together as a conglomerate, Czech and Slovak Federal Republic between 1990 and 1992, the Czech Republic and Slovakia each chose independence in 1993.

However, the most radical process of change in statehood within CEECs definitely took place throughout the Balkans, where the dissolution of Socialist Federal Yugoslavia (in 1991) resulted in almost ten years of radical conflicts between different ethnic and national groups.

Those conflicts included wars in Slovenia (1991), Croatia (1991–5), Bosnia and Herzegovina (1992–5), Kosovo (1996–9), Serbia (2000–1) and Macedonia (2001) – many of which ended with genocide and organised actions against civilian populations as well as with the necessity of external invasions of NATO or peacekeeping missions by the UN. Wars in the former Yugoslavia resulted in deep social, political and economic crises in many of the countries of the area which, paradoxically (and unlike many other areas of CEE), enjoyed a relative prosperity in the communist period. Various mutations of those crises are – with the very notable exceptions of Slovenia and Croatia – largely present in many Balkan states until today. As demonstrated recently by the separatist tendencies in Montenegro and Kosovo (which declared their independence from Serbia in 2006 and 2008 respectively), the instabilities in statehood are also still present in some areas of the Balkan region.

Military alliance with NATO and the economic and political integration with the European Union definitely remained one of the key nodal points of the post-1989 transformation in the CEECs. In the first case, many former Soviet satellites saw NATO as a long-term (and also symbolic) guarantee of peace and stability throughout the region and in the broader, global perspective. For this reason, many of the CEE countries once grouped in the Soviet-dominated Warsaw Pact (dissolved in 1991) clearly opted for NATO membership. The latter was granted to Hungary, Czech Republic and Poland in 1999, while many other CEECs (including Bulgaria, Latvia, Lithuania, Romania, Slovakia and Slovenia) joined the North Atlantic pact in early 2004. In a similar vein, prompt accession to the structures of the European Union was almost unanimously perceived throughout CEECs as a guarantee of long-term economic stability and prosperity similar to that enjoyed by many Western European EU members. For this reason, many CEECs put in their EU-membership bids as early as 1994, followed by almost a decade of strenuous reforms and membership negotiations. In May 2004, eight former CEE states (the Czech Republic, Estonia, Hungary, Latvia, Lithuania, Poland, Slovakia and Slovenia) joined the European Union, followed soon after by other former-communist countries (Bulgaria and Romania, in 2007). Another CEE state, Croatia, currently remains an EU-candidate country.

Finally, it must be borne in mind that, although very successful in its symbolic meaning, revolutionary character, and overall set of state-system, political and economic benefits, the grand transformation in the CEECs has also had many, unintended, side-effects of a different nature. On the one hand, many CEE economies have felt very clearly throughout 1990s and 2000s that their new systems – based on the principles of the free-market and capitalism – are almost fully dependent on broader regional and global economic trends and tendencies. The negative impact of these on the CEECs became obvious on several occasions in late 1990s (in the aftermath of the Asian and Russian financial crises) as well as in the 2000s (in the aftermath of 9/11). On the other hand, or perhaps even more importantly, the very social level has also seen a very clear impact of the grand transformation in the CEECs after 1989. Phenomena such as large-scale unemployment, the creation of new wealth-based social distinctions and divisions, or the arrival of inter-ethnic and intra-societal group conflicts must surely be taken into consideration in this context.

3 The foci of this volume

Keeping in mind the common features of the post-1989 transformation in the CEECs, the present volume provides a set of nationally specific case studies which emphasise the diversity of social, political and economic transformations. In particular, the main aim of this volume is to propose a discourse-based perspective which will explore the discursive and constructive nature of the broad range of social changes in the post-communist countries of Central and Eastern Europe. Thus, through a set of national case studies, we explore the role of discourse in the construction of social and political transformations in Europe before and after the turn of the new millennium.

Our study focuses on the set of changes taking place in a variety of social and political milieus of the CEE countries after 1989. Through our study, we address a number of those changes in a novel way which significantly broadens the paradigm of studying the CEE-specific 'transition' and links the latter with the subsequent exploration of various transformations taking place elsewhere, that is, in different parts of Europe as well as on a global scale. Thus, we want to look at how various forms of social and political transformations intersect and are accommodated in a set of CEE nation-states such as, for example, the Czech Republic, the former East Germany, Poland, Romania, Russia, Slovenia and other Balkan states highlighted in our study. As we approach the transformations taking place in the CEE countries after 1989, we take a diachronic look at various forms of transition which, developed in those countries to date, are reappearing in different social and political contexts. Also, we elaborate how various post-1989 social and political transformations are clearly 'displaced': that is, how they influence the experiences of post-communism within the countries in question as well as in different locations where different social actors need to accommodate (for example, in the case of migration) their experiences of the pre- and post-1989 social and political changes.

Throughout the volume, we concentrate upon a variety of CEE-specific transformations from the point of their foundations, that is, the ever accelerating dynamics of linguistic and discursive practices (see below). Accordingly, contributions to our volume focus on a striking array of discursive practices which are underlying constructions of social and political change – in both 'public' and 'private' spheres as well as in the intermediary semi-public/semi-private sphere. Such a sphere-related view of discourse allows us to focus on various social and political groups who, allowing for their diversified access to power, are either crucial for production and dissemination of various social and political meanings or are, through their lower positioning in social and political organisation, only expected to accommodate and take for granted various views which were produced by those with direct access to power and control ('micro-macro mediation', see below). Thus, on the one hand, we want to focus on a variety of discursively constructed social changes which are rooted in discourses of those who are 'holding power over discourse' (Foucault, 1970 [1984]; Fairclough, 1992) and have direct access to power (for example politicians, key economic establishments, public bodies or the media). On the other hand, we also want to shed light on those groups which have to cope with the everyday implementation of various 'powerful' discourses and who either need to contradict or subsume the visions of social and political organisation constructed in the 'public sphere' (see also Galasińska, 2006; Galasińska and Galasiński, 2007; Galasińska and Kozłowska, forthcoming). Allowing for the cross-national perspective of our study, we want to see whether such processes of 'dissemination' and 'accommodation' of discourses are uniform throughout post-communist societies of CEE countries and whether they differ in a context-dependent (and country-specific) way.

Another feature which is addressed and strongly emphasised in this volume is that of the historical and cyclical nature of discourse. We believe that 'discourses are always connected to other discourses which were produced earlier, as well as to those which are produced synchronically or subsequently' (Wodak, 1996, p. 19; see also Wodak and Krzyżanowski, 2008). As will be shown in a range of contributions to our volume, the principle of 'recontextualisation' (Wodak, 2001; Reisigl and Wodak, 2001) is one of the key features which underlie discursive practices carrying social and political change in the CEECs. Accordingly, several of discourses currently dominant in CEECs are frequently reappropriating various elements of other discourses produced synchronically and diachronically in those countries as well as elsewhere, for example in Western Europe, within EU institutions, and so on. Similarly, we also believe that 'discourse is not produced and cannot be understood without taking the context into consideration' (Wodak, 1996, p. 19). Such a multilevel approach to context allows us, as is portrayed through several contributions to our volume, to examine discourse in a diversified way which allows for linking individual linguistic and discursive practices with the broad context of social and political changes which underlie their (social) production and reception (see also Wodak and Krzyżanowski, 2008).

So far, transformation in the CEE countries has been approached by social-scientific research from a multitude of disciplinary and multi-/interdisciplinary, theoretical and analytical perspectives (and, obviously, one short paragraph is unable to even list the majority of those studies). In works from within social and political theory, the post-communist transition has been studied from the point of view of the state, civil society, organisational patterns, political behaviour, hegemony, globalisation and modernity (see, for example, Holmes, 1997; Sakwa, 1999; McBride, 1999; Kostecki, Żukrowska and Góralczyk, 2000; Bönker, Müller and Pickel, 2002; Clark, 2002; or Outhwaite and Ray, 2005). Importantly, those as well as other general theoretical works (such as, for example, those from within the field of cultural studies, see Kennedy, 1994, 2002; Webber and Liikanene, 2001) were published alongside many strongly analytical studies. Within the latter, a considerable number of studies exploring particular localities and practices was undertaken by ethnographers and social anthropologists (see, for example, Verdery, 1996; Burawoy and Verdery, 1999; Berdahl, Bunzl and Lampland, 2000; Buchowski, 2001; Hann, 2002; Svašek, 2006). Not surprisingly, many of the analytical approaches to the post-1989 transformation in the CEE were focused on the economic aspects of 'market transition' (see, *inter alia*, Wedel, 1998; Mandel and Humphrey, 2002), while one of the most frequently explored newer topics was that of gender relations, which had been previously under-studied in the pre-1989 CEE contexts (see, for example, Funk and Mueller, 1993; Saleci, 1994; Bucley, 1997; Ashwin, 2000; Gal and Kligman, 2000a, 2000b; Krzyżanowska, 2006).

While we endorse the views presented by many of those seminal studies, our inherently constructivist approach to discourse and social change wants to challenge, in a somewhat broader social-theoretical perspective (see Tiryakian, 1995), reductionist and highly normative approaches to post-communist transformation and modernisation in the CEE countries (see, for example, Merkel, 1994; Zapf, 1995). Hence, while still accommodating the concept of transition in the some chapters, we want to depart from the grand-theoretical paradigm of CEE-specific 'transitology' (focusing on transition in the CEE as essentially unique and unprecedented; see Blokker, 2005) and, by developing a 'case-specific and historical-contextual approach' (ibid. p. 503) we will aim at showing how the post-communist transformation and modernisation can be approached from a broader, global perspective.

We also aim to test whether 'diverse processes embracing political, social, economic, technological and cultural change' (Clark, 1997, p. 1), which taken together may be defined as globalisation, do take place in CEE countries and are actually 'there'. By looking at various ways in which a number of general trends such as, for example, how increased human mobility and migration are perceived in the CEE societies, we will be able to point out how those 'global' issues are (discursively) accommodated in the 'local' spaces of post-communist nation states. Thus, we also want to bridge several strands of linguistic and discourse-analytic research on the issues surrounding what is generally defined as 'post-communist transition' in Central and Eastern Europe (CEEC) with approaches to social and political changes taking place in Western Europe. As we see it, the two 'areas' can no longer be treated separately, as has been shown by, for example, several studies on discourses of/about the European Union (see Krzyżanowski and Oberhuber, 2007; Muntigl, Weiss and Wodak, 2000) whose social and political influence and regulatory depth is, by now, spanning through both Western Europe and the CEECs. Hence, the contributions to our volume will also focus on various linguistic and discourse-analytic approaches which aim at breaking the traditional 'East-West' divide, and which want to emphasise that social and political transformations in Western Europe are accompanied by, and inherently linked to, subsequent changes in social and political organisation in the CEECs. By the same token, although focusing solely on social and political changes in the context of very closely defined transformations (that is the nationally specific post-communist transition in the CEECs), several contributions to our volume are not treating those transformations as isolated from other changes taking place in different 'national' and 'supranational' settings elsewhere in Europe and the world.

4 Discourse and transformation in CEECs – outline of the volume

Allowing for the strongly interdisciplinary character of this work, we are aware that this volume cannot effectively produce a single and unified definition of discourse and transformation (as well as of their deeper theoretical and empirical interconnections). However, while keeping in mind the central aim of this volume – that is, the in-depth exploration of the links between discourse and transformation in the context of the post-1989 Central and Eastern European social and political change – we use the following section to highlight how respective chapters approach and link discourse and transformation, in both empirical and theoretical terms. Highlighting the common ground of the contributions, we also point in our outline to the recurrent and common features in the ways in which different contributors approach and explore discourse and transformation and their mutual interdependencies.

The volume opens with a chapter by Michał Krzyżanowski and Ruth Wodak who, by highlighting a critical-analytic approach to discourse and transformation, propose a general theoretical framework of reference (in the form of a *Thesenpapier*) for the contributions presented later on. Hence, in line with the interdisciplinary ambitions of this volume, the first chapter presents Critical Discourse Analysis (CDA) as an interdisciplinary research tradition at the intersection of diverse theoretical and methodological approaches to discourse and transformation, as well as clarifying some of the key standard theoretical notions (social change, modernisation, and so on) which are both indispensable and inescapable in any volume on social and political change. At the general level, Chapter 1 emphasises the necessity of a *context-sensitive* and *interdisciplinary approach* to the multilayered and multidimensional character of modernisation and transformation specific to Central and Eastern Europe. By showing how discourse and transformation can be effectively linked in and through discourse studies, the chapter first theorises key notions in the theoretical exploration and interpretation of social change and then outlines how critically inspired discourse studies contribute to the empirically based examination of diverse forms of 'real-world' social, political and economic changes in CEE. To this end, Krzyżanowski and Wodak also highlight the importance of key analytical concepts of (critical) discourse studies such as context, interdiscursivity and intertextuality.

According to their diverse foci and empirical foundations, contributions in the remainder of the volume are grouped in three parts, dealing with:

- *Transformation(s) of the public sphere in discourses of the media and public policy (Part I: Chapters 2–4);*
- *Transformation(s) of the public sphere in discourses of politics, institutions and economy (Part II: Chapters 5–8);*
- *Transformation(s) of the semi-public/semi-private and private spheres in discourses and narrative experiences of transformation (Part III: Chapters 9–11).*

Part I opens with Chapter 2 on the media and their representation of public policy, in which Brigitta Busch views the media as one of the key vehicles in the transformation of public attitudes towards the role of different languages in the public sphere. Busch links discourse and transformation by showing how the media carry different language ideologies and language-ideological debates and how discourses (re)produced by the media in their practices contribute to the increased dynamics of change in public views and attitudes towards different languages. Busch focuses empirically on the role of the Balkan media when ethnocentric and nationalistic tendencies receded. Drawing on examples from the Balkan area, the chapter raises the question of how the media position themselves with regard to social inclusion/exclusion in the current post-conflict situation. Integrating discourse analytical and sociolinguistic approaches, Busch examines how in the globalised media order of public service, private, commercial and alternative media develop their particular language policies, practices and ideologies. The data used in the chapter suggest that the idea of serving and participating in creating a public sphere defined by national or language boundaries has been losing its impact in CEE contexts where communication flows have become more multidirectional and increasingly pluralistic.

Chapter 3, by Gabrielle Hogan-Brun, focuses on how the education policy of Latvia was mediated by the country's multilingual press. The chapter reinterprets the interplay of forces in educational policy-making surrounding the Latvian 2004 education reform, which aroused discontent amongst its large 'Russophone' minority population whose attendance at (Russian) minority language schools is in any case much higher in Latvia compared to that in Lithuania or Estonia. The author critically examines how the processes of implementing the education reform were framed in different ways by the country's Latvian- and Russian-speaking press at the macro level by moving from a predominantly ethnocentric to a more issue-oriented stance to education as well as an increased focus on (e)quality and the nature of educational provision in Latvia. In her chapter, Hogan-Brun shows that the social changes are rooted in the changing and dynamic discourses of, on the one hand, those who are 'holding power over discourse' (in this case: politicians and the media) and, on the other hand, of those (Russian-speaking) groups who have to deal with the everyday implementation of new visions of the Latvian state, the education system and the public sphere. She thus points to how the connection between discourse and transformation (understood as a unified socio-political change, see also Krzyżanowski, forthcoming) operates within the *micro-macro mediation* at different levels of social and political organisation. All of those levels (in this case – the discourse of the powerful elites and of the broadly defined masses) must be taken into consideration if we are to see how discourse helps legitimise the sometimes forceful transformation undertaken for purely political rather than genuinely social reasons (see also Chapter 1).

In Chapter 4, Igor Žagar looks at how the media reported a refugee crisis that culminated in Slovenia in the first months of 2001. As is argued by the author, the reporting was not focused on the 'problem' of Bosnian refugees who chose Slovenia as their final destination in a similar crisis eight years earlier. Instead, refugees from the former Soviet Union, Asia, the Middle East and Africa were targeted in 2001: it was increasingly asserted that migrants were willing to seek refuge and asylum in the West, and therefore were only using Slovenia as a transit state. Žagar's methodological approach is a pragmatic text analysis which pays special attention to implicit aspects of meaning construction, in interaction or in contrast with explicitly voiced perspectives and with rhetorical goals and constraints. The author shows how the refugees' identity was (re)constructed in Slovenian media discourse and how the latter may be treated as a display of the new anti-immigrant/xenophobic arguments peculiar to the post-communist (and post-Yugoslav) Slovenian context. In Žagar's chapter, transformation does not denote as much the *processes of change* as *their immediate or intermediate results* (or, in fact, side-effects). Hence, the author shows that transformation actually leads to new social phenomena (increased mobility, migration) which necessitate further change in inter-group relations in society. The social and political inability to tackle such causal chains of change leads, as is argued in Chapter 4, to the negative results of transformation such as racism, discrimination and xenophobia. It is within these negative changes that discourse becomes the most salient: by supporting the reproduction of prejudices against different groups it becomes a tool in impairing intergroup relations. Discourse hence takes active parts in the aforementioned small-scale 'chained' changes which are tantamount to the larger process of transformation and change.

Opening the second part of the volume, Chapter 5, by Michał Krzyżanowski, presents a diachronic analysis of Polish post-1989 political discourse about Europe and the EU. The contribution links discourse and transformation via both a theoretical and empirical exploration of the pivotal notion of 'discursive change' (Fairclough, 1992). The latter highlights the 'mediation between discourse and society' (see also Wodak, 2006) and points to the dynamics of discourses which, by reproducing society and culture, also contribute to the process of ongoing social and political change. The chapter focuses empirically on a macro-discursive change defined as the 'Europeanisation of national discourses', which, as is argued in the chapter, has been on of the main forces driving the dynamics of post-communist political discourses in both Poland and other CEE countries. Contrary to many political-scientific (normative) approaches, Europeanisation is viewed in the chapter as a form of discursive change which has been taking place in diverse national settings of the CEE countries in the process of adjustment of their national-political cultures and practices to those known from the (overwhelmingly Western-specific) supranational arena of EU politics. By examining the socio-political ontology and development of the discourse about Europe/EU resulting from the Europeanisation of Polish political discourse, the contribution also highlights a link between socio-political change, discursive change and the dynamics of discursively constructed *collective European/national identities and identifications*.

The following chapter, by Igor Nosál, examines how discourses of childhood, as both a social and political issue, are framed in the Czech Republic by state institutions, political actors, as well as in the alternative discourses of the country's non-governmental sector. The focus on the linguistic aspects of the conflicting dominant and alternative discourses allows seeing the variability of the ways in which childhood as a social category is constructed. The chapter's perspective on post-communist transformation focuses on the power relations in everyday life experience. Thus, by providing yet another account of a CEE-specific *micro-macro-mediation* (see also the chapter by Hogan-Brun), Nosál views the post-communist transformation as not only a process of rebuilding of formal designs of economical and political systems, but primarily as a decentralising and pluralising force in the power relations in everyday life. The chapter links discourse and transformation inasmuch as it also explicates how the studied discursive practices of power-maintenance are negotiated in post-socialist contexts: those practices are, it is claimed, applied not only to govern the children, which are treated as the object of state policy, but also to govern their parents, families and everyday life. Here, the author argues that the governing discourse about children is grounded in the specific cultural field (which is constructed as the 'Czech' cultural identity) located at the intersection of both past (that is communist-era) and present discursive practices.

In Chapter 7, Brian Bennett analyses an ardent debate over the question of liturgical language which convulsed the Russian Orthodox Church in the 1990s. Arguing that the traditional hieratic language of Church Slavonic had become unintelligible to most believers (especially to the many new converts), some reformist clerics pushed to replace or augment it with vernacular Russian. Church Slavonic became a symbolic battleground over which the reformist and traditionalist camps within the Russian Church battled, each side wielding biblical, pastoral and theological arguments. Yet this was not just an in-house debate carried on in obscure ecclesiastical venues; it connected with wider socio-political contestations in post-communist Russia. More specifically, the traditionalist defence of Church Slavonic merged with a broader discourse of cultural preservation. This discourse was articulated by leading cultural figures in the national press, especially in the form of the 'open letter,' a time-honoured convention in Russia. The author carefully examines how this in-house debate over liturgical language spiralled out to assume wider national significance. Bennett's examination of discourses and debates about religion contributes to a better overall understanding of social change and transformation in the CEE in general and Russia in particular. Bennett focuses on the rise of new religious practices as a *result of socio-political change* (just like Žagar, see above). The author thus points to how discourses about religion (that is a space at the cross-section of the 'public' and the 'private') are being effectively absorbed into public debates and appropriated by different public and political actors. Like Busch (see above), Bennett also tackles the role of different discourses in language ideological debates shaping the public spheres in CEE contexts.

In Chapter 8, Helen Kelly-Holmes employs a specifically narrative approach to look at the company histories of 14 'survivor' brands and companies of the former German Democratic Republic (GDR). In the early days following the fall of the Berlin Wall, there was a widespread rejection of the products and brands of the GDR and a rush to purchase and experience their long-forbidden counterparts from the West. Eventually, however, East German brands began to find a voice again. The analysis seeks to answer the questions: How do these texts describe the 'pre-transition' events in the company/brand's history? How are these events ordered? Which are now highlighted, and which are downplayed or even eliminated? What language is used to describe these events? Is the now outmoded lexis of actually existing socialism present or has there been rewording in favour of a more 'market-friendly' Western-like language? How is the transition process narrated? Finally, given that the company history is history as marketing, what identities – GDR-nostalgia; pan-post-communist; regional East German; all German – are constructed textually for these brands and companies in relation to the commercialised post-communist context? Answering these and other questions, Kelly-Holmes analyses company histories in order to see how they function as sub-narratives within the assumed German grand narrative of *transition* (a term the author uses instead of *transformation* – to reflect on its gradual nature; see also the chapter by Krzyżanowski and Wodak) and to explore how they make sense of the process of transition, by framing it within a narrative framework. Hence, just like other contributors (for example Nosál or Hogan-Brun, see above) Kelly-Holmes analyses a peculiar discursive *micro-macro mediation* which is deeply inscribed in the process of transformation. In a broader perspective, the author also tackles the *discursive change* (see the chapter by Krzyżanowski) which, in her case, is studied from a set of field-specific discourses of the economy in the German context.

The last part of the volume – on transformation(s) of the semi-public/semi-private and private spheres as displayed in discourses and narrative experiences of transformation – starts with a study by Cristian Tileagă (Chapter 9) concerning the issue of reconciliation with the communist past in Romania. The author deals with the social production and politics of public disclosure in relation to accounting for 'collaboration' with the Securitate, the notorious Romanian secret service of the communist era. Tileagă's contribution focuses on the confession of a public intellectual (in a letter sent to one of Romania's national newspapers) of being an 'informer'. A discursive-psychological approach is used to consider how 'reconciliation with the past' is accomplished in such a 'text' where issues such as disclosure, subjectivity, remembering, accountability and biography become relevant. The author's aim is thus to locate issues such as public disclosure and reconciliation with the past in the transformations of social, political and moral frameworks brought about by post-communist changes. In his socio-psychological perspective, Tileagă positions discourse as the main tool in the narrative construction of (publically disclosed) private biographies (subjectivities/identities) which are put to unprecedented test in the period of post-communist transformation, understood by Tileagă (just like Kelly-Homes, see above) as a phased process of *transition* from communism to democracy. Studying that transition allows Tileagă to investigate yet another form of *micro-macro mediation,* which, unlike in other chapters, is studied exactly at the point of intersection of the public and the private.

Semi-private discourses of economic migration are then analysed in Chapter 10 by Aleksandra Galasińska, who focuses on an internet forum discussion triggered by newspaper reports and articles on recent Polish migration to the UK (in the aftermath of the 2004 EU Enlargement). The chapter discusses the dynamics of Polish discourses on migration by pointing to the evident discursive struggle between, on the one hand, the new accounts on migration in the early 21st century (post-2004 migrants) and, on the other hand, the 'old' historical grand narrative of Polish migration. Anchoring her study in narrative and discourse analysis, Galasińska investigates what constitutes the post-EU-enlargement narrative of migration, how this narrative is created, and how it is used as a form of negotiation with, as well as resistance towards, the national, historically bounded, decontextualised (as well as, to a large extent, mythical) grand narrative of migration. In so doing, the author links discourses of migration with new translocal discourses of Polish social and economic transformation in the context of the EU expansion after 2004. Thus, like several other authors in this volume (see above), Galasińska analyses a peculiar *micro-macro mediation* which underlies the necessity of approaching transformation from a discourse perspective. The latter is also emphasised by showing how the historical (macro) narratives of different national and other groups are *recontextualised* and re-negotiated in the period of transformation characterised by the new forms of migration and mobility (all narratively co-constructed in the micro discourses in question).

Finally, in Chapter 11, Dariusz Galasiński aims to answer the question of the complex relationship between Polish system transformations and the individual/personal identities of those who experienced (or 'lived through') those transformations. The author is interested in uncovering the ways in which the self is positioned with regard to the transformations by trying to establish where his interview informants (from Polish border communities) locate themselves within the processes of transformation and change and how, in a very personal manner, they respond to those changes. Galasiński's central argument is that, although long-rejected as a political system, communism still persists as a dominant intellectual ideology evidenced in these personal accounts. Thus, it is argued that, despite being eradicated in the public domain, communism still provides the ideological framework within which the private/semi-private discourses of new realities are constructed. Galasiński refers to *discursive change* and *identities* as the central notions that allow for the linkage between discourse and transformation. However, unlike Krzyżanowski (see above), Galasiński focuses on the application of those concepts in the discourses of the private and not the public sphere. Looking at the former rather than the latter, Chapter 11 studies discursive configurations of identities in the 'private' discourses of people who bear the brunt of the transformations. In thus providing yet another take on the *micro-macro-mediation*, the author attempts to answer the questions of the relationship between the processes of transformation in Poland and the identities of those who lived through them.

Note

1. We are grateful to Brian Bennett for his extensive comments on the draft of this introduction.

1

Theorising and Analysing Social Change in Central and Eastern Europe: The Contribution of Critical Discourse Analysis

Michał Krzyżanowski and Ruth Wodak

1 The 'uneasy' social change in Central and Eastern Europe

Although commonly used and theorised,[1] the notion of 'social change' is definitely one of the most problematic concepts in the social sciences. On the one hand, 'social change' has been embedded and discussed in the field of social theory ranging from seminal classics, such as in Marxist conflict theory or in the phenomenology of Alfred Schütz (1962, 1967), up to functionalist and systemic approaches,[2] and insights from social constructivism (Berger and Luckmann, 1966) and the 'structure and agency debate'.[3] However, these approaches have rarely, if at all, applied in practice.

On the other hand, countless empirical studies on new social phenomena (mostly of nation states, but also reaching beyond those boundaries) neglect the distinct macro-scale definitions of social change; instead, such studies tend to describe mezzo/micro causes and effects of social change. Indeed, it has rarely been illustrated how empirical studies of mezzo/micro social dynamics might contribute to rethinking some of the key (macro) theoretical concepts.

An even more differentiated picture emerges with regard to the vast post-1989 socio-political changes in the Central and Eastern European Countries (CEECs). Although several studies linking social change theory and practice in diverse contexts have been proposed,[4] most research on social change in the CEECs has pointed to the fact that neither the usual grand-theoretical approaches, nor the traditional empirical methodologies, could be simply 're-used' to understand and explain the CEE-specific changes. The largest problem, for example, relates to different 'scales' (Jessop, 2002; 2004; 2005) which are to be considered when investigating changes in the CEECs.

Hence, the grand socio-political change in CEECs must be seen from the macro-perspective of processes of globalisation. The transnational change in the post-communist countries (the symbolic 'fall of the Iron Curtain', the emergence of new political and economic orders, and new intra-societal stratifications) certainly requires some grand-theoretical approaches. Moreover, the fact that, ever since the beginning of the 1990s, the majority of the CEECs expressed their will to join the European Union (which in many cases took place in 2004 and 2007) was also a macro-scale political factor which pushed for a unified look at the regulatory processes of the EU-related political and economic adjustment throughout the region. However, there are several unique features of CEECs' transformation which must be considered as well.

Firstly, the CEECs' transformation has yielded a high degree of diversification of different regionally and nationally specific forms of change. The best examples of such mezzo and micro changes which escaped some of the macro theorisation have been, for example, in regional terms, the rise of radically nationalist tendencies in many post-Yugoslav countries in the 1990s, or, in nationally specific terms, the emergence of significantly diversified party-political and economic landscapes in practically each of the CEECs. (NB: Such differentiation of national-political landscapes had significant influence on the different pace of EU-related adjustments and accommodations.)

Secondly, unlike other, previous changes in different parts of the world, the transformation in the CEECs was a case of subsequent and non-simultaneous changes at the levels of politics, economy and society. Accordingly, those who were willing to tackle the CEE-specific social change (perceived as a combination of those three or even more overlapping areas) were forced to examine the far-reaching interdependencies that exist between fields of social, political and economic action (see Bourdieu, 1993; Girnth, 1996) all at once. If they had neglected any of those areas, the analysis would necessarily have stayed incomplete.

Finally, a crucial problem resides in the fact that social change in the CEECs entails a specific 'historical compression' (Ziółkowski, 1999), forcing the post-communist countries to impose forms of social, political and economic transformation at very fast pace, all of which have taken place elsewhere more slowly and over much longer periods of time. Thus, the post-communist countries have experienced transformations specific to different stages of modernity (including 'early modernity', 'late modernity' and 'post-modernity'; ibid., pp. 42–3) simultaneously, thus giving 'an immense role to the transgression interests and imitative values stemming from the attempts to unitarily imitate all of those three phases which, in many respects, were contradictory to one another' (p. 44).

This chapter offers an account of that change from the perspective of Critical Discourse Analysis (CDA). In this context, we first present a way of rethinking the notion of social change in the CEE-specific contexts by deconstructing such concepts as *modernisation* or *transformation*. Then, having provided an outline of how discourse and social change have been approached so far within CDA, we move to selected concepts of the Discourse-Historical Approach to show how they can be applied in the empirical operationalisation of processes of modernisation and transformation in the CEECs in both a multi-dimensional and context-specific way.

2 Unpacking social change through modernisation and transformation

While we have first pointed to several crucial problems which, so far, have been key obstacles to coherent research on social change in the CEECs, the aim of this chapter is certainly not to call for abandoning the concept of social change. Instead, we propose a 'conceptual unpacking' (Jones and Krzyżanowski, 2008) of the concept and plead for the reinstatement and rethinking of the two crucial theoretical notions of *modernisation* and *transformation*; we believe that this may help understand and explain the immense complexity of the processes and factors involved in social change in diverse CEE-contexts.

In its classic meaning, *modernisation* denoted an ideological division of social orders into various 'worlds', which implied their level of development. That division put 'Western' societies in a very privileged position allowing them to take 'modernising actions' (colonisation, *per se* or symbolically), and endorsing a superior position as 'modernisers' of the world through peaceful or sometimes militarily supported policies legitimised through salient values such as the protection of world peace, stability, economic wealth and so on. Within this process, three 'worlds' have been traditionally distinguished (Sztompka, 1993, p. 130):

1. The First World of the developed industrial societies, including Western Europe and the US, but soon to be joined by Japan and the 'newly industrialised' countries of the Far East.
2. The Second World of the authoritarian 'socialist' societies dominated by the Soviet Union, moving at huge social cost along the path of enforced industrialisation.
3. The Third World of post-colonial societies of the south and east often remaining located in the pre-industrial era.[5]

Obviously, the collapse of the Soviet Union and the dawn of democracy in Central and Eastern Europe challenges the existence of the 'second world' and puts the CEECs on the path of increased and accelerated modernisation, since most of them chose to adopt and integrate Western models and patterns of social, economic and political organisation (in various forms) into their newly shaped social systems. By the same token, the 'great change' and transformation of the CEECs additionally fostered the role of the 'west' (that is, Western Europe and the US) as *patrons* of CEE democracies and economies, whilst being a comfortable excuse for their very rushed economic, political (viz. EU) and military (viz. NATO) 'colonisation' and modernisation.

While we discard the classic divisions introduced by modernisation theories, we endorse the recent rebirth of interest in modernisation which focuses on key characteristics of modernisation as a macro theory of social development and social change. The most salient way of perceiving modernisation has been proposed by Tiryakian within his 'new modernisation analysis' (or NMA; see Tiryakian, 1995; also called 'neo-modernisation analysis'; see Tiryakian, 1996). By explicitly and implicitly integrating several narratives on modernisation in late modernity[6] Tiryakian suggests that (1995, pp. 254–6):

- modernisation is neither uniform throughout a given socio-cultural system nor is it continuous, even after a specified 'take-off' stage';
- 'an aspect of the dynamics of modernisation (...) is the cyclical nature of modernisation', 'there are periods of increased activity (...) and

there are other periods where complacency or fatigue sets in with little collective effort at upgrading and renovation';
- processes of modernisation, while historically patterned, are adaptable to a variety of settings, though at the same time they may cluster in a single country or set of countries;
- modernisation is not a single process of system transformation and/or general efficiency upgrading. In a given society, some of its sectors and some groups of actors may consciously pursue paths of modernisation all the time, some may do some of the time, and some may even reject paths of modernisation.

And, as he continues elsewhere (Tiryakian, 1996, pp. 3, 4):

- 'modernisation is always a possibility for actors (...) since actors can avail themselves in deliberate choices of the resources of the human and non-human environment';
- 'The intended upgrading and the intended course of development by actors are always subject to correction from unanticipated consequences and reactions by either other units of the societal complex and/or by external units. Modernisation as an intended process is subject to contingencies that may or may not be provided for by the actors seeking to modernise a given unit or a system of units'.

While the cyclical nature of modernisation, or its 'non-linearity' (Beck, Giddens and Lash, 1994), is a highly contested claim (although, as it seems, it proves to some extent valid in the case of post-1989 Eastern European modernisation where 'faster' and 'slower' stages of development have been visible; see below), another key premise of NMA allows for the fact that modernisation (in its character/pace) is highly context-dependent and cannot be 'measured' with respect to any ideal-typical (and, by now, outdated) models. Another claim, of non-singularity of modernisation within given societies, gives particular agency to those groups of actors who constantly and consciously pursue (or claim to do so) modernising paths; for example, political (and other) elites (see below). Or, as Tiryakian summarises it, 'there are many models of modernisation and since no society can present *the* model of modernisation, it is best for the responsible elites and younger generations in Eastern Europe to shop around for models and implementations' (1995, p. 259).

The concept of *transformation,* however, is a term very often used with reference to current social changes[7] most commonly associated with transformation into capitalist systems, also referred to as 'transition'.[8] Although not congruent with modernisation, transformation is often directly linked to the latter. Michaela Tzankoff (2001, p. 13) states, for example, that transformation has recently been approached from four main perspectives: a) system-oriented and modernisation-theoretical approaches (focusing on the interplays and interconnections between economic and social development); b) cultural approaches (focusing on interplays between religion, culture and social interactions); c) structural approaches (focusing on state-system and social classes); and d) actor-oriented approaches (focusing on actions of particular political actors).

The first and most common approach envisages transformation as 'a set of catching-up processes, the overall aim of which [...] is to reach the state of modern (western) democracies, market-economies and welfare for the widely understood social masses' (Zapf, 1995, p. 69). Additionally, the 'aims of catching-up processes' (*Aufholprozessen*) are 'in principle widely known and are particularly intended by the central actors' (ibid.). Following the modernisation-theoretical approach, 'the socio-economic developments are the most promising basics for the introduction and consolidation of democracy' (Tzankoff, 2001, p. 13), since 'the economic development entails the change of social classes and social structures and therefore it also sharpens the economic conflicts stemming from distribution of resources' (ibid.). Furthermore, the modernisation-like transformation is also supposed to 'be followed by a higher level of education and therefore the democratisation of political culture' (pp. 14–15), which, however, as is widely known from Eastern European examples, does not take place automatically.

Further, transformation is understood as a gradual process which must entail a set of 'steps' or 'stages' which should be fulfilled/followed/ reached in order for the transformation process to become effective (in terms of reaching its pre-planned goals). Therefore, transformation is most commonly envisaged in 'stages' of system development from the authoritarian regime to democracy and portrayed as quasi-teleological (applicable to whatever context). Thus, Wolfgang Merkel, for instance, by referring to the former GDR, defines transformation as based on three main steps (Merkel, 1994, p. 120): 'the end of [the] authoritarian regime, the institutionalisation of democracy, and the consolidation of democracy.' Those stages are additionally fostered/ weakened by three factors which, according to Tzankoff (2001, p. 22), 'influence the course and effect of the process [and include]: a) the aspect of pre-authoritarian experiences of democracy of a society; b) the type and duration of the authoritarian regime; and c) the approach to the consolidated [strived-for] democracy'.

Instead, Tiryakian (1995) views transformation (interestingly, as a concept adjacent to if not synonymous with modernisation) in the concrete setting of post-Soviet transformations in CEE. According to Tiryakian, this transformation starts and still takes place mostly within 'the authoritarian regime itself' (Tiryakian, 1995, p. 253) and entails gradual evolution

> from a highly centralised empire with its own socialist logic of development (or, as it turned out, non-development) to an admission of failure in the economic realm, a brief groping for economic and political modernisation (*perestroika*) and then, a cascade of political events that gave contemporary relevance to Durkheim's pregnant concept of 'collective effervescence'. (ibid.)

Even though Tiryakian assumes that the political field comes into play only in the last stage of this four-stage transformation, economic changes are assumed to have preceded and initiated the need for transformation as such.

Summing up, we argue that the effective merger and recognition of key features of modernisation and transformation constitute a theoretical platform for grasping aspects of salient social change in the CEECs. Through recognising the simultaneity of the cyclical nature of modernisation as well as the linear character of transformation (see Figure 1.1) one is able to understand the complexity of social change at both macro and mezzo/micro levels.

With regard to *modernisation*, it becomes clear that its conceptualisation encompasses the processes of change within particular (small- or large-scale) cycles which allow for the recursivity of patterns of change in different (macro and mezzo/micro) dimensions and on different levels. In the case of the CEECs, the levels (described above) range from the macro cycles of globalisation or trans-nationalisation (for example, with regard to the EU and its Europeanisation, see Chapter 5 by Krzyżanowski in this volume) via the nationally specific mezzo levels to the micro levels of various fields (politics, economy and so forth) which, in turn, are open to the empirical investigation.

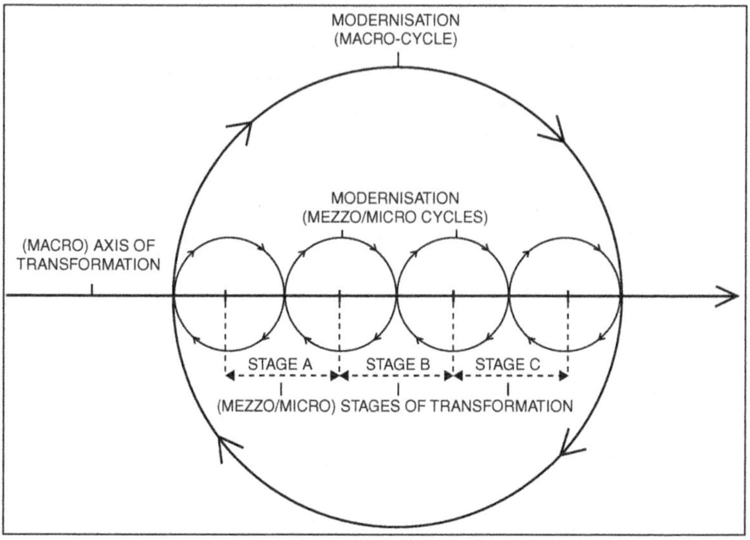

Figure 1.1 Combined and simplified outline of (macro and mezzo/micro) stages of transformation and cycles of modernisation

On the other hand, the cyclical processes of change nevertheless contribute to the longitudinal (historical) change of the macro-systems as well as of their small-scale elements. Macro processes are recontextualised (see below) and implemented on a smaller scale in non-linear processes, which, however, can only be analysed *a posteriori* and not predicted *a priori* (see below). By the same token, we are aware of the fact that many processes of change might also take place subsequently: therefore, after 1989, different mezzo/micro stages of transformation(s) took place in national and regional settings at different times. Such temporal differences may be constituted by various factors such as the impact of a combination of specific historical conditions as well as current (social, political and economic) transformation-related phenomena and resources in the various CEECs. The specific pace of economic and legal as well as political changes caused by the adjustment to EU conditions can certainly serve as an example of *how different stages of transformation differ in diverse settings in highly context-dependent ways.*

3 Critical Discourse Analysis and the study of social change

3.1 Combining cultural political economy and CDA

Processes of social change (in general and in the CEECs in particular) cannot be taken into consideration without relating them to the levels of discourse and text (see Wodak, 2008). Such a premise is not only directed by our belief that 'discourse constitutes society and culture as well as being constituted by them' (Wodak, 1996, p. 18) but is also reinforced by our theoretical assumption that processes of modernisation and transformation must inherently presuppose an in-depth 'mediation between discourse and society' (see Wodak, 2006). Thus, the macro-sociological framing of change must be related in complex ways to the micro level of individual actors; we therefore conceive of each instance of discursive practices as both constructing and reproducing the (changing) social reality in which individual/collective actors are located.

The question remains, however, of how to relate 'the (necessarily micro-sociological) discourse-analytic approach to processes of (macro-sociological) change' (Gruber and Menz, 2004, p. 176). Critical Discourse Analysis (CDA) is certainly a paradigm which has proposed several theoretical approaches on the dialectics between the mezzo/micro-social (discursive) practices and their macro-social and macro-political embeddedness.

In his seminal study on *Discourse and Social Change*, Norman Fairclough (1992) initiated CDA's research on social and political change. Though frequently revisited in recent years, also in the specific context of changes in the CEECs (see Chouliaraki and Fairclough, 1999; Fairclough, 1992; 1996; 2005a; 2005c; 2005d; 2007) and significantly modified by novel theoretical concepts (for example, from the field of cultural political economy) and elaborated with different concepts such as 'semiosis' (see Fairclough, Jessop and Sayer, 2004), Fairclough's overall conception of the relation between language/discourse and social change remains within its first key premises.

Thus, Fairclough in his most recent research perceives discourse as one element or moment of social change, and combines his approach to CDA with a form of 'cultural' political economy. Political economy differs from classical economics in asserting that economic systems and economic changes depend upon, and are closely interconnected with, political forms and systems (Polanyi, 1944). Cultural political economy asserts, in this view, that economic and political systems and changes are socially constructed and also culturally conditioned and embedded; they depend upon and are closely interconnected with particular meanings, interpretations, narratives, values, attitudes, identities and so forth (see Fairclough and Wodak, 2008). Furthermore, these processes of social construction inherently involve discourse – they have a partly discursive character.

Accordingly, in analysing social change, Fairclough considers both *structural* and *strategic* dimensions of changing social orders (Jessop, 2002). Particularly in contexts of crisis and instability, groups of social agents and agencies seem to develop diverse and competing strategies for change, and successful strategies are implemented and can lead to structural change. But from a cultural political economy perspective, strategies are partly constituted as discourses which map accounts of the past and the present and their problems and failures onto 'imaginaries' for the future. Where strategies are successful, their implementation entails dialectical relations and transformations between discourses and other moments of the social: the *operationalisation* of discourses and narratives in wider social and material changes, their *enactment* in new practices, institutions, organisational routines and so on, their *inculcation* in new identities, and their *materialisation* in changes in the physical world (Fairclough, 2001a; 2003; Fairclough, Jessop and Sayer, 2004).

In this way, a broad macro-theoretical framework is proposed which, on the one hand, explains the general logic of social change; on the other, it does not account for the cyclical, non-simultaneous and complex nature of national, regional, or indeed local transformations due to various stages of modernisation (see above).

Hence, as already emphasised by Fairclough in his early study, 'there has been a significant shift in the social functioning of language, a shift reflected in the salience of language in the major social changes which have been taking place in the last few decades' (1992, p. 6). And, he continues, 'many of these social changes do not just involve language, but are constituted to a significant extent by changes in language practices; and it is perhaps the one indication of the growing importance of language in social and cultural change that attempts to engineer the direction of change increasingly to include attempts to change language practices' (ibid.). In his study, Fairclough points to the most salient discursive changes which can be defined as key processes: among these are 'technologisation, democratisation and commodification of discourse' (ibid.) which can be observed subsequently in different national contexts in the period of late modernity (see also Fairclough, 1996; Chouliaraki and Fairclough, 1999; Gruber and Menz, 2004).

More importantly, however, and returning to his early study, Fairclough points to a set of 'minimum conditions' (Fairclough, 1992, p. 8) of a discourse-based approach which is sensitive to social change(s): first, that a discourse-analytic approach must be *'multidimensional'* (ibid.). It should hence enable 'relationships between discursive and social change to be assessed, and detailed properties of texts to be related systematically to social properties of discursive events as instances of social practice' (ibid.). Discursive change therefore appears very close to social change, and the main task of a systematic, discourse-analytic approach to social change consists in deconstructing the interplay between subsequent changes in discourse and in social practices.

Second, a discourse-based approach to social change must be a *'method for multifunctional analysis'* (ibid.) which allows looking into how 'changing discourse practices contribute to change in knowledge (including beliefs and common sense), social relations and social identities' (ibid.). Thus, Fairclough continues, 'one needs a conception of discourse and a method of analysis which attends to the interplay of these three' (ibid.). Third, in his claim for CDA as being a *'method for historical analysis'* (ibid.), Fairclough suggests that 'discourse analysis should focus upon structuring or "articulatory" processes in the construction of texts in the long-term constitution of the orders of discourse' (ibid.). Following Foucauldian conceptions of discourse, Fairclough envisages 'intertextuality' as one of the ways of interpreting/analysing historical change of discourse and its salience for changing social practices.

Finally, a discourse-based approach to social change must be *'a critical method'* (ibid.). As the author suggests 'relationships between discursive, social and cultural change are typically not transparent for the people involved'; and therefore social change is based on the slightly 'unconscious agency' of those who are affected by its outcomes. Thus, bringing in the notion of power in/over discourse, Fairclough postulates that his critical approach

> implies showing connections and causes which are hidden; it also implies intervention, for example providing resources for those who may be disadvantaged through change... [also] it is important to avoid an image of discursive change as unilinear, top-down process [as] there is a struggle over the structuring of texts and orders of discourse, and people may resist or appropriate changes coming from above, as well as merely go along with them (ibid.).

3.2 CDA and modernisation: cycles and vertical orders

While fully endorsing the validity of the four 'minimal conditions' for an approach to discourse and social change as proposed by Fairclough, we claim that several *theoretical and analytical concepts* proposed by the Discourse-Historical Approach (for details, see Krzyżanowski and Oberhuber, 2007; Wodak, 1996, 2001; Reisigl and Wodak, 2001) enrich and elaborate the theoretical and empirical scope by accounting for social and discursive change from context-dependent perspectives of *modernisation* and *transformation* (see below for the latter). While, due to limitations of space, we cannot present here all of the key premises of the Discourse-Historical Approach, we will focus instead on selected claims which help to operationalise and analyse modernisation (in this section) and transformation (in the following one) for particular contexts in the CEECs. And, while we argue that the elements of our approach that are listed below are both equally applicable to the analysis of modernisation and transformation, we present them in relation to their vertical (bottom-up and top-down) as well as horizontal characteristics. The latter, we claim, converge with *the cyclical nature of modernisation* as well as with *the linear-staged approach to transformation*.

Hence, we argue that a fuller account of the cyclical nature of the processes of *modernisation* can be achieved by introducing *vertically ordered levels of theorisation and analysis* which relate macro theories to the levels of empirical analysis at the micro level. Macro theories (of, for example, theorising social change more generally, say in a global or transnational perspective) necessarily need to be operationalised into lower-scale mesotheories (see Figure 1.2). Within that level, it is possible to integrate, for example, theories relating to regional- and national-specific phenomena (such as, *inter alia*, discursive strategies constructing regional and national identities) and to intra-societal differentiation and stratification caused by changing macro conditions, and so on.

Furthermore, a next step links the meso-theories to the level of discourse theory according to the object of investigation (for example, specific forms and contexts of social change in the CEECs). Finally, discourse theory should, in turn, be operationalised into linguistic units by means of different linguistic categories (such as those enumerated in Figure 1.2, including perspectivation, argumentation and so on).

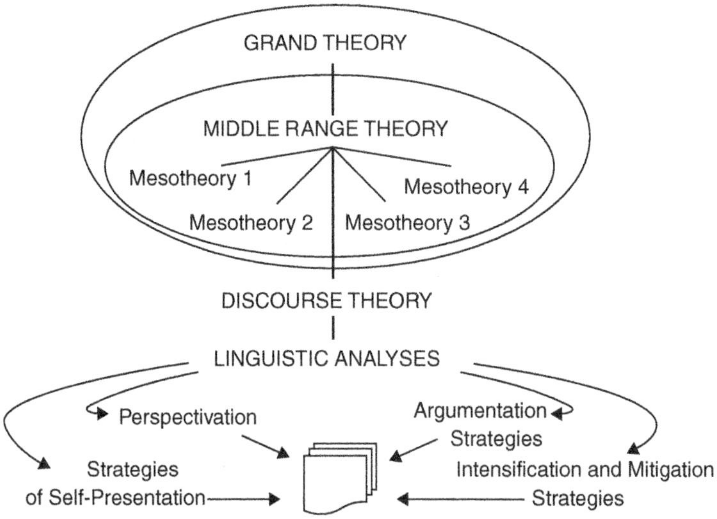

Figure 1.2 Levels of theorising and analysis (Wodak, 2001, p. 69)

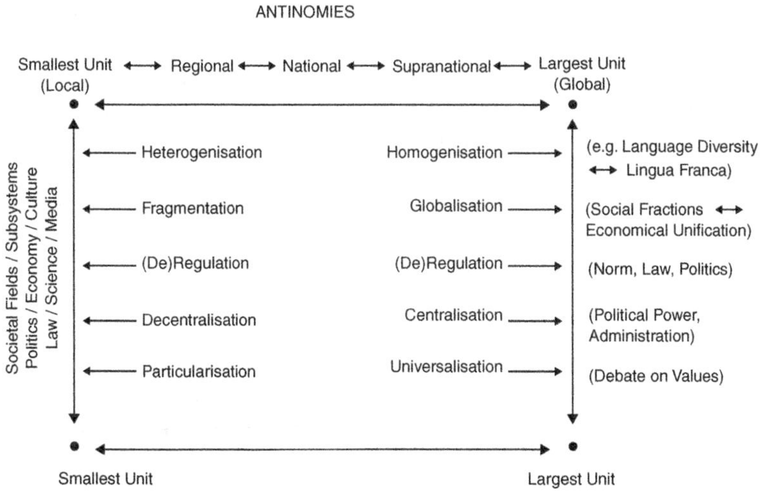

Figure 1.3 Diagram of 'antinomies' (Wodak and Weiss, 2004, p. 233)

As an example for this model, we refer to our assumption on conflicting *'antinomies'* in the discursive construction of European identities (Wodak and Weiss, 2004, see Figure 1.3)[9] which depict the tensions and struggles between global and local social policies and related implementations and change in late modernity in the European Union and Europe. These antinomies are considered to be the main tensions affecting various subsystems of society (or 'social fields') such as politics, economy, culture and law. The antinomies encompass a set of processes and strategies which, located within different levels or contexts, converge with the previous model of theorisation (see below; Wodak et al., 1999; Kovács and Wodak, 2003). Thus, the framework of antinomies can also be applied when considering different levels and stages of change (see Figure 1.3). This framework was originally designed to illustrate processes of 'glocalisation' (see Wodak, 2005; Bauman, 2000; Friedman, 1999; 2000). However, we believe that this matrix can easily be transferred onto the context of glocal interplays in the CEECs (for example, see Busch and Krzyżanowski, 2007; Krzyżanowski 2005a; forthcoming).

It must be noted, however, that while these antinomies may serve as a heuristic in the theorisation of conflicting and non-simultaneous processes of social change, they also serve to contextualise different types of discursive strategies and processes.

In this way, the notions of *context(-dependency)* and *recontextualisation* (of different policies and their discursive implementation) are constitutive for the Discourse-Historical Approach. We distinguish four distinct levels of context (see also Wodak, 2001, p. 67): 1) the broader socio-political and historical context; 2) the extra-linguistic social/sociological variables and institutional frames of a specific 'context of situation'; 3) the intertextual and interdiscursive relationship between utterances, texts, genres and discourses; and 4) the immediate, language or text internal co-text.[10]

Clearly, the first and top level is the one where the antinomies (and related macro-theories of social change) would be located. We assume that large-scale processes influence the framing of individual institutional and situational contexts (second level) constituted by the actors involved in production of discourse, which, in turn, relate to the intertextual and interdiscursive links between texts and discourses (third level). Finally, the co-text designates the features which, though located within the text itself, can be related to the higher levels of context, as has been illustrated elsewhere (fourth level; see also Wodak, 2000; 2008).

3.3 Transformation: towards linear change in/through discourse

Transformation is conceived of as a predominantly linear and staged process: a certain continuity of social change as well as its context-dependent diversification. Thus, discourse must be seen from the perspective of its historicity: it is in synchronic discourses that earlier discourses are frequently 'recontextualised' (Wodak, 2001). The distinctive contribution of the Discourse-Historical Approach thus lies in 'the analysis of historical and political topics and texts' (Wodak et al., 1999, p. 7) and their continuity. Accordingly, the systematic analysis should illustrate how on-going transformation is linked to and draws on previous (historical) stages and discourses in complex ways.

Thus, transformation can be related to the concept of *interdiscursivity*. This concept, based on the notion of *intertextuality* introduced by Bakhtin and elaborated by Fairclough (see above), can be understood as a process which links different discourses (see Figure 1.4). Interdiscursivity, hence, denotes the links between different discourses which can be decontextualised from their original temporal and spatial contexts and can reappear in different historical conditions. However, while discourses appear to be of a more abstract character than texts (or genres or other 'semiotic types', ibid.),[11] the latter are subjected to concrete analysis.

While the concept of interdiscursivity has been applied to the variety of settings in non-CEE post-communist countries (for example,

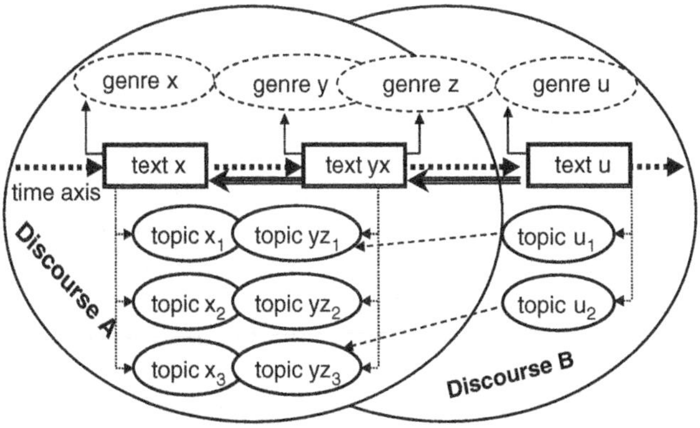

Figure 1.4 Interdiscursive and intertextual relationships between discourses, discourse topics, genres and texts (Wodak, 2001, p. 69; also Reisigl and Wodak, 2001, p. 39)

see Wodak et al., 1991; 1994; 1999), it has also been used effectively to study how, for example, 'neutrality' has changed over time in Hungary and, in comparison, in its 'neutral' neighbour-state of Austria (see Kovács and Wodak, 2003). There, it could be illustrated how discourses on neutrality change at different stages of national transformation (particularly with regard to Hungary and its change from the communist system to its post-1989 social and political set-up, but also in Austria) and how different discourses may be related and linked in a cross-national perspective. Thus, when defining the role and change of discourses at different stages of transformation in other CEE contexts, the diachronic analysis detects which elements of discourses of the communist period before 1989 are still constitutive for the public and private discourses after 1989. More importantly, analysing interdiscursivity reveals that, even within the post-1989 period, distinctive stages of regionally and nationally specific transformation can be distinguished, caused by different social, economic and political context-dependent developments (see Krzyżanowski, forthcoming).

Based on the concept proposed by Pierre Bourdieu (1993) and elaborated by Girnth (1996) and Reisigl and Wodak (2001), *fields of action* prove to be crucial when analysing the elements of transformation within particular fields of society (politics, economy, and so on). In this way, one can observe systematic and non-simultaneous, context-dependent discursive changes in all important domains of society.

'Fields of action' are defined as 'segments of the respective societal "reality", which contribute to constituting and shaping the "frame" of discourse' (Wodak, 2001, p. 66), while 'the spatio-metaphorical distinction among different fields of action can be understood as a distinction among different functions or socially institutionalized aims of discursive practices' (ibid.; see Figure 1.5). Wodak provides an example of the 'field of political action' (ibid.) which can be analytically categorised into 'legislation, self-presentation, the manufacturing of public opinion, developing party-internal consent, advertising and vote-getting, governing as well as executing, and controlling as well as expressing (oppositional) dissent', (ibid.), all of which serve specific functions.

This example illustrates at how many levels and in how many different forms discourses may be produced by means of different texts and genres. It also shows how discourse not only *spreads into* different fields

Fields of action					Field of control
Law-making political procedure	Formation of public opinion and self-presentation	Party-internal development of an informed opinion	Political advertising, marketing and propaganda	Political executive and administration	Political executive and administration
Genres					
– laws – bills – amendments – speeches and contributions of MPs – regulations – recommendations – prescriptions – guidelines	– press releases – press conferences – interviews – talk shows – lectures and contributions to conferences – articles, books – commemorative speeches – inaugural speeches	– party programmes declarations statements and speeches of principle – speeches on party conventions	– election programmes – slogans, speeches in election campaigns – announcements – posters – election brochures – direct mailings – fliers, etc.	– decisions (approval/ rejection) – inaugural speeches – coalition papers, speeches of ministers/ heads – governmental answers to p.q.	– declarations of opposition parties – parliamentary questions – speeches of MPs – petitions for a referendum – press releases of the opposition parties

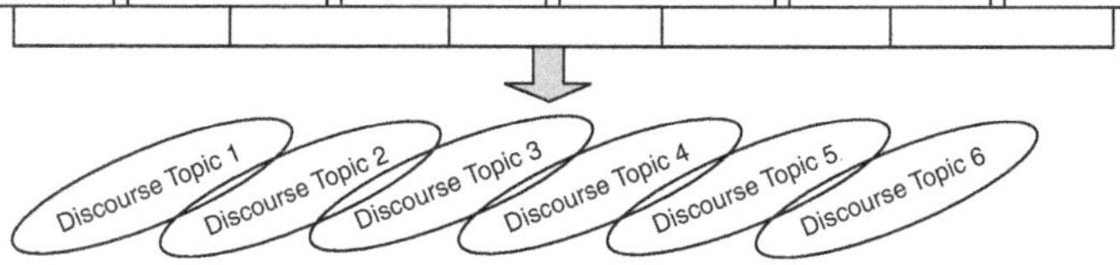

Figure 1.5 Field of politics and its fields of action (Wodak, 2001, p. 69)

of action such as politics, the economy and society, but also how diverse sub-fields of those areas may *contribute to* changing different national (as well as larger- and smaller-scale) discourses, thus contributing to different forms of transformation or, in fact, incepting new stages of the transformation.

Thus, we claim that changes in one sub-field can but need not appear in other sub-fields of one domain (such as politics); moreover, changes in one field need not be accompanied at the same time in other fields (such as, for example, media or education). To add to the complexity, transformations may take place at different times in different regional and local contexts, and different stages can occur simultaneously in various fields in various contexts inside one nation state (see Figure 1.6). We are dealing with linearity, cyclic processes, spatiality and temporality, as well as non-simultaneity and contradictions all at the same time, which explains the complexity of modernisation. Hence, any unidirectional, teleological macro-theory must necessarily stay at a high level of abstraction and presents a huge challenge to an empirically oriented context-dependent operationalisation.

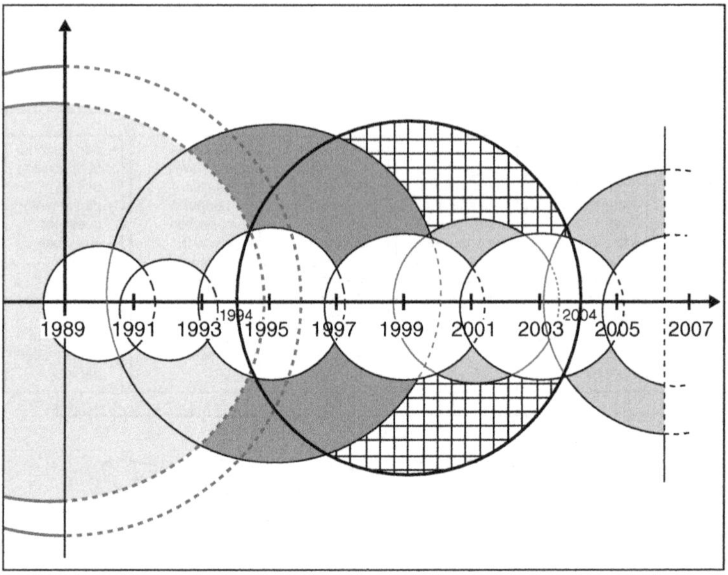

Figure 1.6 Modernisation and transformation in Poland after 1989 (simplified diagram)

4 Modernisation and transformation in Poland: an example

In presenting the complexity of the interplays between modernisation and transformation, we provide a general outline of the post-1989 change in Poland (see Figure 1.6). In this necessarily brief outline, we only consider two selected fields of society: politics (white circles) and economy (grey circles), which are treated here as inherently interconnected and mutually dependent.

The 'size' of the cycles of political change are established according to the parliamentary elections in Poland after 1989 (these took place in 1989, 1991, 1993, 1997, 2001, 2005 and 2007). Those cycles overlap to denote that political change does not take place abruptly (that is, 'on the day of elections') and that it usually takes a period of time until new forms of policies (by the new governments) are introduced and when the previous ones lose their effect or are changed. It is therefore the case that the projection of the cycles of modernisation on the actual stages of transformation (which can be sketched on the horizontal time-axis) remains ambiguous: the stages of transformation are of different length while their definite beginning/end is very difficult to establish.

The cycles of economic change (that is, change in the field of economy) are of different size than their counterparts in the field of politics. The economic cycles are marked by three periods: 1990 to 2000 (the period of considerable economic growth), 1999 to 2003/2004 (the period of economic recession or slowdown, mainly in the aftermath of the 1999 Russian crisis and fuelled by the economic disruption caused by 9/11) and the period since 2003 (economic growth caused by the Polish EU accession, still taking place).[12] Importantly, as in the field of politics, there exists a considerable overlap between different cycles to denote that the economic processes of change (growth/recession) are initiated when the 'previous' cycles are still in place.

An important point must be made about the convergence of such diverse political and economic *micro cycles of modernisation* and the *macro cycles* which influence the former. As we can see in the Polish case, the change in post-1989 fields of politics and economy is influenced by the previous macro cycles. Those cycles include the pre-1989 Polish economy and politics (white and bright-grey circles with dotted borderline) whose ultimate limits cannot be established: their influence on politics and the economy post-1989 was obviously larger in the first years after 1989; however, they can still be considered as influential and active to this day. On the other hand, another type of macro cycle which clearly influences Polish post-1989 politics and economy is related to the 1994–2004 EU-accession process (dark chequered circle). That cycle clearly converged with a variety of nationally internal political and economic actions (smaller circles) while also determining the qualitative and quantitative character of social change taking place in this period.

If one considers all cycles as different *social fields* (consisting, in turn, of diverse *fields of action*), one arrives at a very complex picture: the implemented regulatory (EU) strategies and policies affect different fields and related genres within such fields at different times in different local and regional places and have different spatial and temporal origins. The cyclical nature evolves through non-simultaneity and recursivity; strategies and policies can be repeatedly implemented, changed and reformulated as well (for example, after elections and after new governments have been installed; or because of more global factors which also impinge 'glocally', such as the 'oil crisis' or the 'war on terror').

Due to limitations of space, we can present only selected and indicative texts which point to the ways in which the aforementioned macro and other cycles of transformation in different fields overlap and/or intersect. The examples are taken from different parliamentary speeches on 'The Main Directions of Polish Foreign Policy' and in particular from passages concerning Poland's reforms in the context of the country's accession to the European Union. The speeches were delivered annually in different periods in the Polish EU-accession process (1994–2004, see Figure 1.6, above) by Polish foreign ministers to the lower chamber of the Polish parliament (the *Sejm*; for extensive description and analysis of those speeches, see Chapter 5 by Krzyżanowski in this volume, as well as Krzyżanowski, forthcoming; 2008).

In the first example (see below), the speaker clearly constructs the vision of Polish transformation as encompassing not only the country's politics and the state system ('consolidation of our democratic state') but also Poland's economy; the latter is described both in terms of 'economic progress' as such, but is also later ascribed a somewhat more abstract dimension of 'civilisational development'. Those two overlapping cycles of modernisation within the fields of both politics and economy are clearly subsumed to the macro goal (or, in fact, the macro cycle; see above) of Polish accession to the EU: the stages of transformation and the cycles of modernisation are presented here as an overarching aim for both politics and economy.

Example 1

We see in the [European] Union the most successful answer to challenges facing the Europeans. We treat the partaking in the European Union not only as a guarantee of our economic progress and civilisational development, but also of a consolidation of our democratic state. We are aware that our accession to the Union is determined not only by the success of a process of Union's reform and by the will of its member-states, but also by the level of our preparation to full membership (PS-9: 7).[13]

On the other hand, in Example 2 below, we witness a very similar discursive construction of Polish transformation as consisting of activities in the field of politics as well as of the 'internal-economic reforms'. Unlike before, 'social structures' are also hinted at separately, as is the set of changes and reforms within the 'state structures' (in the field of politics; see above). While the subsequent and overlapping changes in all those fields are, as before, overtly referred to as subsuming to and framed by the macro cycle of Polish EU accession, the speaker later *deconstructs* the field of politics into different sub-fields which must also undergo transformation (note that such emphasis on politics has clearly strategic reasons of positive self-presentation). Those sub-fields include: 'state-structure'; 'diplomacy'; 'government administration'; 'local governments'; 'trade unions'; and 'political parties'. The presence of the trade unions (traditionally located at the cross-section of economy and politics) is particularly salient: it points to the fact that – just as in our model – different cycles of modernisation do overlap, not only at the level of the entire fields (see above) but also within their diverse subfields.

Example 2

Poland's negotiation concerning EU membership will be commenced in a couple of weeks. This decision of the European Union crowns our couple-year-long diplomatic efforts; it also constitutes a positive assessment of the effectiveness of Poles' efforts in internal-economic reforms and in the modernisation of social- and state-structures (...) It is going to be a particularly difficult test for the entire of our state-structure: for diplomacy, for the government administration, for local governments, for trade unions and for political parties. Such is the dimension in which those challenges and opportunities shall be perceived (PS-13: 1).

5 Conclusions

Following Fairclough's (1992) appeal for a contribution by discourse analysis to the study of social change via 'multidimensional, historical, critical, and multifunctional analysis', we have presented above how the Discourse-Historical Approach adds to theorising and analysing social change in detail. In particular, we have illustrated how various cyclical/vertical and linear processes at the level of discourse or within its micro, mezzo and macro contextualisation are related to cycles of *modernisation* and the linearity of *transformation*. By pointing to both vertical and horizontal ordering of discursive processes and strategies, we have argued that the field of discourse studies in general, and of Critical Discourse Analysis in particular, contributes substantially to the understanding and explanation of salient phenomena involved in post-communist transformation and modernisation in Central and Eastern Europe.

Of course, this necessarily brief outline cannot illustrate all the concepts and tools of CDA which could be applied when analysing social change. Thus, by pointing to some of the most important notions which contribute to the analysis of modernisation and transformation, we most certainly have not exhausted the variety of approaches which have been proposed in (C)DA over the years and which, in turn, could be applied when linking micro and macro, discourse and their social, political and economic contexts of production and reception.[14]

In sum, this introductory chapter emphasises the necessity of a *context-sensitive and interdisciplinary approach* which recognises the multilayered and multidimensional character of the unprecedented forms of modernisation and transformation specific for the region in question.

Notes

1. For example, see Appelbaum (1970); Etzioni and Etzioni-Halevy (1973); Boudon (1986).
2. See Luhmann (1995, 1997); Parsons (1964, 1966) and Sztompka (1991, 1993).
3. See Archer (1995; 2003), Giddens (1984) and Mouzelis (1995).
4. See Grancelli (1995), Kurczewska (1999) and Sztompka (1999).
5. Edward Tiryakian argues for two reasons why the original version of modernisation 'that had an initial vogue in the 1950s until about the end of the 1960s' (1996, p. 1) eventually lost its importance. As he claims, on the one hand, the theory 'came under heavy attack from the voices of the Third World – about which part of the world the analysis had been largely preoccupied' (ibid.). On the other, the emergence of the competitive theory of World Systems (initiated by Immanuel Wallerstein and his followers) overrode modernisation by proposing a view on an 'unfolding "mega" process of world-wide capitalistic incorporation, which once achieved [...] would then make possible one further transformation: a global socialist overhauling of the capitalist engine' (ibid.). Importantly, however, many of the elements of modernisation theory have been kept within the field of Civilisational Analysis spearheaded by such scholars as Stein Rokkan, Shmuel N. Eisenstadt or Tiryakian himself (see also Arjomand, 2001; the special issue of *International Sociology* on 'Rethinking Civilisational Analysis').
6. These include Sztompka (1991), Zapf (1990) and Beck, Giddens and Lash (1994).
7. See von Beyme (1994), Merkel (1994, 1999) and Zapf (1990, 1991, 1995).
8. Due to limitations of space, theorising differences between *transition* and *transformation* is beyond the scope of this chapter. For the description of different accounts, see Stark and Bruszt (1998) or Fairclough (2005a). For different conceptions of *transition* see Aligica (2003), Cox and Mason (1999), Kovács (1994), Neuhold, Havlik and Suppan (1995) and Pickles and Smith (1998). More specifically, see Krzyżanowski (2005a, forthcoming) for a new model of 'Triple Transition', which we cannot elaborate here.

9. In Figure 1.3, the order of antinomies which we consider in a top-down (largest-to-smallest) way has actually been placed in a horizontal way for ease of presentation.
10. Based on Wodak (2001), the four levels of context are presented here in a reverse order which directly matches the top-down 'vertical' character of the levels of theorising and linguistic analysis.
11. Here we take Jay Lemke's definition of discourse as a starting point. As he claims: 'When I speak about *discourse* in general, I will usually mean the social activity of making meanings with language and other symbolic systems in some particular kind of situation or setting. [...] On each occasion when the particular meaning characteristic of these discourses is being made, a specific *text* is produced. Discourses, as social actions more or less governed by social habits, produce texts that will in some ways be alike in their meanings. [...] When we want to focus on the specifics of an event or occasion, we speak of the text; when we want to look at patterns, commonality, relationships that embrace different texts and occasions, we can speak of discourses' (Lemke, 1995, pp. 7ff).
12. We are aware that there exist significantly different views as to the macro/mezzo/micro periodisation of economic change in post-1989 Poland (see Balcerowicz, 2000; Kołodko, 2001; Kołodko and Piątkowski, 2002) and CEECs (see Artis, Banerjee and Marcellino, 2006). Therefore, the cycles of economic change in post-1989 Poland should be treated as very general (at the macro level), while we are also aware that this must remain simplistic and cannot take into consideration all macro and mezzo circles of economic growth/slowdown which took place in the period in question. We are also aware that, the economic recession *per se* took place in Poland (as well as elsewhere among CEECs) only in the wake of the 1989 change (within the so-called 'big shock' or 'big bang', see Sachs (1991, 1992, 1995) and Sachs and Lipton (1990) for Poland-related accounts), while in subsequent years we can only speak about a faster/slower, yet steady, period of economic growth (we are grateful to Wiktor Krzyżanowski for his remarks on this point).
13. For the information on applied codes and transcription conventions, see Chapter 5 by Krzyżanowski (this volume) as well as Krzyżanowski (2005a, 2008 and forthcoming).
14. See also Blommaert (2005), Flowerdew (2002), Hausendorf (2000), Hausendorf and Bora (2006) Martin and Wodak (2003), and Lassen, Strunck and Vestergaard (2006).

Part I

Transformation(s) of the Public Sphere (I) – Discourses of Media and Public Policy

2
Reflecting Social Heteroglossia and Accommodating Diverse Audiences – a Challenge to the Media

Brigitta Busch

1 Introduction

One aspect of the recent transformation processes in Central and Eastern Europe was the disintegration of larger political entities into states based on a nation principle. Nationalistic ideologies could to some extent fill the void left after the formerly powerful socialist and communist ideologies had disintegrated. The role of media in ethnic polarisations and conflicts and their participation in spreading hate speech became an important topic on an international level in the 1990s. The transformation of the media systems in the former socialist and communist countries was monitored by European and international institutions which mainly used the Western European post-Second World War media order, based on the idea of a dual media system with a strong public-service sector acting within a national public sphere as a blueprint. At the same time on a worldwide scale globalisation processes already accelerated a power shift from state institutions to supranational and to local bodies. In the media and communication sector this reconfiguration became obvious particularly rapidly. In the late 1980s, a wave of corporate mergers, strategic alliances and the convergence of media, communication and entertainment industries changed ownership structures, contributed to altering information and communication flows and to intensifying the spread of globalised cultural products in the countries of Eastern Europe. The state-centred models employed in the transformation process of the media sector were not only already outdated to some extent, but also their national orientation made them inappropriate for countering nationalistic discourse. The globalised media industries that immediately set out to conquer the new markets opened by privatisation, failed to provide an adequate space for the articulation of civil society.

This chapter focuses on the interplay between media, language and discourse in transition processes. The first section of the chapter gives an insight into the growing field of research concerned with the role of the media in the recent transformation processes. Focusing on examples from the space of former Yugoslavia, the second part examines the role of media in the propagation of a unitary state language as part of a nationalistic discourse. The two following sections are dedicated to media developments that indicate a counter move: media that seek to address the entire former Serbo-Croatian linguistic space, within the Balkan region as well as among migrants in different parts of the world, and media initiatives that engage in opening a space for the heteroglossic publics and weaving translocal connections.

2 Transformation, media and language

In political practice both the media and languages are seen as crucial factors in processes of transformation. Freedom of information and access to information is often considered as a *conditio sine qua non* for political and social change and as prime indicators for a successful transformation process. The tacit assumption that these fundamental rights are guaranteed only to speakers of official languages within a given territory has rarely been questioned, neither in the so-called countries of transition nor in the EU member states. Speakers of minority languages and of languages of migration are still often impaired in their access to media in their language with a national spread. The common state language is still seen as a factor that can foster national unity and provide identification with a state. Although in the past years the Council of Europe and the European Union have increasingly taken up a more active role in conceiving a language policy beyond the individual member state, the field of language policy – especially in domains other than education – remains mainly a prerogative of the nation state.

Media and language policy are interlinked in a multiple sense: which language(s), codes and varieties are being used in the media already predetermines questions of inclusivity and exclusivity of the public sphere and of representation. Media are also powerful actors in the implementation of language policies. Media texts, just like other texts in the public domain, provide discursive and linguistic resources which can be seen as authoritative voice (Bourdieu, 1982) and media serve as fora in which folk beliefs on language, academic expertise in linguistics and political opinions on language can be expressed and language policies can be negotiated. Media discourse is shaped by everyday language practices and in turn contributes to shaping them.

Traditional transformation research has so far paid only little attention to the role of media (Tzankoff, 2001, p. 9) and to the role of language policies and linguistic practices linked to media (Busch, 2004) in processes of social change. Nevertheless, there is now a growing corpus of research into the role of media in transformation, mainly focusing on Central and Eastern Europe. Some of this work concentrates on cultural dimensions such as, for example, the propagation of westernised mass culture in the space of Eastern Europe (Coman, 2000, p. 51). Alternatively, it focuses on the relationship between media and the state, too often still following the theoretical model developed in the US during the Cold War period. This simplifying model is based on a binary opposition between the controlled and state-dominated media in totalitarian systems and the ideal of free and democratic media in systems in which the market is the main regulating factor (Sparks, 2000, pp. 36ff; Coman, 2000, p. 51). This ideologically loaded way of conceiving media change ignores the important impact of oppositional and alternative media, often summarised under the heading 'samizdat'. It also ignores media developments of internationalisation and globalisation that began a long time before the fall of the Berlin Wall. From a Western perspective the transformation process was understood as a process of 'normalisation' and of 'Europeanisation' of the media systems in Eastern and southeastern Europe (de Smaele, 1999), a process that should ideally result in the adoption of (traditional) Western media standards in the countries of transition. Political interventions from the part of the 'international community' took the outdated Cold War models based on Wilbur Schramm's theories of media and modernisation (1964) as guiding principles in media policy and granted highest priority to media privatisation, expecting that such a process would automatically lead to a democratisation of media in the long run.

The Western European model, which served as an export model, foresees the duality between a public-service media sector with its orientations and obligations regarding the national public sphere and a private media sector which, according to modernisation media theories, should guarantee that a multiplicity of opinions and interests are represented in this public sphere. This model was often imposed on the so-called countries in transition without taking already-existing media structures and reception habits into account and without regard to the critique that had already emerged around the concept of the national public sphere. Habermas's analysis of the national public sphere as a mediating instance between the state and society, originally published in the 1960s, received larger attention again after its publication in English in the late 1980s. Feminist studies made the criticism that the public sphere was assumed as a male domain (Young, 1987) and post-colonial studies formulated a similar concern regarding the whiteness of the public sphere (Morley, 2000, pp. 120ff). Habermas (1990/1962) himself revised his model with regard to Foucault's work and acknowledges that he underestimated the existence of counter discourses and publics that were already present in the traditional bourgeois public sphere and that the exclusion of the 'other' was a constitutive feature of the national public sphere. Not only gender, ethnic origin, age and political orientation, but also language, can become such a factor of exclusion or fragmentation of the public sphere or rather an ensemble of public spheres that interact (Busch, 2004). Under the conditions of globalisation or, more accurately, of glocalisation in the media and in cultural production, the question of the public sphere also needs other approaches as media flows have become more diverse and multidirectional and reception habits have been changing considerably with the greater availability of new communication technologies.

In the transformation process in the 1990s the taboo of the inviolability of state borders that had dominated the post-Second World War political order in Europe was abandoned, larger multilingual entities disintegrated into states, which considered themselves as nation states. This disintegration caused new majority-minority relationships and a new definition of status for languages spoken and written in the successor states of entities such as the Yugoslav Federation or the Soviet Union. Languages that had formerly been dominant state languages became minority languages with a low status in certain contexts (Russian in the Baltic states in the 1990s) and former regional or minority languages were raised to the status of official languages (Estonian in the Estonian Republic). Besides the flag, the coat of arms, the national anthem and other insignia, the state language was considered a central element for the affirmation of 'new' national identities. The efforts of imposing a single uniform language on the discursive and on the formal linguistic level were closely connected to processes of delineation and assertion, processes similar to those analysed by Bakhtin in the 1930s in the context of the Stalinist regime (1981, pp. 270ff):

> A unitary language is not something given (*dan*) but is always in essence posited (*zadan*) – and at every moment of its life it is opposed to the realities of heteroglossia. (...) We are taking language not as a system of abstract grammatical categories, but rather language conceived as ideologically saturated, language as a world view, even as a concrete opinion, insuring a maximum of mutual understanding in all spheres of ideological life. Thus a unitary language gives expression to forces working toward concrete verbal and ideological unification and centralization, which develop in vital connection with the process of sociopolitical and cultural centralization.

International politics intervened only in the domain of language policy in the media when access to information was denied or when the exclusion from the public sphere was imposed on the basis of language difference, when the violation of basic rights became too obvious. The Council of Europe, the OSCE, the International Federation of Journalists and a number of private foundations regularly intervened in the so-called countries of transition, criticising in particular the slowness of transformation in the media field, the often exclusionary and polarising media discourse and the univoicedness of state-controlled media. But it was only in 1997 that the OSCE installed the Office of the Representative on Free Media, which was given the role of pursuing questions of media and transformation as well as the role of media in conflict prevention and conflict resolution. Language and the media became a topic in the Office much later with the publication of a comparative study in 2003 (Karlsreiter, 2003).

3 The role of media in the propagation of the state language – reconfiguring the space of former Yugoslavia

During the time of the Socialist Federal Republic of Yugoslavia a sensitive equilibrium between centralist and federalist tendencies had to be constantly negotiated and renegotiated. These centripetal and centrifugal forces were also present in language policies and in the media sector. The number of standard languages into which the South Slavic linguistic space was segmented varied over time: until the Second World War there were three, Slovenian, Serbo-Croatian (which was then also called

Croato-Serbian) and Bulgarian. In 1945 Macedonian was codified and declared the official language in the Republic of Macedonia, in 1954 linguists from the Serbian and the Croatian Federal Republics formulated an accord on the common Serbocroatian-Croatoserbian language which foresaw the equal use of the eastern and Western variant of the common language (Bugarski, 2004, p. 28). The dissolution of the language unity was a long process: already in the 1980s, that is, before the federation disintegrated, linguistic activities tended to emphasise differences, and a series of new grammar books and of so-called differential Serbian-Croatian dictionaries appeared. It is interesting to note that there are considerable differences between these dictionaries not only in the number of lexical items they list, but also in their general orientation; some represent an extreme attempt at purism drawing on lexical items which stem from the language reform introduced by the totalitarian NDH[1] state during the Second World War, others are more 'moderate' (Okuka, 1998, p. 88; Langston, 1999, pp. 186ff). In 1989 Serbia declared the Cyrillic script as the official script in the Republic and started to replace Latin signs in the public space. In 1990, when Croatia proclaimed independence, the Croatian language and the Latin script were anchored in the constitution as the official ones. Bosnia and Herzegovina followed in 1993, declaring Bosnian, Serbian and Croatian as the official languages. Bosnian linguists published grammars and guidebooks for the use of 'correct' Bosnian. In particular, schoolbooks, administrative communication and the media were considered means of propagating the new standards and stressing towards the outside their distinctive and towards the inside their unifying nature. In practice this policy was not so easy to implement as migration and social transformations (such as urbanisation) have led throughout history to the co-presence of different idioms across the South Slavic space, such as the different languages linked to changing state administrations, different liturgical languages and languages of literary production with supradialectal features. Each of these idioms was linked to a network of speakers, and each idiom had a certain communicative efficiency and was attached to different forms of symbolic power. As individuals participated in different networks, considerable mixing and overlapping occurred. Using different idioms was mainly linked to social belonging. During the separation process national belonging and territorial connotations began to dominate over all other connotations (Škiljan, 2001, pp. 95ff).

In the 'Second Yugoslavia' after the Second World War, the media system was highly decentralised, each of the six Federal Republics – the

Republic of Bosnia-Herzegovina, of Croatia, of Macedonia, of Montenegro, of Serbia and of Slovenia – and the two Autonomous Regions – of Kosovo-Methodjia and of Vojvodina – had its own radio and TV station. Press was similarly decentralised, not only on a journalistic level but also with regards to production and distribution. In the 1990s each of the successor states of Yugoslavia could therefore rely on its own elaborate and functioning media system. The main interest of those who came to power in the new states concentrated on radio and TV. The idea was that these media could serve as a means of promoting national unity. These 'national' media, also considered the voice of the government, assumed the role of the propagation of the state languages and saw themselves not only as centres of codification but also as guardians of the 'pure' standard language. The West thought that privatisation would necessarily lead to a greater diversity of opinions in the media, but in fact it was through privatisation that the ethnisation of the media landscape was accelerated, oppositional media were often obstructed or silenced by obscure financial transactions, exclusion from production and distribution infrastructures and so on. In this context the cases of two print media published in Croatia, *Danas* and *Slobodna Dalmacija*, became famous on an international level. Both enjoyed a high reputation for their quality journalism. When privatisation began, the journalists were interested in buying the shares and running the papers themselves, hoping that this could guarantee their independence, but their efforts were obstructed. The media intervention carried out by international organisations in the space of former Yugoslavia was the greatest intervention in this sector since the Second World War. These international organisations were not prepared for a highly developed complex media system that from the 1980s onwards had developed a range of critical quality media which did not fit into the polarised East-West way of thinking (Thompson, 2000, p. 5).

The outbreak of the war interrupted the information and communication flows between the now separated states, and differing views from other parts of the space of former Yugoslavia became difficult to access. State radio, TV and print media close to the ruling parties became weapons in war propaganda. The Balkan Neighbours Project[2] and the research project Media and War (Skopljanac, Brunner et al., 2000) analysed media texts in the 1990s and identified discursive strategies which aimed at fortifying national identities and justifying the drawing of borders. Part of this strategy was linking accents and language use to national or ethnic identities and imposing a 'purified' code. It was not only a question of using the new emerging standards but even more of transporting and amplifying metalinguistic discourses which linked 'correct' language use to national loyalty and stigmatised 'wrong' language use as 'yugonostalgic'. Such metalinguistic discourses, which amalgamated political statements, philological positions and folk beliefs about language, were also spread through language-advice columns which flourished in the media and contributed to create a policing environment.

Examples of ethnicising discourse and hate speech (see Thomson, 2000) linked to prescriptive language use (see Busch, 2004) were discussed for all of the successor states of former Yugoslavia. Two will be mentioned here: in 1993, when the war in Bosnia-Herzegovina was raging, the potentates in Republika Srpska, the Serbian part of Bosnia-Herzegovina, aligned their efforts of 'language cleansing' to the 'motherland' by adopting not only the Cyrillic script, but also by prescribing the ekavian[3] variant for public use. In fact the authorities were well aware that the 'ekavian' variant, which is widely spread in Serbia, was not used in the Serbian part of Bosnia in daily practice. The idea was that the 'ekavica should be given back to the people to which it belongs [...] in order to liberate it from foreign influences'.[4] All media were compelled by law to the exclusive employment of the ekavica and the Cyrillic script. The forced ekavisation ended in a fiasco and in 1998 the Republika Srpska authorities had to revise their decision and re-permit the use of the jekavian variant in the public domain.

Another extreme example of an overtly prescriptive language policy aiming at cementing differences via the media was 'Croatian Radio and Television' (HRTV) in the early 1990s. HRTV produced a handbook that listed desired Croatian and undesired 'foreign' words, oppositional journalists were sacked under the pretext of being unable to speak 'correct' Croatian. Language use in war reporting was strictly prescribed; for example, the Jugoslovenska narodna armija (JNA) had to be called 'Serbian communist occupator' (Thompson, 1999, p. 159). Temporarily state television followed a policy that attempted to make the symbolic boundaries, which had been discursively constructed between the Croatian and the Serbian language, to coincide with communication boundaries. Speakers of Serbian were subtitled into Croatian in TV and in films (Škiljan, 2002, p. 278).

Similarly print media close to the then ruling party HDZ served as a tribune for public debates about language and saw themselves as promoters of the new standard language. There are only very few empirical studies on the effective change of language use in the space of former Yugoslavia and it is difficult to say how much the efforts to promote unitary languages actually caused changes in daily language practices in the public sphere. One of the few is Langston's study (1999) based on a corpus of text samples obtained from different Croatian media in 1996–7, which he compares to samples taken in 1985. He concludes: 'Noticeable changes in lexical usage in the Croatian media have indeed taken place since the break-up of the Yugoslav state, but on the whole they are relatively minor.' (p. 188). It is not surprising that changes mainly concern the administrative and political vocabulary, as there was a profound transformation of the political and economic system. Even the state media, which had been principal actors in spreading metalinguistic discourses aiming at 'purifying' the language, apparently only differed slightly in their daily practice from the private media and from linguistic practices before the war.

4 Diaspora: ethnicisation or maximising audiences and merging linguistic spaces

Although the ruling elites made considerable efforts to silence oppositional and independent media during the period of the war, this turned out to be impossible. Independent and alternative media in particular, and media addressing the diaspora, developed a way of imagining their audiences in a different way from the national media. A broad spectrum of media, print and audiovisual, is published for the diaspora by media enterprises linked to the space of former Yugoslavia. The daily European edition of the famous Sarajevo newspaper *Oslobodjenje* is one of them. Whereas Bosnian papers that were close to the ruling party during the war, such as *Liljan* or *Dnevni avaz*, propagated a new Bosnian standard language, *Oslobodjenje* continued to allow a plurality of voices and styles. Only the pre-war policy of alternating between the Cyrillic and the Latin script was abandoned. It is possible, even today, to occasionally find in *Oslobodjenje* articles written in the ekavian variant which is to some extent afflicted with a more 'Serbian' connotation. But it is also possible to see contributions showing features that are labelled as 'Croatian' (such as the Croatian names for the months – 'lipanj' instead of 'junij'). Similarly, lexical items that carry a 'Bosniak' marker can be seen occasionally. The European edition of *Oslobodjenje* and the Sarajevo edition differ only in 15 per cent to 20 per cent in their content; not only international news and BiH politics but even local *fait divers* remain in the European edition. It is mainly the local announcements and the advertisements that are particular to one or the other edition. In an interview with the author in 1993 the editor of the Frankfurt-based edition pointed out that there was a common language policy and a clear convergence between the two editions as readers in BiH were also interested in the activities of the BiH diaspora throughout Europe and beyond. Considering that roughly 2.5 million of the population of Bosnia-Herzgovina live in the Bosnian Federation and 1.5 million in the Republika Srpska, whereas 1 million live in the diaspora, almost every family in BiH has relatives abroad. For readers outside BiH it is important to see the immediate environment they used to live in or their families and friends are living in represented in the media. It is obvious from the personal advertisements that readers – especially in the diaspora – come from all parts of BiH; the policy of allowing for language variation in the paper opens it up for such a diverse readership. In the beginning the final text for the European edition was sent to Germany where the advertisements for the diaspora were added. Nowadays the journalists outside BiH also participate in the editorial work and the communication flow is not one way between motherland and diaspora but multidirectional; language use represents a multitude of language developments in BiH and beyond.

Commercial interests guide the policy of the 'yellow-press' magazine *Svet plus* which claims to be the diaspora magazine with the biggest circulation between Athens and Stockholm. The magazine belongs to the Coban publishing house, which is located in Novi Sad (Serbia) and produces a whole range of not ostensibly political media titles such as love-story magazines, crossword-puzzle magazines and special-interest magazines. *Svet plus* is a 60 to 70-page publication of which about a quarter is taken up by advertisements. It concentrates mainly on celebrity gossip centred on stars and starlets of the pop music scene from the space of former Yugoslavia. Although the ekavian variant is mainly used throughout the texts, care is taken to address migrants from all parts of the space, for example by reproducing satellite TV programmes from Serbia alongside of those from Croatia or BiH. *Svet plus* caters for different tastes and styles with stories about the Yugo rock music scene from the 1970s and 1980s, stories on nationally oriented turbo-folk starlets and features about sport celebrities from the various successor states. The humour page regularly prints jokes on language use under the heading 'Little Multilingual Dictionary'. They usually begin with the question 'How to say [...] in New-Croatian or New-Bosnian?' or 'How do they say it in Vranjan?' (Vranjan is a small town in Serbia). Similar jokes had already circulated before the 1990s in Yugoslavia when the first purist tendencies could be felt.

A similar strategy of maximising audiences by addressing the whole South Slavic space can be observed with the Belgrade-based company Pink TV. Pink, sometimes referred to as 'Balkan MTV', could profit from the large Serbian home market to build a media empire that reaches now even beyond former Yugoslavia. Soon after the terrestrial programme was launched in Serbia, Pink began to broadcast a satellite programme for the diaspora. A little later it continued with a programme for BiH and a programme for Montenegro, both of which rebroadcast the same main programme from Serbia with localised news and talk-show windows. Pink TV advertises specific cultural practices, values and promotes new trends in fashion and music and reaches audiences from Slovenia to Bulgaria, covering BiH and Montenegro as well as Serbia, and is highly popular among the diaspora.

5 Heteroglossic audiences and transnational media flows

Independent, alternative or civic media, that is, media within the private sector but not with a primarily commercial orientation, played a central role in the transformation process. The idea of providing space for an alternative public sphere and of making silenced voices audible are guiding principles in the way these media approach and imagine their audiences, which ideally become active participants in production and distribution process. The role of the so-called samizdat media as catalysts in moments of change was recognised by international organisations, but their connectedness to community and civic media which developed often as a continuation of samizdat initiatives and the role of a third media sector, outside both the public-service and the private sector, was completely underestimated. During the 1990s support for independent and alternative media in the Balkan area came mainly from NGOs active in the field; the only exception were media that reached a kind of iconic status such as 'Radio B92' in Belgrade. Nevertheless, it is within the third sector of civic media that an experimental space is opening up, allowing the development of new forms of media communication and new language practices.

In the past years there has been a growing number of media which address the otherwise fragmented audiences across the Balkan area in a translocal move. One of these is 'Cross radio'. The 'Cross radio' project mainly promotes programme exchange between different radio stations in the space of the former Yugoslavia and between stations that produce programmes in urban centres with a significant diaspora. 'Cross radio' focuses on culture with the idea of promoting a transnational and thus 'de-provincialised' cultural space. Consequently, different codes and registers can be heard in the programmes, which are re-broadcast by stations from Pristina, via Belgrade, Zagreb, Ljubljana, to Zurich and are also directly accessible to a wider public via the internet. In the print sector there is a range of cultural magazines and periodical publications along similar lines.

In the multilingual area of Vojvodina as well as in the region around Skopje several multilingual media initiatives have been active for some time. Such initiatives as Radio 021 (Novi Sad), urbanNS (TV station, Novi Sad) or Life Radio (Skopje) produce at least some of their programmes in a multilingual format (Karlsreiter, 2003). This means that, for example, Serbian, Hungarian, Slovakian, Romany and Ruthenian can be co-present in one particular time slot. In the multilingual radio programmes different languages alternate, speakers use the language they prefer to speak in and the moderators take care that the programme can be followed by listeners with different language backgrounds. To ensure this they employ different techniques, ranging from direct and complete translations to reframing utterances in a response in a different language or summarising statements in another language. Television programmes can make use of subtitling in different languages and of using voiceover techniques. In multilingual areas such as Vojvodina or Skopje it can be assumed that part of the population has at least some understanding of more than one language. The impetus for the development of multilingual formats originated in an understanding that there was a complete lack of appropriate interfaces between media producing in different languages and often even an unawareness of what media in the respective other languages published. In Macedonia the AIM journalist network has provided translations into Albanian from articles originally written in Macedonian and vice versa. These direct insights into the strands of debate, which developed in the media in the respective other language, helped journalists as well as readers gain a better understanding of the 'other'. Producing multilingual formats is not only a formal question but also has implications for the creation of meaning, for discourse and its reception. Bi- and multilingual media products simultaneously address audiences which are habitually separated; journalists have to keep the interests and needs of both audiences in mind and the positions which are being negotiated have to be acceptable for both.

The most recent example of the central role played by media in the negotiation/language status can be seen in the context of current efforts to promote the standardisation of Romany. In the past ten years the number of programmes and of media in Romany has increased in Macedonia as well as in Serbia. This development can build on previous experiences made during the 1970s and 1980s when Skopje was one of the centres of the codification of Romany. It was only in the 1980s that the Council of Europe asked the member states to recognise Roma as a minority and to grant linguistic rights for the speakers of Romany. Consequently there was a centralised effort to codify a central Romany standard. But the Courthiade grammar – named after its author – was contested by several Roma organisations and did not seem workable because writing practices that drew on the different majority languages of the countries Romany speakers lived in were already established. Until the 1990s Romany was mainly present in school manuals and in local media and did not serve to a larger extent as a lingua franca in communication beyond the local environment. With the increased migration after the end of the two-bloc logic there is now an intensive contact between speakers of different Roma variants in urban centres, who use Romany as the common language. With the spread of the internet in the 1990s the use of Romany in a written form has increased, especially in the Roma email networks. The fact that local media develop more and more translocal connections and exchange relations also contributes to a process of convergence and to what could be called standardisation from below or postmodern standardisation (Matras, 1999). The aim is not to construct a single unified prescriptive standard but to allow a standardisation that is open for variation and that recognises the multivoicedness of society.

6 Conclusions

Discursive strategies in media can emphasise or minimise political and administrative boundaries. They can also accentuate or diminish language differences and through metalinguistic discourses contribute to a climate in which language becomes a symbolic boundary towards the outside and a homogenising means towards the inside. This becomes critical when symbolic boundaries are constructed as obstacles to communication. Homogenisation in language use is much more difficult to implement today under the conditions of globalisation where media flows have become more diverse and multidirectional than in previous times when media were organised around a national public sphere. In audio and audiovisual media different substandards, jargons and codes are a very natural and 'normal' phenomenon; it is the administrative discourse that has become the guardian of the standard.

The example of media and language developments in the space of former Yugoslavia over the past two decades shows contradictions. Forces tending toward a strong national public sphere and the creation of a homogeneous linguistic space were equally present, as were actors that imagined their audiences in a much more diverse way. Critical and independent media had already been established during the last decade of the Socialist Federal Republic of Yugoslavia and played an important role in providing the platform for a non-nationalist discourse during the war, although they were repressed by the respective nationalistic state authorities. To apply a linear time-axis model, which represents the development of the media landscape as a narrative that takes its starting point in a less democratic situation and moves to a more democratic one, would therefore result in a crude simplification. Even in exceptional situations of conflict and nationalistic hubris media developments and language developments cannot simply be analysed within their national framework but must be considered in the context of globalisation. With the increasing multiplication and multidirectionality of communication flows, media production, reception habits and media use have changed significantly. Media in the successor states of the former Yugoslavia have become both more local – including the use of local varieties on the Slavic continuum – and more transnational, because publishers are trying to sell to a market that transcends not only the frontier of the present 'new' nation states but also the old boundaries of the Republic of Yugoslavia in the pursuit of creating a larger South Slavic market.

Parallel to efforts of linguistic demarcation in national media in the successor states of former Yugoslavia emerge developments that regroup the Serbocroat speaking realm into one. Such developments are motivated less by nostalgia than by market considerations. In the commercial realm this strategy is a means of maximising audiences and creating a public for advertising; the linguistic means aim at avoiding language that is marked as a particular national standard. In the sector of civic media this strategy of addressing linguistic space as public in a translocal dimension is understood as a possibility of 'dis-enclaving' the space culturally. Linguistically this is achieved through the direct representation of different voices and discourses with their particular means of expression. For both kinds of media, commercial and non-commercial, the diaspora is an important factor and takes part in the communication flows.

In multilingual situations in which new political borders created new status differences in relation to the official position of languages, national authorities often reacted only with delay or under pressure from 'outside', when they guaranteed access to information and participation in public discourse to speakers of languages that had recently decreased in status and become minority languages. On the other hand, minority media could also show a tendency to retreat into their 'own' universe. The rise of multilingual formats in the media was a response to processes of ethnicisation. Such multilingual formats make use of the multimodal dimension of media communication and make the co-presence of different languages visible; it also has a transformative effect on the discourse itself.

The decentring of standard language is a phenomenon that can be observed on a global scale. Diverse 'impure' linguistic practices – code switching, language crossing, linguistic bricolage – have made their way into the media field and also via the media into other public domains. Transgressing prescriptive linguistic norms and employing codes that combine different elements can function as a means of regrouping audiences beyond the imagined national or ethnic community. Audiences are not necessarily defined on a territorial basis. In the reconfiguration of communication spaces as well as in language policy, centres tend to lose normative power. It is mainly in independent media that the multi-voicedness of society becomes visible in all the three dimensions that Bakhtin (1984, p. 56) described: heterology (*raznorečie*), that is, the diversity of discourses; heteroglossia (*raznojazyčnie*), that is the diversity of language(s); and heterophony (*raznoglossie*), that is, the diversity of individual voices. The creation of open spaces in which the multi-voicedness of society cannot be reduced seems to be of crucial importance in processes of transition because it is in those spaces that subject positions can be developed and power relations negotiated.

Notes

1. The fascist NDH state (Nezavisna Država Hrvatska/Independent Croatian State) introduced a language reform which aimed at marking the difference between a Serbian and a Croatian language. In the course of this reform an etymological orthography was propagated and internationalisms labelled as serbisms.
2. A project which brought together researchers and journalists to monitor print media in Albania, Bulgaria, Greece, Macedonia, Romania, Turkey, Serbia, Montenegro and Kosovo. The aim of the project was to detect stereotypes and prejudices that were present about the respective 'others'.

Until the end of the project, the results were published on a regular basis between 1994 and 2000.

3. Ekavian and jekavian relates to the reproduction of the old Slavonic sound 'Jat', which can be reproduced as 'e' or 'je' as, for example, in the word for river: 'rijeka' (jekavian) or 'reka' (ekavian).
4. Alternativna informativna mreža (AIM), 13 September 1993. This example is also discussed by Bugarski (1995).

3

Contesting Social Space through Language Education Debates in Latvia's Media Landscape

Gabrielle Hogan-Brun

1 Introduction

During the course of Latvia's move from Soviet authoritarian rule to democratic government since the early 1990s, the speed of socio-political and economic change resulted in societal tensions that also strongly affected the country's educational domain. Looking at the latter, this chapter explores the role of discourse in the construction of Latvia's social and political transition. More specifically, the discursive 'link between the politics of education and the transformation of the educational system' (Mebrahtu et al., 2000, p. 15) is analysed in this demographically heterogeneous setting.

The concept of 'discourse as a form of social practice' (Fairclough and Wodak, 1997, p. 258) is key for the perspective represented in this chapter. In line with that conception, the chapter aims to explicate that there exists a particular relationship between a particular discursive event (the studied Latvian educational reform), a situation (the divided attitudes of Latvians and Russophones towards the reform), an institution (Latvia's government through the Education Ministry behind the reform) and the (deeper) social structures which frame it. Focusing on the dynamics of the intersection of the political and the social in Latvian post-communist transformation – based on the example of the country's educational policy – the analysis will show that the social changes analysed are indeed rooted in discourses of those who are 'holding power over discourse' and who have direct access to power (in this case politicians and the media;

see also the introduction to this volume). On the other hand, this chapter will shed light on those groups (that is, Russian-speakers) who have to deal with the everyday implementation of various ('powerful') discourses and who are either driven to contradict or to accept the visions of social and political organisation constructed by the politics and the media (see the introduction to this volume).

This chapter also follows the field-oriented division of the social space. According to Pierre Bourdieu (1973), the political field plays, to a great extent, a determining role in all other social strata. In the Baltic countries, and particularly in Latvia, the two main (Latvian and Russian-speaking) communities continue to largely coexist side by side. The political field has intervened directly, since the restitution of independence, in an attempt to redraw the divided social space. Here, education has been used as an important means of re-centring the cultural capital of the dominant group (the ethnic Latvians) upon the sizeable Russian-speaking section of the school population, with the political aim of transferring social capital through objects such as books, qualifications and, symbolically, the titular language. Consequently, schools and universities were deployed as key agents in the (re-)production of dominant social realities through cultural practices during the various phases of transition across the Baltic. For Bourdieu, the intercourse between institutions, and their values and regulations, constitute another metaphorical space that is interactive, flexible and fluid. But the dynamics of the forces that operate within this space can be subject to changes, especially in periods of conflict, or during processes of political and social transformation, such as occurred in the Baltic. Below we shall explore the media's role of meaning-making in this central metaphorical space in which we can identify the discourses of (educational) institutions and other agents on the one hand, and the discourses of government ministries and departments as the fields of power as well as related practices and values on the other.

2 Reforming education in context

The Baltic countries have experienced profound social reforms to rebuild their democratising societies since their political reorientation that started in the late 1980s.[1] As one of several interdependent central social sub-fields, education has featured as a principal transformative vehicle to overcome the limitations of the Soviet past. Key features of educational transition across Central and Eastern Europe include the following characteristics: a) introduction of the national curriculum;

b) decentralisation of the administrative system; and c) elimination of the state monopoly of schooling (see also Mebrahtu et al., 2000, p. 14).

Reforms, however, can fail when they are piecemeal, since their implementation often requires flexibility at state and local levels. Moreover, as we shall see below, legislation does not tend to translate into systems overnight, for the response of the public to imposed policy change can be multi-faceted and complex. This applies particularly to processes of educational transition in countries moving from authoritarian rule to democratic government, where the shift in ideology tends to result in conflicts that emerge between the political and the social arenas as attempts are made to put policy into practice (McLeish, 1998, p. 20). Increasingly, governments are called upon to coat their policy discourses in inclusiveness, affirming differences, particularly of ethnic identity (Osborn, 2005, pp. 21ff), and to provide opportunities for stakeholders to actively help mediate policy change. This trend is more evident in Lithuania, and to some extent also in Estonia, than in Latvia.

A number of publications exist, with varying focus, on educational transition in Central and Eastern European post-communist settings. Early work dealt with economic change (Phillips and Kaser, 1992), privatisation (Beresford-Hill, 1997), and wider aspects of transition processes in education systems (McLeish and Phillips, 1998). A subsequent volume, on educational transformation and societies in transition against the background of globalisation, is Mebrahtu et al. (2000). In the run-up to accession to the European Union, reviews of national education policy in Estonia, Latvia and Lithuania were carried out within the framework of the Baltic regional programme of the Organisation for Economic Co-operation and Development (OECD, 2001a; 2001b; 2002). Whilst these reports offer a synthetic picture of the main processes of educational transformation in these countries, they also expose the need for an extension of comprehensive comparative research across the Baltic. More recent studies on education in the Baltic multilingual settings are by Hogan-Brun and Ramonienė (2003; 2004). Adrey (2005, pp. 460ff) presents a critical review of post-1991 language-in-education policy reforms in Latvia, which we shall now focus on.

Owing to Latvia's greater demographic heterogeneity, the process of education reform and its implementation there was complex. Although the principle of providing teaching through the medium of the mother tongue is being upheld generally, educational policies in support of cultural and linguistic diversity ended up being less liberal there than is the case in both neighbouring republics (see Hogan-Brun, 2007; Hogan-Brun and Ramonienė, 2004). According to the Latvian government, more teaching through the medium of Latvian was deemed to be necessary to ensure that the numerous Russian-speaking residents learn Latvian and integrate (see also Galbreath and Galvin, 2005). These are mostly Soviet-era immigrants from Russia, but also from Ukraine and Belorussia, who together amount to approximately 36 per cent of the overall population. Hence, a major education reform was pushed through in 2004 (Estonia also had plans to introduce this by 2007; see Hogan-Brun, 2007) with the aim to further consolidate the position of the dominant group (the Latvians) and its (official state) language within this divided social space.

According to an amendment to the 1998 Education Law,[2] 60 per cent of the curriculum in all public (minority) upper secondary schools now has to be taught in Latvian, in addition to Latvian language and literature classes. The reform came into effect on 1 September 2004, also allowing schools to offer subjects pertaining to minority identities, culture and language in other languages, mainly Russian.[3] With these new regulations, and through the Ministry of Education, an attempt was made to strengthen the vision of the dominant group on the configuration of social space in society by determining the range of its social capital to be transmitted as part of the curricular activities expected from schools.

These new rules became the subject of heated debates in Latvia, which produced a growth in inter-ethnic tensions. Galbreath and Galvin (2005, p. 453) argue that the style in which the policy was implemented was partly the result of the Soviet legacy of 'show politics' on post-Soviet policies. This linkage with a previous discourse points to the process of recontextualisation (Wodak, 2001) in a different political field of action, with discursive practices, reappropriating various elements of other discourses, carrying social and political change.

Resident Russians contested the amended law, maintaining that these changes would undermine their culture and language. During EU accession negotiations, they seized the opportunity to appeal in Brussels for minority rights, demanding Latvia's ratification of the Council of Europe Framework Convention. Moscow's attempts to instrumentalise the situation further inflamed exchanges between Latvians and Russians.

3 Pre-reform discourse

The aforementioned changes were particularly controversial in the eyes of those numerous resident Russian-speaking parents whose offspring attend Russian-medium schools (these constituted 40 per cent of all national teaching establishments in 2004). The Russian-language press initially claimed that the education reform was an 'assimilating Latvianisation' attempt (Reports,[4] 5 May 2004). It printed repeated calls by the Head of the Latvian Association for the Support of Russian-Language Schools for a moratorium on the reform until minorities' schools, students and parents were fully prepared for its introduction (*Час (Čas), Телеграф (Telegraf), Вести сегодня (Vesti Segodnya),* in Reports, 7 May 2004; *Вести сегодня (Vesti Segodnya),* in Reports, 10 May 2004; *Вести сегодня, Телеграф (Telegraf),* in Reports, 13 May 2004; *Вести сегодня (Vesti Segodnya),* in Reports, 27 May 2004). With the debates surrounding the reform mounting, a range of public anti-reform rallies started to take place. Stressing that it was unacceptable for students to be involved in these protest actions during scheduled lessons, Latvia's President Vaira Vīķe-Freiberga ordered security organisations to deal with disturbances and the violation of rights during the protests against the educational reform (*Вести сегодня (Vesti Segodnya), Телеграф (Telegraf),* in Reports, 6 May 2004). These developments showed how, due to the interconnectedness of socio-political variables, shifting ideologies can result in conflicts that emerge between the political and social arenas as attempts are made to put policy into practice (see McLeish, 1998, p. 20).

The state, as the main locus of the public discourse, was called upon to explain and justify its actions. Persisting with the progress of the reform, the government commissioned a range of opinion polls in May 2004, according to which it appeared that most of Latvia's minority schools were ready for the change and that there was no reason why the transition to tuition in Latvian could not be realised by 1 September 2004. Several public figures (the 'actors'; Blommaert, 1999, pp. 8ff) were firmly positioned in the foreground with a range of statements prepared to underpin the progress of the reform and to offer some flexibility regarding its implementation. According to the Prime Minister, Indulis Emsis, who was also drawn into the public debate, several political parties were using these education issues in their own self-interest, thus preventing the development of a constructive dialogue between the government and the minorities in the area of the education reform (*Latvijas Avīze,* in Reports, 12 May 2004). His adviser was reported to have added that, from the point of view of state security, it would be dangerous to yield to pressures from the Russian community, that insufficient preparedness of the education reform's implementation had created a political climate for mass political movement, and that the main task had now become to discourage political consolidation of the Russian community on the basis of the education reform (*Latvijas Avīze*, in Reports, 18 May 2004). The Special Task Minister for Society Integration, Nils Muižnieks, was reported to have added that the reform was essential for the interruption of the reproduction of the Soviet system, which had divided society on the basis of language knowledge (ibid., 12 May 2004).

Latvia's attempt to redraw its social space through educational policy-making was paralleled by EU accession negotiations, which themselves had significant repercussions on local language-regime politics. Areas of concern under Western monitoring related to issues such as education, language proficiency testing, occupational restrictions, naturalisation and citizenship rights. Hence language ideological debates regarding minority (language) and citizenship rights tended to be played out in a wider arena, frequently attracting the attention of international commentators (cf. Adrey, 2005; Hogan-Brun, 2005c).

Reporting on official decisions and ensuing debates as illustrated in the above press extracts, Latvia's media were drawn in heavily on the meaning-making of discourses with respect to the interplay of forces surrounding the education reform. An in-depth pre-reform press analysis of the dynamics of forces within this space between institutions, rules and people's practices is given in Hogan-Brun (2006). This shows how the process of policy implementation and accompanying debates were framed in different ways at the macro level by the Latvian- and Russian-medium press, with diverging slants on events that in turn impacted on the polarised target groups. The division of Latvia's press into two barely related information spaces was initially identified in Latvia's first mass-media content analysis in 1998. This highlighted that the intermediate stratum of people who participate in both fora (that is, reading the press in both languages) is very small, and that the opinions of these persons are rarely represented in the public media (Zepa, 2003, p. 93).

Intensified by the existence of these closed information spaces, the overall picture that emerged in the abovementioned press analysis was that newspapers reflected an ongoing discrepancy between language policy (as laid down by law) and actual beliefs, needs and practices within Latvia's two main language groups. Yet, contrary to expectations raised through the portrayal of the education reform by the media, it turned out that most Russophone parents eventually decided to send their children to minority schools at the start of term in September 2004. We may infer from these obervations that, while most resident Russian speakers read the press and vote for politicians who defend their interests, they in fact tend to make individual decisions in real situations and consider pragmatic orientation as an option. Such behaviour can reflect, in Bourdieu's words, 'doxic attitudes' that explain the ways in which subjects adjust themselves to ideology's rules. Hidden by the smooth working of habitus, this can help people to accommodate, but may indicate a great deal of internal tension caused by internalised contradictions (Bourdieu, 1994, pp. 276ff).

4 Changing post-reform media discourse

Recent press coverage shows that the nature of the media discourse has changed during the two years following the reform. Moving from a predominantly ethnocentric to a more issue-oriented stance towards education, Latvia's newspapers now tend to display an increased focus on (e)quality and the nature of educational provision within the country. Exchanges that are taken up by the press point to the continuing contesting nature of the metaphorical space that exists within the cultural field in interactions between institutions, rules and people's practices. We shall now explore how and to what extent Latvia's Russian- and Latvian-medium press has re-conceived its role in this changed context.

Several communication strategies were developed to justify the reform and deal with counter-arguments, initially with some degree of caution. On taking over as Minister of Education, Baiba Rivza stated in an interview with the private television channel LNT that it was too early to speak about the results of the education reform at minority schools. Maintaining that the minority education reform was necessary to prepare students for enrolment and studies at universities (which by law function in Latvian) she forecast that, since the process had started just a year previously, the actual results of the reform could be seen only once pupils studying today in the tenth grade graduate (*Телеграф (Telegraf)*, in Reports, 20 April 2006).

These were delayed comments that followed the dissemination of results from a joint study by the Member of Parliament Yakovs Pliners, and Jelagava City Councillor Valeriys Buhvalovs (both members of *For Human Rights in United Latvia*[5]), on the implementation of minority education reform. According to this, the level of academic attainment of minority secondary school students has dropped since the reform, and many of the affected establishments do not have enough bilingual teaching aids, such as books, dictionaries and reference literature. Their research also claims that school directors and representatives of educational administrations believe that ninth-grade students, who are subject to the reform during the following year, are not ready for the requirements set by the reform (*Час (Čas)*, in Reports, 4 February 2006). Subsequently, the MP and his colleague presented their newly published book, on *The Quality of Education at Russian Schools Undergoing the Reform*. Based on data collected at Russian schools, their findings point to an increase in the workload of pupils. The study also claims that the number of students needing to repeat a grade as well as that of school drop-outs has grown. Furthermore, Pliners was reported to have said that, '[while] officials assure that the situation in bilingual education is normal, their conclusions are based on the polling results of school directors who may well not disclose all the information' (*Час (Čas)*, in Reports, 8 May 2006).

These publicly disseminated findings elicited a number of public statements by a range of actors from different arenas within education. The Education Minister was reported to have announced that a special agency monitoring the quality of minority education had been formed in order to improve the situation in the future. Further, responding to a memorandum issued by the Latvian Association for the Support of Russian-Language Schools (LASHOR in its Russian acronym) that stated that the government had stopped maintaining a dialogue with NGOs on minority education issues, she admitted that some of the indicated complaints were well-founded, and stressed that it was very important to foster a continuing dialogue with all stakeholders, including school children (*Час (Čas)*, in Reports, 18 May 2006). Latvia's Prime Minister, Aigars Kalvitis, added in an interview with *Latvijas Avize* that the government did not foresee any 'softening' of the minority education reform, and that its implementation would continue (in Reports, 29 May 2006). *Neatkarīgā* subsequently featured an article by Evija Papule, the Director of the State General Education Evaluation Agency (which is under the Ministry of Education and Science). This stated that all minority schools now had submitted their first reports on the implementation of the reform. It also provided information showing that while schools did experience problems with material and technical resources, this was apparently counter-balanced by improved attitudes towards the reform among parents, students and teachers (in Reports, 19 June 2006). *Telegraf* followed this up, publishing various opinions by people in the teaching profession, including school directors, concerning the education reform in minority schools. They confirmed that in general, students and teachers were managing the reform successfully, but that more focus should be placed on the frequently observed low quality of teaching and the lack of suitable study aids for minority schools. Still, according to a statement by a representative of the Centre for Curriculum Development and Examination, the results of the school year 2005–6 showed that the level of Latvian language proficiency skills among students had improved (*Телеграф (Telegraf)*, in Reports, 22 June 2006).

Both Baiba Rivza and Evija Papule subsequently positioned themselves centrally in the foreground to publicly comment on the quality of education in (bilingual) minority schools. In an interview on quality assurance, which was featured in *Vesti Segodnya*, they stressed that monitoring the implementation of the education reform in minority schools had revealed that the academic achievements of students subjected to the reform were indeed at the same level as that by pupils who were not subjected to the reform. The minister added that the results of the former were in fact even better in several areas than those of students attending schools with Latvian as the main language of instruction (*Вести сегодня (Vesti Segodnya)*, in Reports, 27 June 2006). This claim was not followed up in the press and would have needed further clarification.

Another sensitive issue aired in the press was related to assertions that a number of Russian-medium primary schools were experiencing problems in recruiting enough children to make running their classes worthwhile. Stating that there was a growing tendency among pupils from Russian-language establishments to start attending Latvian-medium ones, Riga City Council representative Guntis Helmanis argued that some of the Russian institutions in Riga were faced with the prospect of imminent closure because of a decreasing student-intake level. It was also reported that one school in Riga providing studies in Russian was caught cheating with its purported number of enrolments in order to receive state funding (*Час (Čas), Вести сегодня (Vesti Segodnya)*, in Reports, 18 April 2006). The Department of Education was quick to start auditing the actual number of students in several Russian-language schools (*Час (Čas), Вести сегодня (Vesti Segodnya)*, in Reports, 10 May 2006).

A more pressing matter that dominated the media during the second half of May 2006 was concerned with the fact that fresh initiatives were underway trying to change the status quo of the newly introduced education reform. The immediate trigger was a conference on 'Law on National Minority Education: Yesterday, Today, Tomorrow?', organised by the political party 'The Concord Centre' in cooperation with several Russian NGOs. Weighing up past and present legal norms concerning minority education in independent Latvia compared to international experience, participants discussed the drafting of a project on minority schools. The head of LASHOR, Igors Pimenovs, informed the audience that such a document had already been elaborated, and that this had the potential to soften the impact of the current education law. Its likely effectiveness was disputed by a representative of OKROL (The United Congress of the Russian Community in Latvia), who felt that the present government would not be likely to accept the draft (*Час (Čas), Вести сегодня (Vesti Segodnya), Latvijas Avize,* in Reports, 15 May 2006). Promptly, on the next day, the Education Minister was reported to have discussed with Pimenovs the possibility of relaunching activities of a working group who had started to work in 2004 on a project entitled 'The National Minority Education Institution Law' (*Latvijas Avize,* in Reports, 16 May 2006). This was followed up immediately with widely publicised news that the political union 'For Human Rights in United Latvia' (FHRUL) had in fact elaborated draft amendments to the current Education Law (*Час (Čas), Вести сегодня (Vesti Segodnya), Latvijas Avize, Rigas Balss,* in Reports, 17 May 2006). With reference to these amendments, Pimenovs subsequently informed the *Telegraf* that they were mainly proposing that school self-administration boards should be granted authority to determine which subjects could be studied in Latvian and which in a minority language, and that students ought to be allowed to choose the language of the final state exams (which, according to existing regulations, had to be in Latvian) (*Телеграф (Telegraf),* in Reports, 18 May 2006). On the same day, and backed by Saeima's rejection of these draft amendments to the Education Law, Rivzha maintained that the education reform was going well and informed *Čas* that she was not going to reopen the law on Ethnic Minority Schools (*Час (Čas),* in Reports, 18 May 2006). At the start of the new academic year, however, she was seen to be prepared to renegotiate on her original position, stating that now, students of minority secondary schools were allowed to take the final common secondary school examinations either in their first language or in Latvian (*Diena,* in Reports, 1 September 2006).

As debates on the issue of the proposed amendment to the education law began to decline, related press interest subsided. A postscript in two Russian-medium outlets reported on suggestions that the envisaged changes were a provocation and attempt to decrease use of the Latvian language in schools (*Час (Čas), Вести сегодня (Vesti Segodnya),* in Reports, 19 May 2006). Five weeks into the first term of the new school year, *Vesti Segodnya* again took up the case, printing an article by Jakovs Pliners on the situation in Russian-language schools. In it, he criticised the regulations of the 2004 minority education reform, particularly the requirement to teach more classes in Latvian, and asserted that the Education Ministry's policy was trying to push the Russian language out of Russian schools (*Вести сегодня (Vesti Segodnya)*, in Reports, 2 October 2006).

Other educational issues that were occasionally picked up by the press served to offer readers a degree of distraction, which possibly may have also led to some reflection. There was some coverage on (e)quality in, and the inclusion of, other communities in the nature of educational provision in Latvia. Thus, quoting the Head of the Riga Jewish Community Education Support Fund who said that the future of the Jewish community depended on the quality of education in school, *Vesti Segodnya* announced early in the year that a new Jewish school was to be opened in the capital on 1 September 2007, with the financial support of several international Jewish organisations (*Вести сегодня (Vesti Segodnya)*, in Reports, 6 April 2006). Elicited by a draft national program 'Roma in Latvia', *Latvijas Avize*, on the other hand, briefly focused on the integration of Roma children in mainstream groups. A Roma cultural representative was quoted as saying that issues faced by the Roma community in Latvia[6] required immediate solutions, and that it was crucial that the Roma receive education to improve their job prospects and ensure better living conditions (Reports, 19 August 2006). Earlier, it had published a review of a book entitled *Roma Study at My School*, which had been produced as part of a PHARE project on 'Roma in Local Society and at School' (Reports, 10 June 2006). There was also some media attention on three Somalians who had started to attend a Latvian school from 1 September 2006. The director of this establishment was reported to have mentioned that their enrolment provided other children and teachers with an opportunity to learn about and get to know another culture (*Телеграф (Telegraf)*, *Diena*, in Reports, 12 September 2006). Against this background, *Vesti Segodnya* subsequently printed an interview with a participant of a LASHOR-supported conference on 'A Model of Intercultural Education for Latvia' who stated that, since Latvia was a multi-national, multi-linguistic, multi-cultural, and multi-religion country, this also needed to be reflected in education (*Вести сегодня (Vesti Segodnya)*, in Reports, 21 September 2006). This selection of newspaper extracts serves to illustrate that both the Latvian and Russophile constituencies are intent on exploiting the topos of multiculturalism for their own ends.

Outsiders' opinions on ensuing reform issues were now relayed through the press to a lesser extent than had been the case during the months preceding the implementation of the 2004 education reform (see Hogan-Brun, 2006, pp. 330ff). One chosen protagonist was the OSCE (Organisation for Security and Co-operation in Europe) High Commissioner on National Minorities Rolf Ekeus, who was widely reported on in both press camps to have stated that he supported the implementation of monitoring procedures for the quality of education in Latvia's national minority schools. He was quoted as saying: 'My task is to follow that the reform in minority schools [will] not deteriorate the quality of education' (*Час (Čas), Вести сегодня (Vesti Segodnya), Latvijas Avize, Diena, Neatkarīgā,* in Reports, 22 April 2006). *Vesti Segodnya,* on the other hand, exploited the comment by Jacques Legendre, the French representative of PACE (the Parliamentary Assembly of the Council of Europe), on the necessity for schools not only to teach the state language, but also to develop and preserve the students' native language. The context was a report on the usage of the native language in European schools that also contained information about the situation on minority education reform in Latvia (*Вести сегодня (Vesti Segodnya),* in Reports, 28 April 2006). The Russian Ambassador to Latvia, Victor Kalyuzhniy, also came into the media limelight when meetings were held with the Education Minister Baiba Rivza and the Special Assignments Minister for Social Integration Karina Petersone. Their discussions on the role of ethnic minorities in the development and implementation of the minority education reform and on possible solutions to particular problems were reported to result in a promise by the two officials that a comprehensive report on the results of the reform would be prepared and that the state was planning to organise more Latvian-language courses (*Вести сегодня (Vesti Segodnya), Latvijas Avize,* in Reports, 12 May 2006). In a previous interview with *Čas,* Kalyuzhniy was said to have remarked that intergovernmental relations between the two countries (Latvia and Russia) were affected by expressions of Russophobia, which risked perpetuating the division of society along ethnic lines (*Час (Čas),* in Reports, 19 April 2006). In contrast to pre-reform press coverage, this was now not supplemented by reports and news of Moscow's views on Latvia's newly implemented minority education policy.

5 Widening the perspective: social space, media, challenges

Our analysis of selected newspaper extracts from Latvia's media landscape shows that the interplay of forces surrounding the education reform, while still prevalent, has abated since its implementation in 2004. However, the press remains divided into two, hardly related information spaces, which is likely to perpetuate the existence of diverging views on particular issues in each media group. Furthermore, there are no discussions in newspapers about the role and meaning of education, and about their relations with culture and identity. It has been suggested (Zepa, 2003, p. 93) that these closed information models, which point to the absence of a constructive dialogue, do not facilitate a solution to problems, and hence offer a prototype of a potential future society consisting of two distinct communities.

This lack of a dialogue between the two major communities (ethnic Latvians and Russophones) is reflected in their diverging attitudes towards language and education. It could be argued that the discrepancy exhibited in Latvia between official language policy and actual beliefs, needs and practices within the two language groups may well persist for some time to come. Yet, increasingly, it can be observed that Russophone parents, in trying to adjust themselves to the rules of the dominant ideology, are starting to send their children to mainstream schools (mainly for pragmatic reasons), thus re-evaluating their position within the country's social space through education. Covered by the working of the Bourdieuan habitus, this behaviour may result in internal tension caused by internalised contradictions, both in the guardians and their offspring during their years of formation.

Latvia's divided social space is likely to continue to exist, metaphorically, in its media landscape too. As Bourdieu puts it, in the field of cultural production practitioners are 'holders of the [...] instruments of diffusion' (1998, p. 1). Since journalism is always dependent on external forces (ibid., p. 53), the dominant group(s) will always try to exercise control over what meanings are generally available or privileged. In Latvia's case, the two separate (Latvian- and Russian-medium) press constituencies harbour different principles of vision and division of the social space within the country. In the eyes of the editor-in-chief of the Russian-language newspaper *Čas*, Ksenija Zavgorodska, '[t]he Russian press is more than just a press. It is a political party. Thousands of people in Latvia are deprived of voting rights[7] and the only place where they can express their opinions is Russian newspapers' (*Час (Čas), Вести сегодня (Vesti Segodnya),* in Reports, 22 June 2006). At the time of writing, the newspaper *Čas* printed the opinions of several MPs about the role of the Russian-language press in today's Latvian society. According to this, some believed that the coverage of national events was not sufficient and argued that the Russian-medium press was influenced by Russia's policies. Others, confirming that the Russian-language press writes about the issues that Russians want to read, felt that it played a crucial role in uniting the Russian-speaking community in Latvia (*Час (Čas)*, in Reports, 29 September 2006). These statements attest to the existence of, and ostensibly also need for, divided information spaces for Latvia's newspaper consumers. Different understandings about history amongst the two main social groups still seem to fundamentally affect the diverging orientations of the country's largely split society.

In conclusion, and as has been widely suggested over a considerable span of time (see, for example, *Вести сегодня (Vesti Segodnya)*, in Reports, 23 February 2006; *Телеграф (Telegraf)*, in Reports, 1 June 2004; *Latvijas Avīze*, in Reports, 18 May 2004), the country's integration process (that was promoted under EU membership-accession negotiations) was halted in the runup to the implementation of the minority education reform. Mirroring the renewed social cleavage, Latvia's divided press has echoed opposing attempts to redraw the social space within the country. However, rather than reacting to ongoing events, journalists ought to become willing and able to provide more critical analyses of social, political and cultural issues in order to scaffold the publics.

Notes

1. For more detailed Baltic-wide information the reader is referred to the following literature: Hogan-Brun (2005a); Hogan-Brun (2005b); Galbreath (2005); Gerner and Hedlund (1993); Hiden and Salmon (1991).
2. The full text of Latvia's Education Law can be retrieved from: www.minelres.lv/NationalLegislation/Latvia/Latvia_Education_excerpts_English.htm
3. For more information on curricular details of the 2004 education reform in Latvia see Hogan-Brun (2006, pp. 322ff). The socio-political context of this reform was treated in Adrey (2005), and in Galbreath and Galvin (2005). Aija Priedīte, the former Director of the National Program for Latvian Language Teaching (NPLLT; available online at www.lvavp.lv), provides insights into issues surrounding the education reform from an insider's perspective in her analysis of language attitudes and practices in Latvia (Priedite, 2005).
4. This was extracted 18 months after the implementation of the education reform (covering the period between 6 January and 3 October 2006) from the online version of the 'Integration and Minority Information Service Reports', which is produced by the Latvian Centre for Human Rights and Ethnic Studies. These reports are compiled from three Latvian-medium newspapers (*Diena, Neatkarīgā, Latvijas Avīze*) and three additional Russian-medium newspapers (*Телеграф: Telegraf; Вести сегодня: Vesti*

Segodnya, Час: Čas), which are all published in Latvia. According to the World Wide Media Guide, neither the content, politics nor credibility of any of these newspapers have been rated yet (*see* www.mondotimes.com/1/world/lv).

5. For Human Rights in United Latvia (FHRUL) is a left-wing alliance of several political parties in Latvia and was established in 1998. Co-directed by Tatjana Ždanoka and Jakovs Pliners, and emphasising issues important to the Russian community, it is supported mainly by ethnic Russians and other non-Latvian minorities. It promotes the introduction of Russian as a second official language in Latvia, wants stronger ties with Russia and requests the granting of Latvian citizenship to all residents of Latvia.
6. According to current figures provided by the Latvian Institute (www.li.lv/en/?id=75), the Roma community amounts to about 0.5 per cent of the overall population. The same percentage is also given for resident Jewish people.
7. So-called non-citizens in Latvia do not have the right to vote in municipal and state elections. In 2006, approximately 18 per cent of the total population (slightly less than half of ethnically non-Latvian population) had no Latvian citizenship. For more information on the conferral of citizenship and on the status of non-citizens in Latvia see Hogan-Brun et al. (2007, pp. 542ff).

Online sources

Education Law of the Republic of Latvia. Retrieved: 24 July 2008, from www.minelres.lv/NationalLegislation/Latvia/Latvia_Education_excerpts_English.htm

Integration and Minority Information Service Reports, Latvian Centre for Human Rights and Ethnic Studies (eds). Retrieved: 4 October 2006, from www.humanrights.org.lv/html/about/us.html (Here referred to as Reports).

Ministry of Education and Science. Retrieved: 8 June 2004, from www.izm.lv:8080/en/default.htm

Ministry of Foreign Affairs of the Republic of Latvia. Retrieved: 22 July 2008, from www.am.gov.lv/en/policy/4641/4642/4643/

National Program for Latvian Language Teaching (NPLLT). Retrieved 22 July 2008 from www.lvavp.lv

The Latvian Institute. Retrieved: 1 October 2006, from: www.li.lv/en/?id=75

The Worldwide Media Guide. Retrieved: 22 July 2008, from www.mondotimes.com/1/world/lv

Newspapers

Час (Čas). Retrievable from www.chas-daily.com/win/2004/09/28/index.html?

Diena. Retrievable from www.diena.lv/

Latvijas Avīze. Retrievable from www.latvijasavize.lv/

Neatkarīgā. Retrievable from www.nra.lv/

Правда (*www.Prawda*). Retrievable from
www.mywebsearch.com/jsp/GGmain.jsp?PG=SEAS&SEC=DNS&ptnrS=ZSzeb012&st=dns&searchfor=www.prawda.newmail.ru
Телеграф (Telegraf). Retrievable from http://rus.delfi.lv/news/press/telegraf/
Вести сегодня (*Vesti Segodnya*). Retrievable from http://rus.delfi.lv/news/daily/vesti/

4
The (Re)construction of Refugees in Slovenian Media[1]

Igor Ž. Žagar

1 Introduction: refugees and/or 'illegal migrants'

When in the beginning of 1992 war broke out in Bosnia-Herzegovina, 'the refugee tide (...) overwhelmed our moral obligations as well as the capabilities of an economically exhausted Slovenia' (*Delo,* 28 April 1992).[2] Even renowned intellectuals with leftist political orientations cautioned that Bosnian refugees made us face 'the choice between humanitarianism and accountability to our own country (so that we do not end up as a "dumping-ground for the leftovers of ethnic cleansing")' (*Delo,* 30 March 1993). The refugees from Bosnia-Herzegovina were reportedly 'causing more and more disturbances', they 'disrupted the routines and customs of the local population', 'increased tensions between nations', and were 'potential criminal offenders'. Not to mention the fact that their health was 'already seriously undermined', so that we could not rule out the 'outbreak of smaller-scale epidemics', and that their 'civilizational and cultural level and behavioural patterns were different'.

For the Slovenian reader at the beginning of the new millennium (1999–2001), these labels must have looked as if they were taken from the morning newspaper. And yet, all of them date from the time when Marjeta Doupona Horvat, Jef Verschueren and I were preparing the first draft of *The Rhetoric of Refugee Policies in Slovenia* some 15 years ago.[3] Our conclusion at that time was that the refugee question was successfully defined as a 'problem' (both in terms of numbers and in terms of a threat to the public order) (Doupona, Verschueren and Žagar, 1997, p. 214). In other words, *a crisis was constructed* in such a way that the deviation from certain principles passed easily as exceptional measures which did not in themselves break a more fundamental, and supposedly stable, system. The refugee population was subject to *other-categorisation* as a group of people hardly worthy of the kind attention given to them by the generous people of Slovenia. Thus refugees were blamed for not working, while being forbidden to work. Segregated education was instituted and abandoned at will. And refugees were said to be completely free, while their every movement was being regulated.

In the present chapter, I would like to re-examine and re-interpret some of these ten-year-old claims and conclusions in light of the latest 'refugee crisis' that culminated in the years from 1999 to 2001. This time the 'problem' was not the Bosnian refugees, who chose Slovenia as their final destination, but refugees from the former Soviet Union, Asia, the Middle East and Africa, mostly seeking refuge and asylum in the West, and therefore using Slovenia mostly as a transit state.

This paper situates itself within the long tradition of studies on racism and xenophobia in general. More particularly, it aligns itself with studies investigating the role of discourse in the reproduction of racism and xenophobia, as well as those investigating racism and xenophobia in the media (for different approaches see Reisigl and Wodak, 2001; van Dijk and Wodak, 2000; Weiss and Wodak, 2003; van Dijk, 1984, 1987, 1991, 1993; Blommaert and Verschueren, 1994, 1998; Blommaert, 2005; Taguieff, 2001).

The basic methodology used throughout this paper will be pragmatic analysis. Pragmatic in this context should be understood in its widest interdisciplinary sense as a functional (that is, cognitive, social, and cultural) perspective on language and communication (Verschueren, 1999), and more specifically, a critical discourse analysis (among others see Fairclough, 1992, 1995; Wodak and Meyer, 2001; Weiss and Wodak, 2003). I concentrate particularly on the analysis of implicit meaning (see also Grice, 1989; Blommaert, 2005) and agent analysis (van Leeuwen, 1996), with particular attention being paid to the (criteria of) use of passive and active constructions, singular and plural, and grammatical person(s).

The aim of such an approach is to show how the identity of 'old' and 'new' refugees was constructed and reconstructed in the Slovenian media, and to uncover some of the implicit mechanisms (and techniques) behind these constructions. The second part of the paper focuses on the specific mode of representing immigrants,[4] the mode I call 'racism in velvet gloves', which is absent from the presentations of Bosnian refugees. But before I go into more (analytical) detail, let me briefly outline some of the basic elements of the criminalisation and creation of otherness[5] as it was formed and practised within the

Slovenian context from a more philosophical and sociological perspective.

In contrast to the case of Bosnian refugees (see below, as well as Doupona, Verschueren and Žagar, 1997), the Slovenian public sphere's reaction to the 'new wave' of refugees would suggest the development of some new aspects and dimensions to the process of criminalisation and other-categorisation of immigrants that were not present in the years before 1999–2001. In terms of criminalisation, in these years it consisted of three elements. First, the immigrants were represented as potential criminal offenders, similar to the case of Bosnian refugees. Second, the representation of these immigrants created the impression that they had a non-legal or even criminal position by persistently referring to them as 'illegal migrants' or 'illegals' (see sections 5 and 6 below). A third element, however, was added – which served as a sort of justification for the first two elements – that represented immigrants as violators of the asylum procedure (requesting asylum while intending to continue their journey further to the West). The second and the third elements were new (in relation to the Bosnian refugees), so the process of criminalisation became more complex, but at the same time more explicit as well. This third element, which also served as justification for the first two, proved to be quite a useful 'tool' for the authorities and the media, justifying the deportation of immigrants and a more strict asylum policy. Namely, it is not unusual for (criminal) offenders who are not citizens of the country in which they have committed an offence to be deported from the country. In this regard the deportation may give the appearance of something that is legally correct and justified, and therefore reasonable and acceptable in public opinion. In this case, the Other is represented as dangerous and threatening and therefore is excluded. As Rancire notes (2005, p. 137), the adjective 'illegal' connects

> the figure of a foreigner to the figure of an offender. Thus, the exclusion of immigrants is easily represented as completely natural, on solid legal grounds, and without any explicit trace of xenophobia.

In the sections that follow we will examine how these rather abstract categories were realised in practice, first in 1992–3,[6] and then in the years from 1999 to 2001. But before we proceed, it may be necessary to explain why I link the process of other-categorisation and xenophobia to the (post-socialist) processes of transition and transformation.

When we speak about ex-socialist countries, Yugoslavia is a very special case, incomparable to others. Not only because it tried to develop its own way of socialism, named *samoupravljanje* (self-management), but also because it was a state consisting of six smaller states called 'socialist republics': Slovenia, Croatia, Bosnia and Herzegovina, Serbia, Montenegro and Macedonia. These six socialist republics, which were allowed relative political autonomy, were very different as far as their history, language, religion and ethnic identity (let alone economic development) were concerned. Let me sketch the background of what used to be Yugoslavia (a theoretically and politically rather tricky business in such a limited context).

In six (socialist) republics, there were six official nationalities (with numerous minorities), four official languages, and three major religions. While Slovenia was ethnically rather homogeneous, Croatia had a large Serbian minority, and Bosnia and Herzegovina consisted of three (officially) equal nationalities: Serbs, Croats and Muslims. Serbia, on the other hand, also comprised two 'autonomous regions': Vojvodina (with more than 20 ethnic groups) and Kosovo (where the majority of population was Albanian). The official language in Slovenia was Slovenian with Catholicism as predominant religion. The official language in Croatia was Serbo-Croatian, a language 'created' after the Second World War from Croatian and Serbian, two Slavic languages very similar in structure. Nevertheless, Croatians, who are mainly Catholic, would refer to their language as Croatian, while Serbs, who are mainly Orthodox, would refer to their language as Serbian. With Bosnia and Herzegovina things became really complicated: the official language was still Serbo-Croatian, while there were three nationalities (Serbian, Croatian and Muslim), and three religions (Orthodox, Catholic and Muslim). All these differences (I'll leave complex cases of Serbia (with Kosovo), Montenegro and Macedonia aside) were kept together with the help of the Yugoslav constitution, and the topos of *bratstvo i jedinstvo* (brotherhood and unitedness) – promoted by the President, Josip Broz-Tito – permeating every pore of the social(list) life. After President Tito's death in 1980, the (mostly nationalistic) tensions began to grow rapidly: between Serbs and Croatians in Croatia, between Serbs, Croatians and Muslims in Bosnia and Herzegovina, and in Serbia, between Serbs and Kosovo Albanians on the one side, and between Serbs and the population of Vojvodina on the other. Slovenia was the first one to secede from Yugoslavia in 1991 though it didn't take part in any of the abovementioned nationalistic tensions: Slovenia didn't have its own Other; its Other was the rest of Yugoslavia. Until today (the end of February 2008), the process of disintegration resulted in seven new countries (Slovenia, Croatia, Bosnia and Herzegovina, Serbia, Montenegro, Kosovo, Macedonia) in which seven (supposedly different) languages are spoken (Slovenian, Croatian, Bosnian, Serbian, Montenegrin, Albanian, Macedonian). From all that we could conclude, in the case of former Yugoslavia the main current of transition wasn't an economic, but a national(istic) one. In other words: the transition took the form of battle for the nation state first, while the economy was left waiting.

2 Bosnian refugees as 'temporary refugees'[7]

When Croatia and Slovenia seceded from the former state of Yugoslavia in 1991, a war broke out. Although in Slovenia this war only lasted for about ten days, one of the immediate consequences was the considerable flow of refugees from former Yugoslav republics. At first there were Croatian refugees in the summer of 1991, but they stayed in Slovenia for a relatively short time. When Bosnian refugees started to arrive in April 1992, much more public attention was focused on them. Many of them stayed in Slovenia for several years because of the protracted state of war, and in mid-1996 there were still 11,780 Bosnian refugees in Slovenia. Let us examine the reaction of the Slovenian public to this influx of Bosnian refugees and how this reaction was rhetorically legitimated.

Quite surprisingly for a newly independent state, one yearning for democracy and human rights, a hierarchy of values was quite quickly introduced. *The newly independent country's responsibilities towards its own citizens were valued more highly than its responsibility to 'others'.* This attitude can even be found in the discourse of Mirko Jelenic, secretary-general of the Red Cross of Slovenia at that time:

> I think that we have already exceeded this limit and it is a high time somebody helped us. At any rate I think that it would not be a catastrophe if Slovenia closed its borders. We are a sovereign country and every government makes use of this measure to protect its own citizens (*Slovenec*, 29 April 1992).

Instead of according the highest ranking to its concern for people in need, the secretary-general of the Slovenian Red Cross focuses on the right of a sovereign state to close its borders in view of its duty to 'protect' its own citizens. Such an attitude clearly shows that the perspective of the Slovenian state is taken here rather than the perspective of the refugees or of an organisation designed to help them.

It therefore should not surprise us that leading politicians and even intellectuals held similar opinions. During a seminar held in Trieste in March 1993, Dr Lev Kreft, a member of parliament for the Party for Democratic Reconstruction (later the United List of Social Democrats, and now Social Democrats), declared:

> 'We are faced with the choice between humanitarianism and responsibility to our own country, so that we do not end up as the "dumping ground for the leftovers of ethnic cleansing",' deliberated Dr Lev Kreft, the vice-president of the National Assembly, as he called attention to the dilemma we are faced with: 'shall we be the first country to become placed safely and snugly within the fortified walls of developed Europe, or an unstable military frontier and a sanitary cordon just outside the fortified walls of Europe' (*Delo*, 30 March 1993).

3 'Tides' and 'waves' of refugees

A common feature of the representation of 'temporary refugees' (in 1992–3) and of 'illegal migrants' (in 1999–2001) in Slovenian media is the metaphor of a natural disaster. *Delo*, on 28 April 1992, reported:

> ... the *tide* of refugees that has already *swamped* our *moral obligations* and the capacities of a Slovenia which is already economically exhausted, now calls for new measures despite the infinite readiness [of Slovenia] to do everything within its capacities (emphasis added).

What we see here is the construction of a metaphor. The word choices *val* (tide) and *preplaviti* (to swamp) are combined with the past tense *je preplavil* (swamped) and a temporal adverb *ze* (already), creating the image of an uncontrollable natural force that can hardly be tamed by human efforts. The 'moral obligations' have all been fulfilled and all the 'capabilities' have been spent. The conclusion thus becomes obvious: there is nothing more that an 'economically exhausted' Slovenia can do.

Curiously enough, when speaking about the number of Bosnian refugees, the media – with very few exceptions – simply adopted the state's point of view, as in the following quotation:

> We can accept 15,000 refugees at the most and the government has been calling attention to this problem for some time now. The number of refugees is already almost as much again (*Slovenec,* 30 April 1992).

It is more than evident that this delimitation is foregrounded as an independently established 'fact' and not revealed as an embedded element in what the government is 'calling attention to'. This could be interpreted as a strong process of identification with the nation and the national, on the part of the journalists, under circumstances that were perceived as a threat (or a 'threat') from the outside. We were witnessing, as will be shown, the same process eight years later with the so-called 'illegal migrants'.

4 Refugees as criminals

The refugee waves, which were flooding the country, also underwent a process of abnormalisation and criminalisation. Let us have a look at the following quotation from *Vecer*:

> As a matter of fact, these refugees *cause more and more disorder, disturb the customs* of the town and certain educational and sports establishments – in short, they are causing *increased tension between nations* in Jesenice, which, given the number of inhabitants from former Yugoslav republics, could grow in scope. It is true that the fears of inhabitants lack an entirely rational explanation, as the refugee center has never housed any other refugees. However, it is also true that in Jesenice the *number of conflicts related to nationality issues* is increasing, while *bomb threats* are becoming a reality. Last week unknown individuals destroyed Cedo bar and a nearby shop; *violence* in the town is on the increase and it is high time minister Bavcar and the Office for Refugees began considering how to establish control over *those refugees* hosted by [local] families. Before it is too late (*Vecer,* 4 November 1992, emphasis added).

The mere presence of foreigners in the above passage is described as abnormal and problematic. And the step from abnormalisation to criminalisation is achieved by means of anaphoric reference (see the emphases) which silently establishes referential identification between the 'refugees' and the 'unknown individuals' who destroyed a bar and a store. And, by an even more far-fetched extension, between the refugees and the even lesser known human agents behind 'threatening with bombs'.

If Bosnian refugees were not represented as potential criminal offenders (a description that potentially applies to every human being), a simple feeling that they are somehow 'different' was often taken as sufficient argument for segregation. What follows is an extract from a letter written to the Ministry of Education and Sports by parents from a school where Bosnian children had classes (in the afternoons) as well as Slovene children (in the mornings):

> ...The children [refugee children] might have had a medical check, but *it is known* that the check was not in accordance with Slovene standards and with the check undergone by our children. As long as we do not have the results of the check confirming that their health is 'OK', the same as the health of their teachers, we do not intend to start any serious discussion about these possibilities. *We know* what the state of the health of refugees unfortunately is.
>
> ...The quality of the facilities and teaching aids in our school is not as good as those in other schools in the area. Is this the reason why you want to cram refugees into our buildings? Because it will not do any more damage to our school? Therefore, you are aware that their *level of civilisation* and *culture* and *behavioural patterns* are different. We do not allow our children to be under the same roof as refugee children if they can be separated, as they are in other places (*Dnevnik,* 4 November 1992, emphasis added).

It is worth noting how the supposedly poor medical condition of the refugee children is 'described' exclusively in terms such as 'it is known', and 'we know', without a single concrete reference. The only argument (or 'argument', to be more precise), substantiating claims about the bad medical condition of the refugee children is the reference to their different 'level of civilisation', 'culture' and 'behavioural patterns'. But then again, these references are completely underspecified and taken for granted.

5 From 'temporary refugees' to 'illegal migrants'[8]

Around 1999, Slovenia was confronted with a new 'wave' of refugees, this time mostly from the East, the Middle East, Asia and some parts of

Africa. Curiously enough, the expression 'temporary refugees' was not used this time. Instead, the media spoke about *illegal migrants, illegals, immigrants, emigrants, asylum seekers, aliens,* or the peculiar Slovenian category *prebezniki*[9] that exerted 'pressure on our borders' in 1999, 2000 and 2001. And this 'extraordinary strain' on Slovenia's borders was also accompanied by an interesting transformation and recasting of the historical account: Bosnian refugees, whom eight years ago the media and state institutions described in the disqualifying terms quoted above, suddenly turned into 'our people'. Of course they are 'ours', the argument went, 'after all we used to be citizens of the same country'. However, just eight years before the media had claimed that 'even though' Bosnians and Slovenians had lived in the same country, Slovenians were not obliged to accept them. In 1999 refugees suddenly became so much 'ours' that the media virtually never used the term 'refugees' for so-called 'illegal migrants' in Slovenia, regardless of the fact that the use of the term 'refugee(s)' would be in perfect accordance with the Geneva Convention (adopted in 1951) and the New York Protocol (adopted in 1967). Between 1999 and 2001, when Slovenia was used mostly as a transit state for refugees from Romania, Iraq, Iran, Turkey, the Federal Republic of Yugoslavia, Macedonia, China, and some parts of Africa, only Bosnian refugees deserved to be called refugees, that is, only those who *fled from* the war in Bosnia-Herzegovina.[10] All the others were simply 'illegal migrants' (or even less).

In this second part of the chapter, I will first try to shed some light on the expressions the Slovenian media (and the Slovenian public in general) used in connection with the newly arrived refugees. Then (concentrating on an article published in the main Slovenian daily *Delo*), I will try to show how xenophobia did not necessarily need to use the vocabulary that was employed in connection with Bosnian refugees eight years previously, but could proceed in a much more subtle way.

6 Illegals, foreigners, and other 'four-letter words'

For the Slovenian public at the turn of the millennium, *refugee* is obviously not just a legal term – above all it is loaded with emotions. Therefore, it cannot be applied to just everybody, particularly not to the unknown, uninvited arrivals with 'vacant gazes' and 'unknown intentions' who sneak into the country on all fours, covered in mud and dirt. These people can only be *prebezniki*, people who fled to Slovenia for unknown reasons and intend(ed) to continue their journey towards the most frequent destination, the West.

The word *prebeznik* is derived from the verb *prebezati,* meaning *to arrive to another place by fleeing.* In contrast to *bezati,* where the usual implication is to *run away from danger* (see note 5), *prebezati* does not imply any specific cause for fleeing. Moreover, it is commonly used in the sense *to desert/deserter* as well. Also, it should be distinguished from the term *pribeznik.* While a *pribeznik* flees to a certain place (usually seeking refuge), a *prebeznik* just flees (over some territory), with no explicit destination in mind. *Prebezniki* thus became a label for the category of people who found themselves on Slovenian territory almost accidentally, by mistake one could say, and who violated Slovenian laws because they crossed the border illegally. The Slovenian public obviously did not want to see that *prebezniki,* the same as refugees, *flee from* something, seeking refuge. This assumption is (additionally) confirmed by the fact that out of several terms available, the media and, consequently, the Slovenian public, chose the one that placed stress primarily on chance, instability, precariousness and the shortness of their stay in Slovenia. The semantically very similar term *pribezniki* did not meet with wide acceptance precisely because it too explicitly implies that one has arrived at the final destination and intends to stay there. The essential difference between the two terms stems from the prefixes *pre-* and *pri-* when combined with the verb *bezati*: while the former suggests chance, instability and shortness, the latter draws attention to intention, permanence and duration.

Nevertheless, the term *prebezniki* retains at least a minimal reference to the destiny and situation of those people who mostly fled from a politically or economically uncertain future in their home country. By contrast, *ilegalci* (illegals), a term often used by Slovenian media[11] when referring to 'illegal migrants', openly classifies them as criminals. This classification is done in two steps.

First, as already mentioned, 'illegal migrants' was the 'official' expression used by Slovenian authorities. Note that they did not use the expressions *immigrants* or *emigrants,* expressions that (implicitly) refer to the status of the person who is migrating. Instead, they used the expression that puts emphasis on the *process of migration.* Since Slovenia usually was not their final destination (at least not initially), such a choice of words may seem quite appropriate and acceptable. But then who can decide whether a certain migration is legal or illegal, when and on what grounds? Crossing a border without valid documents may indeed be illegal, but that has nothing to do with the act or process of migrating as such. If a person wants to leave her/his country, she/he does not need any approval from the authorities. That is simply one of her/his (human) rights.

Second, 'illegal migrants' are shortened to 'illegals' (quite a usual procedure in the everyday use of language). But, *illegals* are primarily people who have committed some illegal or unlawful act, that is, people who have violated laws in some way. And the term *illegal* in no way alludes to the fact that such a person seeks refuge and is fleeing from some kind of danger. A person (or institution[12]) who (that) sees these people as 'illegals' only sees them as violating laws and therefore eliciting corresponding treatment, which usually implies the use of repressive methods and special means.

It is somewhat surprising that among the widely accepted terms used for the people who illegally crossed the (Slovenian) border was the term *tujci* (foreigners).[13] Of course they are 'foreigners', as much as anybody else is who crosses the border legally with a valid non-Slovenian passport. Foreigners – a legal category – always existed and they always will. And foreigners are both: people possessing a valid passport and those without it. If such a general and (supposedly) neutral term suddenly starts to be applied to people who illegally cross Slovenia's borders, then it must indicate some basic uneasiness and ambivalence in the attitude of Slovenians toward foreigners in general. As long as they arrive in Slovenia with valid passports in their pockets they are acceptable and Slovenian public opinion proudly speaks of 'traditional Slovenian hospitality'. But as soon as they 'sneak' into Slovenia, scrambling through some muddy ravine in an attempt to reach the West, this traditional hospitality shows its other face, *intolerance and dislike.* The more technical term for this type of attitude is *xenophobia.* Of course, Slovenians try to avoid this term, as I have already pointed out in connection with the term *refugee.* Some words may carry a lot of weight, and this weight may occasionally be just too heavy.

7 Removing foreigners

Apart from a (sometimes unbearable) weight, words also have their own history and meaning, independent of the history and meaning *we* are willing to ascribe to them. Around the year 2000 the Republic of Slovenia, supposedly a social state, governed by the rule of law, and a state that signed international conventions on the protection of human rights and refugees, established the 'Centre for the Removal of Foreigners'.[14] For those who find such a choice of words completely natural, let me point to a few things. This term is most often used when we (try to) remove insects, filth, litter or garbage, stains, heaps of snow, peels, pipes, stalks, tumours or some other malfunctioning or useless body parts (if we can not cure them, that is). In short, not only do we remove things that are redundant or getting in our way, we also want to get rid of them once and for all. Societies that consider themselves 'civilised', or at least want to be seen as such, usually do not remove people. To talk about such things is done in bad taste and has even become kind of unfashionable – at least since the end of the Second World War – to name a couple of reasons (in case nothing more essential or rational comes to your mind). No doubt many criminal organisations deal in the removal of people, but governments, at least most of them, do not belong to this type of organisation (or at least they (say they) do not want to). Unwanted foreigners are usually *deported*, a (legal) term that is widely in use, implying a forced departure from a country. They could also be *returned* or *turned back*; however, *removal* suggests (implies) that the most likely places they could be found after such an act are in dustbins, sewers and chimneys.

Slovenia, obviously, does not remove unwanted foreigners in such an absolute and total way. And, of course, it *was* probably just the choice of words that *was* slightly awkward and clumsy. But this is *precisely what I would like to emphasise*: when government officials come into positions to take the word(ly) equilibristic as something natural, as something that is not only their job, but rather something that they are – so they believe – called to do, the *basic meanings of words* become dependent only on their goodwill. Apart from that (their goodwill), there can only be slips of the tongue, misunderstandings and malevolent imputations. Yet, if we give in just another fraction, and allow that the Centre for the Removal of Foreigners *was* only clumsiness or misunderstanding – does not this 'clumsy' choice of words say more about what its author had in mind and actually wanted to say? Do not such 'misunderstandings' (at least) hint at how the 'problem' was in fact understood?

8 Refugees as waste

Such examples of the inappropriate use of words might, of course, be just 'misunderstandings'. However, I am afraid that the 'removal of foreigners', at least in this case, does not point to any clumsiness or misunderstanding but to an increasingly global, indisputable and profound conviction that, after all, we are not all equal. The evidence that corroborates this claim of inequality comes from a seemingly completely different sphere of activity. In the search for ways in which to use the fats that are a by-product of processing the waste parts of potentially 'mad' cows into bone meal, there was a serious proposal to use them to make soap for less developed countries. And this proposal was advanced in Slovenia. Very innovative, one could say, and in perfect accordance with the EU mentality that inspired some countries to quite openly suggest that BSE-infected beef should be exported to countries struck by famine. This plan could also produce some beneficial demographic effects (if I am permitted to express some bitter sarcasm here).

Obviously, there is still (and all the more) a deep gap between 'us' and 'them'. And the only place we can analyse how 'we' see 'them' is in speech, language, tongue. However, we have to be careful as well. A tongue is a sly and tricky thing. It is always there for us to do with as we wish, neglected and squashed in its teeth-chamber, stretched and strained, used to negate and to deny or, when urged to, kept tightly shut in the mouth. And despite all of this flexibility, despite the mighty elasticity, stretchable all the way to the stiffness of the ineffable, the tongue keeps its pockets of meaning, a kind of palimpsest field that enables us to dissect and analyse each and every kind of speech – be it sophisticated academic diction or vagrant babbling and gibbering.

9 Xenophobia as 'simple reflexes'

And this is exactly what I will try to show in these last sections of this chapter. I will concentrate on one text from the column of Dr Alojz Ihan in the Saturday supplement of the national daily newspaper *Delo* (10 February 2001, p. 32). The column, titled *(Ob)vladamo* (which could be translated as '(Put) under control' or 'We manage') is dedicated to 'illegal migrants', and is an exemplary case of how this 'problem' can be treated differently – namely, between the lines, without using any explicit discriminatory expressions.

In the first part of his text, Dr Ihan claims (among other things) that the right place for the introduction of a 'cosmopolitan atmosphere and racial tolerance' is in the city. 'In a city,' he continues,

> a variety of nations and cultures *even* feels relaxing but in a village it is different. When you meet someone in a village, you should greet him, look into his eyes and know him, or else it becomes awkward – *some ancient defence mechanism activates within the individual. I do believe that kind rustic women burst into tears when they see a chocolate-coloured African in the fields. But I do not believe we are talking xenophobia here, just simple reflexes* (emphasis added).

Since I am a philosopher, allow me to be somehow naïve and wonder (as philosophy is allowed to – and even must – do) about certain things Dr Ihan has written. Namely, I really wonder why kind rustic women should burst into tears when they see a 'chocolate-coloured African' in the fields? They may be surprised or dazzled when they suddenly see a black person where mostly white people live, but why should they burst into tears? What happened, after all, was that they had seen a person of a different colour, nothing more. And that person (according to Dr Ihan's dramatisation) did not do anything to them – did not threaten them, attack them or hurt them. That person was just there, that is all.

10 Linguistic construction *ex nihilo*

But, was he or she really 'there'? Nobody – be it the media or *vox populi* – has ever reported a crying rustic women gazing at 'chocolate-coloured Africans' wading the furrows. However, Dr Ihan used various linguistic (and argumentative) means to make his entirely hypothetical and made-up story sound intriguing, believable and convincing:

1. Instead of, '*if* they see…in the fields', which would be clearly hypothetical, within the register of probable, and not (yet) accomplished, he writes, '*when* they see…in the fields', clearly implying that he is writing about something that had happened or happens all the time, on regular basis, or at least often;
2. He uses the plural, 'kind rustic *women*', instead of singular, 'a kind rustic *woman*', as if there had been more similar cases;
3. Last but not least his narration begins with 'I do believe', and continues, '*I do believe* that kind rustic women burst into tears when they see a chocolate-coloured African in the fields'.

But, what exactly do we believe when we say 'I do believe…'? Usually something not proven beyond any doubt, something we have heard about, and think that it could or should be true. If we could prove or demonstrate what we claim to believe, if we saw it or heard it ourselves, we would not only *believe* it, but *know* it instead.

The yarn about the wailing rustic women staring at the black gent in the fields is therefore put before the reader as a fact (already) overheard by the author, as a piece of hearsay widely talked about. The use of plural (rustic women…), and the particular choice of time and tense (when...) make the story even more credible. Yet, that is not all. The real beauty of 'I believe that...' lies in its mitigating role: when somebody says that he/she *believes* something, it only means that he/she *thinks* that something could be true, but by no means is the *claim made* that he/she *knows* it really is so. Which is a handy and cosy rhetorical strategy as the speaker can easily renounce his standpoint, if necessary.

The question remains, however; why does Dr Ihan *believe* that kind rustic women weep at the sight of 'chocolate-coloured Africans'? Because of 'simple reflexes', says he, not xenophobia. What kind of 'simple reflexes' he had in mind, he did not bother to explain. Which is unusual, because:

1. Those reflexes are supposed to be 'simple'; and therefore,
2. easily explicable, especially when the person talking about 'simple reflexes' holds a doctorate in medicine (as Dr Ihan does).

That is, if we are in fact speaking about reflexes at all. It is much more likely that we are dealing with a special 'argumentative' technique, made up for the (common) folks, where we put forward a conclusion and hope that our listener will not bother to ask for the argument, given that no such argument actually exists. Or does there?

11 Xenophobia as 'ancient defence mechanisms'

At the beginning of the quoted fragment Dr Ihan claims that there are differences between a city and a village. 'When you meet someone in a village, you should greet him, look into his eyes and know him, or else it becomes awkward – some ancient defence mechanisms activates within the individual,' he claims. Yet, if it is so that when you meet someone in a village, you should greet him and look him in the eyes, why did Dr Ihan's rustic women not do that? Why did they not look the 'chocolate-coloured Africans' they found in the fields in the eyes and greet them? Why did they burst into tears instead? Could it be that the order of events in Dr Ihan's description of human relations in the country is in fact *the opposite of what he wants his readers to believe*: that you should *first* know someone, and *then* greet him/her (and look him/her in the eyes)? And, if you do not know that person, you simply do not greet him/her. And, on top of everything, if that person's skin is of a different colour from your own, you even start crying.

But then, if it is so, there is absolutely no difference between Dr Ihan's village and Dr Ihan's city, where we usually only greet people we know (only that we do not cry as much when we see 'chocolate-coloured Africans', 'lemony Japanese' and 'ruby-red Indians'...). That, of course, thwarts his main distinction between a village and a city – the distinction on which he founded his whole heartbreaking tale, featuring tearful rustic women and strangely coloured aliens creeping all over Slovenian soil.

12 Construction of normality

Let us sum up: Dr Ihan *postulated* a distinction between a city and a village to point out how human relations in the city are different from those in the village. Fear, distrust and tears are the elementary features of the village locals when encountering an alien. The distinction set by Dr Ihan, in his words and with his arguments, *proved non-existent and groundless* in the end – following his own line of argument, his own setting and his own dramatisation.

All that we are left with in the end is a bad taste in the mouth and an unpleasant feeling that Dr Ihan's writing is no more but a 'simple reflex', nicely wrapped into harmonious sweet-talk that one can consume with their Saturday-morning coffee and a hot croissant. And that is exactly how xenophobia is generated and maintained: not with loud manifestations and militant slogans, but with soft words, *describing* an image of normality. Only that the image in question is really being *constructed,* not described.

13 Conclusion

There were three major findings during the course of this paper. First, both 'refugee crises' – the one from 1992 to 1993 as well as the one from 1999 to 2001 – have a common background: they are described in terms of natural forces ('waves', 'tide'), even natural disasters ('floods'), as something people can hardly control. Second, natural disasters and threatening natural forces are ideal grounds for reinforcing the disparity within the Self–Other relation (see Section 1), and, consequentially, possible other-categorisation and criminalisation. Again, both these strategies were at work in both 'refugee crises'. Third (and this element only appeared in the 1999–2001 'refugee crisis'), once the belief in uncontrollable natural forces (quite naturally and spontaneously) had been established, which in turn gave rise to other-categorisation and criminalisation, nothing more was needed to facilitate the maintenance of this belief than simple *narrative*. This narrative came mostly in the form of reports or recounting of past events using neutral, simple, everyday grammatical features as their building blocks. What has been shown in this paper, particularly in the second section, is that grammatical features are in no way neutral and simple; that appropriate (mis) use of conjunctions, tenses and grammatical numbers can turn something fictional and hypothetical into real and experienced (Section 10). And that with the appropriate (mis)use of prefixes (lexical/discursive) and aspectual elements (especially in Slavic languages that have very ramified morphology), we can impute intentions to people (even groups of people) we do not know and we have never met (Section 6).

Notes

1. I would like to thank Michal Krzyżanowski and Aleksandra Galasińska for their valuable comments on an earlier version of this chapter, as well as Sabina Autor for her help with some of the technical aspects of it.
2. The Slovenian newspapers quoted in this chapter are: *Delo* (*Labor*), *Dnevnik* (*Daily*), *Vecer* (*Evening*), and *Slovenec* (*Slovenian*).
3. For more detailed information, see Doupona, Verschueren and Žagar (1997).
4. For discussion on immigrants and related topics, see: Mezzadra (2004a, 2004b), Brysk and Shafir (2004), Cohen (2006), Pajnik and Zavratnik Zimic (2003), Rundell (2004); for Slovenia and Eastern Europe, see Milohnic (2002) and Pajnik, Lesjak-Tusek and Gregorcic (2001).
5. For discussion of other(ness) and related topics, see: Balibar (2002, 2004), Rancière (2005), Mastnak (1995), Sumic-Riha (2005), Riha (1995), Reisigl and Wodak (2001), Caldas-Coulthard (2003), Reisigl (2003), Wodak, de Cillia, Reisigl and Liebhart (2003).
6. Much more exhaustive analysis of this period can be found in Doupona, Verschueren and Žagar (1997).
7. For the history of the label 'temporary refugees', see Doupona, Verschueren and Žagar (1997, pp. 200–3).
8. See also Žagar (2003).
9. This expression will be explained later in the text.
10. The Slovenian word for a refugee is *begunec*. It is derived from the verb *bezati* (to flee, to run away from danger, escape) which, in turn, is derived from the noun *beg* (flight, escape). In contrast to the English term, it does not place explicit stress on 'seeking refuge'.
11. Two major dailies (out of three), and news programmes of the national TV were systematically scanned from November 2000 to March 2001.
12. Slovenian police are still using the term 'illegals' on their website (www.policija.si/si/).
13. Although the term '(illegal) aliens' is often used in English in similar contexts, the Slovenian 'tujci' is closer to the English 'foreigners'.
14. In Slovenian, *Center za **odstranjevanje** tujcev.*

Newspaper sources

Delo, 28 April 1992, 29 April 1992, 30 March 1993
Dnevnik, 4 November 1992
Slovenec, 29 April 1992, 30 April 1992
Vecer, 4 November 1992

Part II

Transformation(s) of the Public Sphere (II) – Discourses of Politics, Institutions and Economy

5

On the 'Europeanisation' of Identity Constructions in Polish Political Discourse after 1989

Michał Krzyżanowski

1 Europeanisation, discourse and identity

As is frequently suggested, *Europeanisation* 'has gained widespread currency amongst scholars as a newly fashionable term to denote a variety of changes within European politics and international relations' (Featherstone, 2004, p. 3). Perceived in such terms, Europeanisation has been used to describe diverse processes taking place 'when something in the domestic political system is affected by something European' (Vink, 2002, p. 1), or, referring strictly to the Europeanisation caused by the development of the European Union, it has been approached 'as domestic change caused by the European integration' (ibid.).

Particularly within the realm of political science, Europeanisation has been studied widely from the point of view of diverse (national) policy fields which underwent a substantial change in the process of their adjustment to the respective areas of EU policies (see, for example: Mény, Muller and Quermonne, 1996; or Green-Cowles, Caporaso and Risse, 2001). Interestingly, though not as much as in the case of the so-called 'old' member states of the European Union, Europeanisation has also been considered from the point of view of its salience in the 'new' (mostly CEE-located) EU member states, particularly those entering the Union in 2004 (see: Grabbe, 2001; Mungiu-Pippidi, 2006; Weinar, 2006). Within the studies focusing on Europeanisation in the CEE, attention has frequently been directed to the 'adaptational pressures depending on the accession deadline' (Gwiazda, 2002, p. 11) which means that the new EU members had to adjust to EU legislation (seen holistically as the EU *acquis communitaire*) at a much greater pace than was possible in case of the 'old' EU members.

However, while the process of Europeanisation and the resulting 'adjustment' of national practices have been examined from a policy perspective, little attention has been paid to the process of Europeanisation in the sense of adjustment or alignment of discourses at the national level to the extra-national (or European) ones. Accordingly, only selected studies have focused on the problem of the 'Europeanisation of discourse' in diverse national settings. For example, Meyer took on the problem of the Europeanisation of national media discourses in several European countries to show diverse 'adaptations in media coverage which are crucial to the thesis of a gradual Europeanisation of national debates about political issues' (2005, p. 122). In a similar vein, della Porta and Caiani have focused on the Europeanisation of Italian public discourses to assess 'the impact of Europeanisation on national actors by focusing on their public discourse on European issues' (2006, p. 78). However, those and other studies linking discourse and Europeanisation (see also Rosamond, 2000) have approached the level of discourse in a rather superficial manner without taking a look at how the process of Europeanisation of national discourses may influence the change and transformation of discursive patterns of identity constructions in the studied contexts. Additionally, I would claim that the mere 'talking about Europe' analysed in those studies is not what should be considered as *de facto* indicative of Europeanisation.

This study aims to make up for the said deficiencies and propose an examination of the Europeanisation of national political discourses from the point of view of: a) their qualitative aspects; and b) their influence on the (subsequent) constructions of different forms of collective identifications in post-communist or Central and Eastern European contexts/countries. Therefore, Europeanisation is viewed here as a form of *discursive change* (Fairclough, 1992) which has been taking place in the diverse national settings of the CEE countries in the process of adjustment of their national-political cultures and practices (to those known) from the supranational arena of EU politics. Europeanisation is hence seen as a discursive change which results from 'a significant shift in the social functioning of language' (Fairclough, 1992, p. 6) and which, in turn, shows that the diverse practices embedded within the macro-scale, socio-political transformation taking place in the CEE countries prior to their EU accession 'increasingly include attempts to change language practices' (ibid., see also Fairclough, 1996, 2005d). Further, it is also argued that the changing language practices resulting from the Europeanisation of discourse also entail a change to the diverse forms of discursive construction of identities (see Wodak et al., 1999), which, embedded within the discourse changing under the transforming political conditions, have also undergone a substantial modification and became gradually de-nationalised or 'Europeanised' (see also Krzyżanowski, 2003).

In this study, I address a set of discourses embedded within (political) actions leading to Polish EU membership (within the years 1994 to 2004)[1] to show how, on the basis of the same 'object of reference' of Europe/EU, various identities came to be constructed within the Polish public discourses of that period. Thus, this work aims to show how 'the national meaning of Europe' (Malmborg and Stråth, 2002) was changing within Polish politics in the 1990s and early 2000s by oscillating between the historically conditioned visions of Polish 'nationhood' and its newly conceived post-1989 'Europeanness'. This work postulates that, in the multitude of identifications that appeared in Polish politics within the post-communist transition after 1989, a variety of 'shifts' and 'changes' took place to add to the general discursive change which can be considered as *the Europeanisation of Polish political discourse*. One such context-dependent 'shift' – highlighted here empirically – was from Europe being a 'nation-external' object of *national identifications* to becoming the object and point of reference for strictly political and institutional *European identifications*. As we can see from the analyses presented below, on the one hand, Europe is juxtaposed with 'the national' and portrayed as just a 'means' of achieving national goals within discourses produced and received within the national arena (such as the 'programmatic speeches' on Polish foreign policy analysed below). On the other hand, Europe becomes the main 'goal' of political action and the key object of (political) identification in the discourses produced by Polish politicians in relation to their involvement at the supranational level of EU politics (see the analysis of interviews with Polish members of the recent European Convention below). Hence, as is postulated in this study, the meaning of Europe has shifted in Polish post-1989 politics from being a national project in political discourses produced within the Polish national political arena to becoming the supranational/European reality in the discourses produced at the 'European level': differently put, the meaning of Europe shifted from its rather imaginative and neutral meaning (with no *de facto* impact on identity) to something real and integrative (and with clear implications for identity formation). By analysing that shift (as well as several other micro-shifts in discourse), this study deconstructs the ways in which several, very often competing and contradictory, 'national' and 'supranational' identifications were formed in various contexts understood here as different 'sites of production of discourse' (van Dijk, 1985).

2 The discursive construction of identities in the field of politics

The claim that (collective) identities are discursively constructed and are discursive in character is central to this study. Like Stuart Hall, I claim that all identities are 'constructed within, not outside discourse [while] we need to understand them as produced in specific, historical institutional sites within specific discursive formations and practices, by specific enunciative strategies' (Hall, 1996a, p. 4). Identities are hence seen here as 'points of temporary attachment to the subject positions which discursive practices construct (...) they are the result of a successful articulation or 'chaining' of the subject into the flow of discourse' (ibid., p. 6). Furthermore, it is postulated here that the main assumptions behind the idea of 'discursive construction of national identity', elaborated by Wodak et al. (1999), are viable and can be extended onto other-than-national collectivities. In line with Wodak and her collaborators, it is assumed here that identity is a form of socially created discourse (on the macro level) born out of interdiscursive connections of public and private discourses (on the mezzo/micro level). Further, (collective) identity is dynamic and, hence, it is constantly restructured, renewed and reshaped in social and historical processes, and while being a form of a text itself, it can also be reflected in the texts produced by both individuals and groups who are perceived as 'members' and 'representatives' of a particular collectivity.

Secondly, following Brubaker and Cooper, special attention is devoted here to the identity-constitutive processes of *identification* which: a) 'involve identifying oneself (or someone else) *as* someone who fits certain description or belongs to a certain category' (2000, p. 17); or b) 'require identifying oneself *with* another person, category, or collectivity' (ibid.). However, because this study highlights the discursive construction of identities and identifications in various instances of 'political discourse' (see also Rancière, 1995), it raises the question, in line with Brubaker and Cooper, of whether the actual identifications of politicians *with* respective collectivities (be they broadly 'understood' national collectives, or a narrowly understood political collective of supranational, EU-ropean politics) do display personal preferences or can be generalised as 'embodying' some general, collective tendencies. It is argued here that a clear distinction between the individually conditioned and collectively typical (discursively constructed) identifications is immensely difficult to draw. For this reason, this work also endorses the claim that most collective identities are actually 'invented' and 'projected' onto various collectivities by selected individuals in what is commonly defined as 'identity politics' (Calhoun, 1994; Wodak, 2002). In this vein, this study attempts to delineate the ways in which various identifications are discursively formed within the groups who are responsible for the design and implementation of various forms of collective action and self-definition. That group might be defined as 'carriers of identities' (Giesen, 1993; see below) and in the present case includes mainly politicians. The latter are envisaged here as those who carry 'power over discourse' (Wodak, 1996; see also Foucault, 1984 [1970]) whose sometimes very personal and political-opportunistic aspirations and motivations may be transformed and projected onto the large masses of national collectivities.

Groups carrying the power over discursive constructions of identities are defined as *'Trägergruppen'* or 'carriers of identity' (Giesen, 1993)[2] and are viewed here as responsible for the construction of (collective) identities by means of different 'codes' or 'schemata' (ibid.) It is through these codes that the 'carriers' construct collective visions of the social reality in the process of communication with broadly understood masses. Eisenstadt defines these 'codes' as effects of

> a combination of the promulgation and institutionalisation of models of social and cultural order with attempts to control the production and flow of resources [through which] ontological and cosmological premises and conceptions of social order prevalent in any society influence the definition of the major arenas of social interactions and the structures of preferences (1998, pp. 230–2).

Differently put, those who have access to, and power over, determining the codes are also those who influence the shape of the collective identity of a certain collective the most. Like Giesen (1993), this study endorses the view of these codes as disseminated by particular social groups which allows for the social-wide propagation of certain simplified visions of reality and the ways in which the latter can/should be organised. Put differently, social reality cannot be constructed nor 'experienced without codes' (ibid., p. 30) while 'the codes of social classification make up the core of construction of togetherness (*Gemeinschaftlichkeit*) and otherness (*Fremdheit*)' (pp. 30–1).

The key graspable, analytic category which can help securely operationalise the 'codes' is that of 'discursive dimensions' (Weiss, 2002; Wodak and Weiss, 2004). The latter have been proposed as both analytical and interpretative categories in the analysis of recent 'programmatic' speeches of key EU politicians within the so-called 'Future of Europe Debate' (see Krzyżanowski and Oberhuber, 2007; Oberhuber et al., 2005). In the their original sense, discursive dimensions constituted a set of both semantic and rhetorical frames of the discourse of EU politicians and officials which underlay their conceptions of institutional and socio-political order of the supranational reality of the EU.

As it is argued, both codes and discursive dimensions ascribe a fundamental role to social and political 'actors' (Giesen's *Trägergruppen*) who are 'in charge' of the social/political construction, reception and distribution of codes and discursive dimensions. Secondly, both the former and the latter are concepts which are very similar in their character: just like the codes, discursive dimensions mirror certain organisational forms and operate as ideational models of constructing the (institutional and political) reality of Europe/EU. While those models can in fact be perceived as certain codes which co-construct the EU institutional reality, they also possess the 'legitimising' force (quite similar to that ascribed to codes) within which dimensions can be used to justify certain visions of Europe/EU and their implementation 'in action' at the European level. Obviously, since not only 'European' but also 'national' discursive dimensions of identity constructions are analysed in this study, it needs to be mentioned that this work postulates the extension of the concept of discursive dimensions to other than European or supra-national spaces[3] in which they were originally proposed.

3 Empirical data and categories of analysis

The analysis of the Polish post-1989 political discourse about Europe/EU (and of constructions of identifications and socio-political change therein) is performed here on two corpora, which are defined as the *national corpus* and the *European corpus*.

The national corpus comprises a set of 20 parliamentary speeches on 'The Main Directions of Polish Foreign Policy' which were delivered by Polish foreign ministers to the lower chamber of the Polish parliament (*Sejm*) between 1993 and 2004 (two speeches per year leading to Poland's

EU membership).[4] The foreign policy speeches are selected for the analysis in order to examine the constructions of national and supranational identifications within genres typical for the expression of 'national role' and of 'national interests' in the international (including EU-ropean) politics. Delivered by a 'national' politician (government official) to the 'national' parliament, these speeches helped analyse how the role of Europe/EU changed in discourse and became a dynamic point of reference for the construction of national identifications through various elements/references typical for the discursive construction of national identity (such as, for example, references to 'national uniqueness', 'national mission', 'national role', and so on).

On the other hand, the European corpus consists of four, semi-structured interviews (duration of 30 to 120 minutes) with Polish members of the European Convention working between February 2002 and July 2003 under the official name of the 'Convention on the Future of the European Union'.[5] The interviews in the European corpus were conducted on various occasions between December 2002 and January 2004, at the premises of the European Parliament in Brussels, where the interviewees were either still acting as members of the European Convention or, later on, as the 'Observers to the European Parliament from the EU-Accession States'. The analysis of interviews with Polish members of the Convention makes it possible to trace the dynamics of Polish political discourse within the 'European arena', that is, within the entire period of the (by then) first and unprecedented involvement of Polish politicians in the European bodies such as the Convention. The analysis also allows for examination of how the first Polish politicians involved in European politics constructed a variety of both national and European identifications when discussing, to a large extent, issues similar to those described within the speeches of the national corpus (such as, for example, 'the Polish role in the EU', 'the future of the EU', and so on). In order to assess the uniqueness of the discourses and discursive dimensions developed by Polish politicians, the elements of discourses examined within interviews with Polish members of the European Convention are also, as much as possible, compared to outcomes of analyses of 28 interviews with politicians from other EU countries, from (then) EU-accession countries and/or EU institutions (also involved in the EU Convention; see also Krzyżanowski, 2005a, 2005b; Krzyżanowski and Oberhuber, 2007).[6]

While the comparability of the two analysed corpora is not straightforward, that is, they were collected during significantly different time spans (of ten and three years) and comprise significantly different genres (parliamentary speeches and interviews), the two sets of data are juxtaposed here primarily in order to contrast the different discursive behaviour of Polish politicians in the two arenas concerned (that is, national and European). Also, although observed in the process of the in-depth analysis, the genre-specific features of the analysed texts are not analysed here due to limitations of space and the specifically discourse-oriented (and not text-specific) analysis.

The methodological framework applied in this study is based, in general, on the 'Discourse-Historical' or 'Viennese' school of Critical Discourse Analysis.[7] Accordingly, this contribution focuses on a broad catalogue of categories of analysis proposed by Wodak et al. (1999) and includes: a) discursive strategies; b) argumentation (topoi); c) metaphors; and d) personal deixis and other forms of linguistic realisation. Due to limitations of space, only one of the selected types of analytical categories specific to the Discourse-Historical explorations can be approached here in a detailed way.[8] Therefore the following analysis focuses on key arguments (topoi) of the analysed discourse and highlights the key argumentation-specific aspects thereof.

Within the presented analysis of *argumentative patterns*, the main focus is on topoi considered here to be 'parts of argumentation which belong to the obligatory, either explicit or inferable premises [and] are the content-related warrants or "conclusion rules" which connect the argument or arguments with the conclusion, the claim' (Reisigl and Wodak, 2001, pp. 74–5; see also Kienpointner, 1992). In other words, topoi shall be considered as certain 'structures of arguments' which need to be 'realised' by the construction of argument leading to a particular (logical and intentional) conclusion (see also van Eemeren, Grootendorst and Kruiger, 1987). One example, drawn from the analyses presented later, might be the '*topos* of national uniqueness' which will (logically) lead to several conclusions including, for example, justification of national actions, presentation of a unique national role, and so on. There also exists a further differentiation between topoi in regard to their type and relation to context: there are topoi which are treated as 'formal', and which are based on the set of 'classical' topoi or 'loci' (such as the topoi of 'difference', 'analogy', 'example', 'equality', 'consequence', and so on; see Kopperschmidt, 1989). On the other hand, there are also topoi which are context-dependent (or content-dependent; see Kienpointner, 1992) and which are 'unique' and 'typical' for the aims, contents and contexts of the analysed texts.

4 Analysis

The analysis of topoi in the 'national' and in the 'European' corpus allows for the identification of two different and highly diversified lists of premises used to structure, respectively, the parliamentary speeches and the semi-structured interviews (see Table 5.1). The lists of the topoi identified in the respective corpora differ primarily in size: there are seven topoi identified in the national corpus and 12 in the European corpus. The European corpus is therefore, in terms of the number of arguments used, far more diversified than the national corpus.

4.1 Analysis of the national corpus

The list of topoi identified in the national corpus is, in its entirety, characterised by arguments which favour nationally specific 'issues' which, respectively, form an array of national identifications. Among these, the *topos of national uniqueness,* frequently paired with *the topos of definition of the national role* appears to have the main role: within this topos the Polish exceptional role *vis-à-vis* the EU is argued for and

Table 5.1 Outline of topoi identified in 'national' and 'European' corpora

Topoi in the national corpus	**Topoi in the European corpus**
Topos of national uniqueness	*Topos of diversity in Europe*
Topos of definition of the national role	*Topos of European history and heritage*
Topos of national history	*Topos of European values*
Topos of East and West	*Topos of European unity*
Topos of past and future	*Topos of Europe of various speeds*
Modernisation topos	*Topos of core and periphery*
Topos of the EU as a national necessity	*Topos of European and national identity*
Topos of the EU as a national test	*Topos of Europe as a Future Orientation*
Topos of the organic work	*Modernisation topos*
Topos of Polish pragmatism and Euro-realism	*Topos of the Polish national mission in the European Union*
	Topos of joining the EU at any cost
	Topos of preferential treatment

portrayed. Correspondingly, the *topos of national history* is invoked to support the said uniqueness of Poland and portray Polish collectivity as exceptionally experienced throughout its history, and, therefore, as able to substantially contribute to the creation of the new Europe and its identity (see Example 1, below).

Example 1

As General de Gaulle said, 'one's geography cannot be changed and one can only change one's geopolitics'. Two dictators, Hitler and Stalin, changed our geography. Yet, with help of democratic institutions of the West and also thanks to a democratic rebirth in the East, we have been changing our geopolitics on our own in the recent years. Our current endeavours to join NATO and the European Union, our efforts to create new shapes of the regional politics, shall be seen as crucial, yet only as fragments of construction of a new, just and solid-based European order (PS-13: 2).

The fact that it is the *national* and not any other form of history which is eventually invoked in discourse constitutes an attempt typical of the constructions of national identities and identifications. In turn, the *topos of East and West* emphasises another strictly national aspect of the first corpus in question. It includes a set of elements of pre-1989 political language which very strongly emphasised the differences that existed between Europe's East and West and which reinforced the divisions introduced by the post-Second World War geopolitical order. Accordingly, this topos seeks a unique placement of Poland above the divisions of East and West, and thus (heading back into the *topos of national uniqueness*) reinforces Poland's attractiveness *vis-à-vis* the European Union: it argues that Poland has a unique role as a 'bridge' between Europe's East and West. Then, the *topos of past and future* also constructs Polish national identifications, yet within the dichotomy between collective 'scope of experience' and 'horizon of expectations' (Koselleck, 1989). While this topos is used to emphasise that the Polish past might have been troubled and negative (which is thus also constitutive of the uniqueness of Polish collective experience), it insists that the Polish 'European' future will be almost entirely positive and peaceful.

Unlike the previously elaborated topoi, the *topos of modernisation* clearly stands out and reaches beyond the constructions of national identifications. It focuses mostly on presenting the European Union as carrying some unique modernising force which would help reform

Polish state and society. The topos of modernisation is therefore frequently tied to the *topos of the EU as a national necessity* and to the *topos of the EU as a national test* of which both construct the 'power' of the Union over Poland in a similar way. By implying that the Union is characterised by some unique principles and standards of social and political organisation (a form of 'legitimation through standardisation'; see Weiss, 2002), the topos of modernisation, contrary to the previous ones, constructs a very positive image of the Union to the detriment of Poland, which is portrayed in a negative way. Poland appears here as a country which is underdeveloped and which accordingly needs to 'catch up' with the rest of the Western world, which the EU collectively stands for.

Example 2

> On the other hand, it does not mean that our restructuring effort shall be abandoned. It [MK: the restructuring] is inevitable for us, irrespective of the fact whether we join the Union or not. I am afraid that the current [state] structure and efficiency will not take us too far. Hence, irrespective of everything, certain reforms must be in progress (PS-10: 14).

The last group of topoi which can be distinguished in the 'national' corpus consists of the *topos of the organic work* and of the *topos of Polish pragmatism and Euro-realism*. The former is a historical topos – which has been present in Polish public discourses since its inception in the national positivist and romantic literature of the 18th and 19th centuries (see Romaniszyn and Nowak, 2003) – and emphasises the need for domestic reforms and collective 'groundwork', all of which must be undertaken irrespective of the country's external situation (see Example 2, above). In turn, the topos of Polish pragmatism and Euro-realism is a typically EU-member-state-like topos, comparable to the similar one identified, for example, in British national (public) discourses (see Mautner, 2000; Statham and Gray, 2005). This topos postulates that Poland must remain conscious of the non-ideal character of the EU as the object of collective aspirations and motivations: it emphasises that Poland must always remain watchful of its national interests irrespective of the developments within the EU. Interestingly, while these two topoi are significantly different in their historical and political ontology (one is clearly 'national' and the other strictly 'EU-bound'), they can both be linked and grouped here through their very distinct and common feature. Namely, they both avoid essentialising the Union as a national 'must' and act very strongly in favour of national, instead of European, identifications. Both of these topoi also assume that the EU is just one of the possible options of Poland's development which, although being clearly attractive and profitable, shall not 'wipe out' the national character and uniqueness. Finally, both of those topoi also point to the realm of the nation state as a space where the social and political activity must occur and which shall, accordingly, remain the main object of collective identifications and aspirations.

4.2 Analysis of the European corpus

Unlike in the national corpus, where the majority of topoi argued for 'national uniqueness' and for retaining the role of the nation state as the main object of collective identifications, the vast majority of the topoi identified in the European corpus deal strictly with European issues and argue for the increased role of the supranational European space. Hence, in the European corpus, we can observe a significant shift towards constructing predominantly European rather than national identifications. Within this shift, we can observe that some strictly 'European' topoi clearly replace the 'national' ones enumerated in the 'national' corpus (see above). The *topos of European history and heritage* is one such topos which, replacing the previously used topoi of 'national uniqueness' and of 'national history' (see above), helps the interviewees to construct arguments in favour of an exceptional history shared by all Europeans, beyond their nation states, as well as in favour of some unique (cultural, religious, linguistic) heritage 'possessed' by the transnational European space (see Example 3, below).

The group of the European topoi (see Table 5.1, above) including the *topos of diversity in Europe*, the *topos of European values*, and the *topos of European unity*, marks the development of other strictly supranational topoi which are deployed to exclusively construct a set of European identifications. Although still carrying some 'touch' of the national issues used to strengthen the arguments constructed within these topoi, all of them share one predominant feature: they are all used to support the unquestionable role and achievements of the EU. Accordingly, those topoi are deployed to portray EU-rope in exclusively positive terms and to elaborate on its features such as 'diversity', 'values' and 'unity'. Those features are said to make EU-rope exceptional and unique, in particular with respect to some frequently unspecified 'others', and help define a unique form of a EU-ropean identity which is also viewed as a form of a 'European spirit' (see Example 3).

Example 3[9]

> one may look at Europe as at a common heritage (.) of culture (1.5) even of religion (3.0) a community of values or even of spirit (1.5) [EW: 385–400].

Although the previous group of topoi appears to be strongly European and marks a significant shift towards constructing some uniquely European identifications, it might still be argued that the arguments constructed on this basis result from some strictly national experiences. For example, the topos of European values is developed to support the Christian-European values which were largely defended by Polish politicians in the 2002–3 European Convention (see Krzyżanowski and Oberhuber, 2007). Thus, we witness a set of strictly European topoi which might be treated as, at least to some extent, based on national experience and motivations. Contrary to the previous group, another set of topoi, including *the topos of Europe of various speeds* and the *topos of core and periphery* (see Example 4, below), cannot be described in that way and must be defined as strictly European. Namely, both of these topoi, are clearly recontextualised from the large-scale discourse of the 'Future of Europe Debate' (see above) – structuring the debates in the European Convention. Accordingly, since they are used by national politicians – irrespective of how much they were involved in the EU-ropean politics – the use of the topoi of various speeds and core and periphery becomes illustrative of the strength of the EU-ropean discourses which easily penetrate and conquer some previously strictly national ways of thinking.

Example 4

> unfortunately (.) I have the feeling it will be the case (...) that will be the result (.) of introducing in the majority of decisions (.) the qualified majority decision (.) and that will cause in a natural way (.) the search for common decisions (.) by SMALLER part the number smaller than twenty-five and that will near groups of countries (.) according to interests according to (.) viewpoints (↓) and we will perhaps have the various SPEEDS (.) and we have to get ready for that [JO: 96–105].

The following two topoi – the *topos of national and European identity* and the *topos of Europe as a future orientation* – constitute a distinct group and share a common feature: they both construct a binary opposition between the image of the 'national' as past and 'old' and the 'European' as 'future' and 'new'. In a similar way, the *topos of national and European identity* is particularly illustrative in presenting the struggle which inherently exists between the national and the European identifications. It also takes for granted the existence of national identities and presumes their eventual decline in the wake of ever stronger supranational identifications embodied by the European identity. Interestingly, within the topos, all interviewees assume that, in a more or less distant future, the 'European identity' will become an element of their reality just like the national identity. Similarly, the *topos of Europe as a future orientation* is a clear continuation of the previously strictly national topos of past and future. However, the distinctive feature of the inherently European topos of Europe as a future orientation is that it is only focused on presenting EU-rope as a certain process (see Abélès, 2000) which is uniquely directed towards the 'future'. The fact that, compared to its national counterpart, this topos does not deal with the 'past element' any more is illustrative of a symbolic deficiency of the EU: the latter does not have any distinct past which could be constructive for its identity.

The *modernisation topos* is the only one of the previously elaborated 'national' topoi (see above) which is effectively reappropriated and recontextualised in the 'European' discourse. Just as before, that topos still portrays the EU as a modernising force which helps reform Poland and which enables the latter to 'catch up' with the West or with the rest of the EU and their standards of social and political organisation. The fact that this topos is equally present in both 'national' and 'European' discourse clearly signals that: a) Polish reforms are still 'in the making' at the time of 'production' of the analysed European discourse (that is, the years 2002–4); and, that b) in the discourse, the EU is still perceived as the key to Poland's 'national' (domestic) modernisation and development. Within the realisations of this topos in the 'European' discourse, Polish involvement in the Union is portrayed as substantial for *'the change to the inside image of our country'*. Also, in a typical modernisation-specific jargon, Polish involvement in the EU shall help Poland *'to take over mechanisms and standards'* (see Example 5, below).

Example 5

In Poland we have forgotten that (.) it is a very serious enterprise and yy yy only being in this family (.) will let us (.) with its support to much faster (.) CHANGE (.) the inside image of our country (↓)(.) to take over mechanisms and standards (↑)(.) much sooner than it would be the case if we stayed outside the EuroPEAN Union [EW: 660–665].

The group incorporating the last three topoi identified in the 'European' corpus can be named as the group of 'national' topoi in the 'European' discourse. This group includes the *topos of joining the EU at any cost*, the *topos of the Polish national mission in the EU* and the *topos of preferential treatment*.

Opening up this group of topoi, the topos of joining the EU at any cost helps to construct an array of arguments which support the idea that Poland should first join the Union – whatever the requirements that must be fulfilled and the promises that must be made – and begin some clear defence of its national interests only afterwards, that is, when an EU member. While this topos carries a set of some clearly opportunistic and unrealistic premises, it is overshadowed by the one goal of joining the EU and therefore constructs the EU as a certainty and as an unquestionable target of Polish national-political actions. Through the unique role that it ascribes to the EU, the topos is easily linkable with the topos of modernisation which, in a similar vein, presents the EU as a certain national imperative.

The *topos of Polish national mission in the EU*, then, is perhaps the most peculiar of all of the 'European' topoi (see Example 6, below). While it clearly replaces the topos of national uniqueness which previously overshadowed the national discourse about Europe/EU (see above), it makes the Polish role in the European Union somewhat different from how it was postulated before. Namely, it seems that in the national discourse, characterised by the very strong and frequent usage of the topos of national uniqueness, the speakers still widely believed that the role of Poland was unique and that the exceptional contribution of Poland to the Union could span from the most abstract issues (such as consciousness, experience, national heritage and the like) out to some very down-to-earth areas (such as geopolitics, the economy, and so on). However, in the 'European' corpus, the interviewees became disillusioned with, for example, Polish uniqueness in economic terms, and therefore opted to construct the national role of Poland in the EU around Poland's *mission*, which, however, is defined in purely abstract and rather unspecified ethical and moral terms.

Example 6

But there is this feeling which Poland has always had (↓) I am not saying that it is like in the literature yy like a mission yy that that

> that yyy as if (.) though I think it was not also coming out of the blue and it is coming out of a feeling of responsibility and I am counting on that (.) that such a feeling of responsibility and solidarity with others with weaker ones will stay with us (↓) and and when we enter [MK: the EU] there that we will not suddenly start to push away anybody around who is poor (.) although it will be a DIFFICULT challenge (↓) [DH, 195–200].

Finally, the *topos of preferential treatment* also heads into the same line of arguing and implies that, due to its exceptional mission and national uniqueness, Poland must be treated by the EU in some special, less-demanding way. Thus, since it postulates some unique features which Poland has and which predispose the country to be treated differently than, say, other EU-candidate countries, this topos must be defined as partially recontextualising several elements of the *topos of national uniqueness* identified in the first corpus. However, as this topos is constructed in a rather ambivalent and unclear way, since it postulates the preferential treatment of Poland on the basis of rather abstract and 'imagined' features of the country (such as the national mission), this topos must be seen as inextricably linked to the topos of Polish national mission in the EU elaborated before.

5 Conclusions

The analysis presented here emphasises that diverse *discursive dimensions* (or codes) of talking about Europe/EU and the nation state among Polish politicians have undergone a substantial change in the period in question encompassing Poland's' EU-accession process (1994–2004). As has been depicted, that change is of a mainly discursive and qualitative character and amounts to what can be called the *Europeanisation of Polish political discourse*. The described discursive change boils down to creating new ways of perceiving and conceiving of the nation state (that is, Poland): the latter clearly loses its multidimensional importance emphasised formerly in the discourses produced within the national arena (and analysed here using the example of a set of parliamentary speeches on Polish national foreign policy). On the other hand, as could be observed in the texts of our European corpus, the said change in Polish political discourse also includes a consequent introduction of various ways of conceptualising and describing Europe/EU into discourse produced within, and clearly directed at, the supra- or extra-national arena of EU politics.

Examined diachronically, the said Europeanisation of discourse appears to be a gradual process of a highly complex character. As one can observe in the analysis, descriptions and conceptualisations of Europe/EU in discourse rarely *replace* references to the (Polish) national collectivity or to the Polish nation state in a one-for-one manner. On the contrary, in the process of the Europeanisation-specific adjustment of the national discourse to the new supranational conditions, many of the arguments previously used to describe the nation state (even if by means of referring to Europe/EU) are in fact *transformed, recontextualised* or *reappropriated* in the newly enacted discursive practices – and deployed to construct the unique agency of the supranational (EU-based) political actions. The presented analysis depicts how, located at the level of discourse, different arguments are constructed by means of various references to, on the one hand, (Poland and Polish) national collectivity or to the (Polish) nation state and, on the other hand, to Europe, the EU or to the supranational European space. As has been shown, those specific argumentative constellations contribute to the diversified constructions of different forms of identifications *with* different objects (that is, with Poland or Europe/EU), while one could observe that those identifications have clearly been constructed 'within, not outside discourse' (Hall, 1996a, p. 4).

In line with the analysis, one could see that the national and European identities and identifications that were examined were by no means limited to any of the 'institutionalised arenas' (Triandafyllidou and Wodak, 2003) pre-assigned for their social and political functioning. Thus, despite being clearly directed at different objects and issues (Polish nation state or Europe/EU in respective discourses, corpora and arenas) both national and European identifications were formed within both the national and European arena. Thus, the discourse analysed here must be considered as a certain open, identity-constructive space which escapes its physical limits (of Poland, or Brussels) and is only tied to those individuals who are the carriers of politically conditioned identifications and who carry them from one arena to the other – from national to European contexts of production and reception of discourse.

Finally, it is worth stressing that identifications with nation/nation state (that is, Poland) and Europe/EU were constructed by means of the largely similar discursive dimensions (Weiss, 2002; Wodak and Weiss, 2004). In both of the analysed discourses/corpora, the said discursive dimensions were constructed on the basis of references to *ideational issues* (by highlighting such abstract features of Poland and

Europe/EU as their identity, their specific mentality and consciousness but also their history, tradition, heritage and so on) as well as to their more concrete, *institutional and organisational aspects* (such as geopolitics, economy, concrete plans of reforms and policies, and so on).[10]

Thus, one may argue, it is exactly the use of the largely similar discursive patterns and dimensions that is deployed to describe both Poland and Europe/EU that clearly facilitates the described Europeanisation of discourse described in this chapter. In other words, that specific form of a discursive change is possible mainly because the features once ascribed to the nation state (such as, for example, its identity) are multi-directionally recontextualised at the level of discourse and are later being deployed to portray the new political reality of Europe/EU. It is argued that, although analysed here in relation to the Polish example, such a process of discursive change understood as *Europeanisation of discourse* is not limited to Poland but may also be observed in other CEE contexts: in particular in the CEE countries oriented towards European integration and aspiring to EU membership.

Notes

1. Due to the limitations of space, it is not possible to describe in detail the political actions analysed in this study and constituting the macro-contextualisation of the discourses analysed below. A detailed description of those actions can be found in a broader analysis of the issues addressed here (see: Krzyżanowski, forthcoming).
2. See also Giesen (1999), Eisenstadt (1987, 1992, 1998) and Eisenstadt and Giesen (1991, 1995).
3. The concept of discursive dimensions has been elaborated further in other 'Discourse-Historical' studies such as, for example, Krzyżanowski and Oberhuber (2007).
4. The speeches were obtained (in the form of Hansard transcripts) from the official archive of the Polish parliament (www.sejm.gov.pl).
5. The interviews were conducted within the research project 'The Discursive Re-construction of European Identities' (funded by the Austrian National Bank – Jubiläumsfonds der Österreichischen Nationalbank, project number 10.222) which I carried out (together with Florian Oberhuber and Ruth Wodak) at the Research Centre 'Discourse, Politics, Identity', University of Vienna, between 2003 and 2005.
6. See Busch and Krzyżanowski (2007), Krzyżanowski (2005a and 2005b), Oberhuber (2005), Oberhuber et al. (2005).
7. For further details, see the contribution by Wodak and Krzyżanowski in this volume (Chapter 1).
8. See Krzyżanowski (forthcoming), for an extensive analysis according to the remaining categories.

9. The name-codes applied in the transcription of the semi-structured interviews have been derived from the names of the interviewees (EW = Edmund Wittbrodt, JO = Józef Oleksy, DH = Danuta Hübner). Transcription symbols:

SYMBOL	FUNCTION
(.)	Short pause
(6.0), (8,0), (9,0), ...	Longer pause (six seconds, eight seconds, nine seconds, ...)
(unread. 6.0)	Unreadable elements of speech
[	Overlapping speech
Mhm. Eeeeeh	Para-verbal elements
((leans back)),((laughs))	Non-verbal behaviour
[Heimat]	Elements of original language (difficult to translate)
I would not say so	Normal speech
THIS	Accentuated/stressed element of speech
(↑)	Rising intonation (if significant)
(↓)	Falling intonation (if significant)

10. The adjectives 'ideational' and 'organisational' are adopted from the description of discursive dimensions proposed by Weiss (2002) as well as by Wodak and Weiss (2004).

6
Governing Abandoned Children: The Discursive Construction of Space in the Case of 'Babybox'[1]

Igor Nosál

1 Introduction

In 2004 a Czech civic organisation that cares for abandoned children created the project Babybox-Statim. The aim of this project was to install special boxes for abandoned babies (so-called babyboxes) in the walls of some hospitals in the Czech Republic. New mothers in a desperate situation could anonymously leave their children in these boxes and the unwanted child would get immediate medical attention and necessary social care. The civic organisation Babybox-Statim wanted to save the lives of babies who would otherwise be left in crisis, abandoned or even killed.[2] Similar boxes for abandoned babies are already functioning in several Western countries. For example, more than 70 babyboxes exist in Germany (they are known there as '*Babyklappe*').

The Babybox-Statim project faced strong opposition from the state administration of the Czech Republic. The project was criticised by the Minister of Health, MUDr Milada Emerová, as well as in a report by her adviser and the chairman of the Czech Society of Social Pediatrics, MUDr František Schneiberg, who wrote that the project supported criminal activities. On 31 January 2005 the Ministry of Health sent its statement to Babybox-Statim, in which it deemed the use of babyboxes illegal. The media reported that police detective Alena Plšková ordered other police officers to prosecute mothers who left their babies in babyboxes. Czech president Václav Klaus also expressed his anxiety in newspapers, saying that help for women who gave birth secretly supported 'irresponsible behavior of parents' and that babyboxes are 'at least disputable'.[3]

Babybox-Statim, however, did not give up the project and opened its first babybox on 5 May 2005 at the private clinic GynCentrum in Prague. It appealed for support to medical and legal professionals, as well as to members of parliament and senate. The position of the Ministry of Health towards Babybox-Statim was criticised by the Foundation of Children at Risk (*Fond ohrožených dětí*) and other civic organisations. Babybox-Statim was eventually supported by many doctors and lawyers, as well as by some politicians. The Institute of State and Law (*Ústav státu a práva*) at the Czech Academy of Sciences prepared expert analysis on the demand for the project, and reached the conclusion that the project did not violate the law. It criticised attempts by the Ministry of Health to criminalise the project, and revealed support among the majority of the public, who took part in the debate. Finally, in February 2006, a new Minister of Health, David Rath, declared that he would not further obstruct the operation of babyboxes in the Czech Republic.

The discussion around the Babybox project may appear marginal and distinct from usual ways of thinking about post-communist transformation in 'transitology literature'. My aim, however, is to point to the lack of attention to the 'local texture and on-the-ground experience' (Berdahl, 2000, p. 3). The literature on the post-communist transformation mainly concentrates on macro-social changes in political and economic systems and institutions. The micro-social level of transformation and the studies of promoting changes in everyday life are not yet much studied. As Daphne Berdahl states:

> Because of a predominant focus on large-scale economic processes, political elites, and evolutionary trajectories, much of the established 'transition' literature explains little about how people have actually experienced the dramatic political, economic, and socio-cultural changes since collapse of socialist rule (2000, p. 3).

My perspective on post-communist transformation focuses on the power relations in everyday life experience. Thus, post-communist transformation is not only the rebuilding of formal designs of economic and political systems, but in the end it also brings deep liberal changes to the heart of power relations – it decentralises and pluralises the power relations in everyday life. I see the post-communist transformation as a radical pluralisation of power relations in discourses and practices which dismantles the state-socialist governmentality. As Bauman (1992a) points out, individual choice in the communist East used to be permanently and firmly limited by the patronage state. The social system now needs to dismantle state-administered patronage – that coercively imposed trade-off between freedom and security (ibid., p. 163).

The aims of my research are the following:

1. My main task is to answer the question of *continuity and discontinuity of state-socialist regulative power* concerning the *dominant discourse* in the sphere of state administration. Instead of the macro-social themes of political and economic transition, I focus on manifestations of 'governmentality' in post-communist everyday life, in the usage of dominant power discourse in the practices of modern 'biopower', and the governing of abandoned children. I intend to explain the relation between discourse, knowledge and power in the events of the micro-social sphere (the case of Babybox-Statim). I also attempt to show how the dominant discourse maintains 'the patronage state' (Bauman, 1992).

2. Analysis of texts published in 2005–6 will demonstrate how the state administration's discourse reacted to this attempted social innovation, and how this discourse presented itself as the dominant power and governing discourse. My analysis concentrates on the *discursive representations of space* in the debates surrounding babyboxes and abandoned children. As a sociologist I analyse this discourse as a form of productive power and the discursive construction of space as a manifestation of 'governmentality' which defines, creates, and sustains the institution of childhood. This discursive aspect of space helps detect the exclusive and inclusive strategies of *the dominant discourse* and its power effects.

3. Although my main interest is in the dominant discourse, I will also sketch an 'alternative' construction of space, that is, the discursive manifestations of the opposition to these power practices as *counter-discourse*, created in the new sphere of 'sub-politics' (in the nongovernmental sphere of civil society). My aim is to show how this counter-discourse opposes the regulative power of the dominant.

2 The theoretical framework

This draws from several sources. The most important is Foucault's theory of discourse and its application to the analysis of power relations (Foucault, 1975; 1976; 1997; 2002). Second are theoretical works on social changes in late-modern society, particularly the theory of sub-politics by Beck (1992; 1997).

The most important of Foucault's works for this chapter are those where he elaborates his ideas of discourse and power, particularly the notions of disciplining the body, power over the population ('biopower'), and the idea of 'governmentality' that he laid out in the last years of his life. Power, according to Foucault, reveals itself in the governance of behaviour in the manner of Christian pastoral guidance and governmentality.

Foucault often defines governmentality as the 'art of government' in a wide sense, that is, with an idea of 'government' that is not limited to state politics alone. Governmentality includes a wide range of control techniques, and applies to a wide variety of objects, from one's control of the self to the 'biopolitical' control of populations. Governmentality applies to a variety of historical periods and to different specific power regimes. That is why it can be used not only in reference to 'neoliberal governmentality' (as it is often used by other scholars and by Foucault himself), which refers to societies where power is de-centred and its members play an active role in their own self-government, but also in reference to authoritarian or 'state-socialist governmentality', which refers to societies where power is highly centralised and its members play the role of passive objects of governance. A particular form of governmentality is characterised by a certain form of knowledge ('*savoir*'). In the case of 'state-socialist governmentality' (a kind of governmentality based on the predominance of state action and the restriction of individual and civic activities of 'self-regulation', as well as of market mechanisms) the knowledge produced allows the construction of patronage state-regulated selves.

In the work of Foucault, this notion is indeed linked to other concepts such as biopolitics and power-knowledge. For Foucault, biopolitics means the style of government that regulates populations through biopower.

Biopower contrasts with traditional modes of power based on the threat of death from a sovereign. In an era where power must be justified rationally, biopower is wielded through an emphasis on the protection of life rather than the threat of death, the regulation of the body, and the production of other technologies of power, such as the notion of sexuality. The regulation of customs, habits, health, reproductive practices, family, 'blood', and 'well-being' would be straightforward examples of biopower, as would any conception of the state as a 'body' and the use of state power as essential to its 'life'. Hence the relationship conceived between biopower, eugenics and state racism. Foucault's research on the medical practices and theories of Social Darwinism as well as 'the defence of society' led him to the conclusion that 19th-century techniques of discrimination, isolation and normalisation prepared the way for ethnic cleansing and concentration camps. It was because of 'the gigantic shadow' of Nazism and Stalinism that the question of techniques of power and governance were actualised (Foucault, 1997). This is why Foucault's ideas are so useful for research on the heritage of totalitarian 'state-socialist governmentality' in the discourse surrounding 'babyboxes' for abandoned children in Czech post-communist society. Foucault's perspective may prove very useful for research on the transformation of care for children at risk, and particularly regarding the question of continuity and deconstruction of totalitarian control over populations, especially discursive practices with children (and their parents), and within the field of child-welfare policy.

The second stream of theoretical inspiration flows from Ulrich Beck's notion of 'sub-politics'. Beck sees sub-politics as one of the new sites for effecting social transformation in contemporary 'reflexive modernity', which has, he suggests, taken over the role of what was previously undertaken by central agencies, including the state in many cases. Such sub-politics create a social order of 'reflexive modernity,' where authority is perennially under scrutiny and 'all forms of hierarchy are routinely challenged' (Taylor, 1999, p. 133). Sub-politics, the 'shaping of society from below', cover the activities of various groups and individuals which take place outside the apparent political structure. Such groups include a wide range of professional and organised groupings inside research institutes, organisations and industrial plants as well as citizen action groups, individuals and collectives.

Beck's theory of reflexive modernisation outlines a picture of a complex society which changes partly by some autonomous processes that flow from past consequences of industrial, technological and economic change. This often happens ahead of any planned governmental activity: sub-politics is, or more cautiously, could become (among several other possibilities), the civil society that takes its concerns into its own hands in all areas and fields of action of society (Beck, 1997).

3 Sources and method of analysis

The sources of my paper consist of texts that express opinions on the Babybox-Statim project, published in 2005–6.[4] These are official documents (written by the Ministry of Health and Statim), accounts of expert research (in the fields of law and medicine), articles in published and internet media, and journalistic commentary and essays. The producers of these texts were representatives of the state administration, experts, activists from the NGO sector, and journalists.

In the analysis I divided the texts into two groups according to the 'emplacement' of utterance in the discursive space. The section 'Dominant Discourse' contains extracts of texts from the governmental sphere of state administration. These are the texts of MUDr Milada Emmerová the Czech Ministry of Health Care and MUDr František Schneiberg (adviser to the Ministry and Chairman of the Society of Social Pediatrics) and extracts from 'The Ministry of Health's Declaration Concerning the Intention of the Foundation STATIM to Establish 'Babyboxes' for the Anonymous Abandonment of Children along the Walls of Clinics for Gynecology and Obstetrics'. Section 5, 'Counter-Discourse', contains extracts of texts from the non-governmental sphere of NGOs, academic institutions and the media, all of which situated themselves as independent from the state. I will provide specific utterances to illustrate the discursive strategies and constructions typical of particular groups of utterances. The *key textual elements* of particular discursive strategies in the following extracts are in *italics*.

In this analysis I applied the method of Foucauldian discursive analysis (Foucault, 2002; Carabine, 2001) and the principles of Critical Discourse Analysis (Fairclough, 2001c, 2003). My interest in discourse is more influenced by Foucault's idea of discourse as productive power, and less with the way that discourse is structured and governed by internal rules, that is, the linguistic analysis of the nature and processes of discourse itself. This perspective is shared by many sociologists and other social scientists. The sociological perspective questions how people, groups and institutions mobilise meanings, how some interpretations become dominant, and whose interests they serve (compare Wetherell, 2001, p. 25). Foucault turned his attention to the relation between discourse and power in social reality. As Wetherell emphasises, 'it has been recognized that control over discourse is a vital source of power and also there are limits to this control because meanings are fluid and escape their users and can be mobilized and re-worked to resist domination' (ibid.). For Foucault, discourses are essentially productive. They produce the objects of which they speak – madness, punishment, sexuality or childhood (or in this case the spatial circumstances of an abandoned child's life). In the sense of productive power, discourse can be defined as 'consisting of groups of related statements which cohere in some way to produce both meanings and end effects in the real world, i.e., the idea of discourse as having force, as being productive' (Carabine, 2001, p. 268).

I suggest in my research that discourses are constitutive, productive and that they take part in the rapid processes of post-communist social change; they construct a particular version of the transformation of childhood (including the re-construction of social space for abandoned children's lives) and, finally, they have real power effects. They define *normality* and establish what 'truth' is at particular moments. In case of the Babybox-Statim project, the discourse about babyboxes produces a particular 'truth' of abandoned children which seeks to invalidate other images of abandoned children and their childhood. Different discursive strategies serve to establish such 'truth'. A *discursive strategy* 'refers to the ways that a discourse is deployed. It is the means by which a discourse is given meaning and force, and through which its object is defined. It is a device through which knowledge about the object is developed and the subject constituted' (Carabine, 2001, p. 288). So in the case of my research, discursive strategy is a device through which babyboxes for abandoned children and other related spaces are put into discourse.

I have adapted Foucault's concept of *normalisation*. The relationship between normalisation and discourse is that discourses convey a message about what is the norm and what is not – in effect, they establish the norm (Carabine, 2001, p. 277). I apply this to the Babybox-Statim project and suggest that in this context discourse operates in three main ways. First, in constituting appropriate and acceptable spaces (physical, emotional, social, political and historical space) in the context of care for abandoned children. Second, as operating in a regulatory capacity through which not only is normal space established and secured, but also the bodies of abandoned children and their parents (mothers/fathers) are disciplined and controlled. Third, the normalisation of space is instrumentalised in order to control and discipline other actors, such as those who rescue and take care of abandoned children.

We can find specific representations of different spaces in utterances about the Babybox-Statim project. Here one sees the space of the babybox itself as well as various social, legal, political and historical spaces that have become the objects of normalisation in the context of care for abandoned children. Thus what I mean by space is not only the geographic and physical aspects of a certain place, but also wider ideas about social, political and historical realities. It is possible to follow normalisation policies as the inclusion or exclusion of various spaces via utterances. The discursive practices of normalisation use certain discursive strategies (for example, *the strategy of medicalisation*) and certain files of knowledge (for example, *pediatric discourse*).

The contemporary 'discourse' on abandoned children in fact consists of various different discourses. One can trace certain professional discourses as legal, medical or psychological, which operate with a certain arsenal of knowledge. Another analytical perspective is political. The dominant discourse is present within the texts of state administration and state organisations. Counter-discourse is localised mainly in the texts of non-governmental and civic organisations, scientific institutions and independent commentators on social affairs. In this perspective one can describe the discursive space as a battlefield where the 'dominant discourse' attempts to sustain its hegemony and legitimise the power interests of the social actors who reproduce this discourse. The 'counter-discourse' is constituted against the power effects of this dominant discourse; it attempts to question its claims to hegemony as well as the interests of the social actors who uphold it.

4 The dominant discourse

4.1 The discursive strategy of medicalisation

Abandoned children and their mothers are situated in the dominant discourse primarily within the 'normal' space of medical surveillance and the state system of institutional care. While abandoned children are represented as primarily biological objects and metaphorically constructed as 'ill bodies' (or potentially ill bodies), their world is subjugated to the space under medical surveillance and state control.

Extract 1 (key textual elements in italics)

It is always a question, from whom a mother wants to hide her birth. From the child??? No, rather from her social surroundings. For this she still has a possibility, one which does not endanger the child or the

> mother, and is provided by *fourteen existing child and baby asylums.* They are able to accept the mother who wants to leave her child after giving birth. They give her asylum before the birth, *prepare her for the birth,* and *make agreements for her birth* with a nearby hospital. From the hospital the mother goes home, while the child stays in the institution. After six weeks the mother signs the agreement that gives her child up for adoption. The child is not put at risk of being left wherever and whenever. The *child's medical history, as well as his mother's and family case history, are known. In this way the workers of the institution are able to make a developmental diagnosis and prognosis for the child,* which is the most important information demanded by adoptive parents in the future. Therefore the Society of Social Pediatrics did not greet with enthusiasm the new law about anonymous births; however, even this law is much more friendly and sensitive to the child than the proposed concept of the babybox.
>
> **Source:** Schneiberg, F. (2005a) 'The Attitude Towards the Establishment of Babybox in the Area of the General University Hospital Clinic for Gynecology and Obstetrics.'

This criticism of babyboxes is based on the concern that it eliminates the possibility of complete medical surveillance. The dominant discourse claims to be an important mediator between the needs of the abandoned child and the demands of the society that will take care of it (social workers and adoptive parents).

4.2 The discursive strategy of nationalisation

The medicalisation of space does not concern only these special micro-spaces (asylums for children or hospitals), but also the macro-space of the nation state. The dominant discourse pictures the patronising power of the state, which is also intended to protect the nation against the 'infection' of abandoned children. Medicalisation thus uses the strategy of pathologisation of excluded objects (children from babyboxes) by reducing abandoned children to 'ill bodies', the illness of whom is unknown. The discourse of state administration emphasises in various ways the 'high standard' of health care in the Czech Republic and juxtaposes it to 'other states':

> **Extract 2**
>
> *In the Czech Republic* the problem of unwanted pregnancies as well as the provision of care for children without families is solved well

> enough *nowadays,* in contrast to *other countries, including those of the EU* (possibilities for contraception, abortions, sterilization because of health reasons, the possibility of discrete births as well as anonymous births according to law No. 422/2004 Sb., the possibility of using the hospital and specialized institutional care (baby and children's asylums), the opportunity for immediate care for children, which is provided by the foundation for children at risk, non-state asylums, support for planned parenthood etc).
>
> ...In the case that 'babyboxes' are established, that *would induce acceptance of births outside of healthcare institutions and that would mean that the high level of prenatal care in the Czech Republic would grow worse.*
>
> **Source:** Ministry of Healthcare (2005) 'The Declaration of the Ministry of Healthcare Concerning the Intention of the Foundation STATIM to Establish "Babybox" for Anonymous Abandonment of Children on the Wall of the Clinic for Gynecology and Obstetrics.'

The babybox is presented in this context as a threat to the Czech population. It is important to notice however, that the image of a high standard of Czech healthcare continues the earlier praxis of communist states to make a shop-window of excellent care for children, to make this achievement a part of the ideology of national pride, and thus to legitimise the socialist system as the most humanistic one. National statistics of infant mortality would be at risk from the 'ill bodies' from the babybox. The priorities of medical surveillance are detectable in the hierarchical order of possible solutions which may solve the problem of unwanted children. First, medical preventive and exterminatory interventions that protect favourable national health statistics are mentioned. Thus one of the power effects of the dominant discourse is the praxis of eugenics.[5] The possibilities of care for abandoned children at the end of the list are ordered in such a way as to put the state-run institutions in the top position and the non-governmental ones in the very bottom.

Using the discursive strategy of medicalisation, babyboxes are excluded as a place of infection and genetic danger for the whole population. The babybox, portrayed as a dangerous place from which sick and alien elements could be brought into the Czech nation, is also discursively constructed via a negative spatial metaphor. František Schneiberg, Ministry adviser and Chairman of the Society of Social Pediatrics, explicitly calls babyboxes a 'black box'.

Extract 3

Even if I do not mention the fact that the babybox would be used *by mothers who are drug addicts, and that those children will most possibly have jaundice and in this way they will be hardly adoptable*, there still remains the question, if our state has an interest in creating a possibility *for foreign mothers to come to the Czech Republic in order to give birth to handicapped babies* and then leave them in babyboxes. If we allow an increase in the number of abandoned babies, *we will open a 'black box'.*

Source: Schneiberg, F. (2005b) 'Speech by MUDr František Schneiberg'

4.3 The discursive strategy of bureaucratisation

Regulated space in the dominant discourse is constructed by connecting medical surveillance with state control. The discourse constitutes bureaucratised space as normal:

Extract 4

... If the foundation STATIM wants to protect children in the spirit of this law, *it must have adequate legitimacy for this.* As far as I know, *STATIM does not have such legitimacy, and the General University Hospital does not have it either.* Therefore, *they may be sanctioned for abuse of the law mentioned above.* If they ask for such legitimacy, I suppose *that they would not get it for the intended activity, which is the establishment of a babybox.*

Source: Schneiberg (2005a)

Here the representative of the medical administration self-confidently relies on the image of a coherent and totally ruled society in which there is no other way of social action than the bureaucratic one, and no bureaucratic institution which would not share his opinion and support non-governmental activity. The non-governmental project is excluded as unsuccessful in advance.

The author continues in his construction of the image of civil society as a superfluous element which bothers the effective and rational governance of experts and officials:

Extract 5

The authors who argue that 'Babyklappe' exists in *Germany and other countries* forget to add that *this happens in the conditions of some social*

> *tolerance, and not because these institutions are grounded in the local legal order. Babyboxes are not legalized,* while the state *cannot* take part in these activities for the reasons mentioned above (see the Agreement on the rights of children). The account which was recently accepted by colleagues from *Germany and Austria states that experts and the state strive to obstruct the occurrence of new 'Babyklappe'* and to *eliminate the existing ones,* and they do it *for the sake of the child's rights.* If the state takes part in the 'creation' of children without a past, of individuals who will have in the future many personal problems because of their unclear identity, it would act in contradiction to the Agreement on the rights of children, and that would be socially unacceptable. *These colleagues were very surprised that the establishment of babyboxes is being considered in our country.*
>
> **Source:** Schneiberg (2005a)

The macro-space of contemporary Western societies is constructed as an anarchic space that is not fully regulated by the state (in contrast to 'our' Czech society). The anarchic (non-legal) social space created by 'social tolerance' enables the activities of NGOs, which take care of children in babyboxes (*Babyklappe*). This 'social tolerance', which allows NGOs to give 'non-legal' aid to abandoned children, is interpreted as a threat to the interests of children and as a 'socially unacceptable' phenomenon. Thus 'social tolerance' and an autonomous civil society, which used to be presented in post-revolutionary political debates as an important aim of the post-communist transformation, are presented by the dominant discourse on abandoned children as a threat.

4.4 The discursive strategy of 'otherisation'

The strategies which constitute 'normal' space work together with the strategies which exclude other spaces. The excluding discursive strategy of *otherisation* represents babyboxes as a 'foreign', 'immoral', 'pathological' and 'dirty' space.

One method of otherisation is to connect the babybox with foreigners and foreign countries:

> **Extract 6**
>
> It is possible to suppose that *'babyboxes' would be misused* first of all *for the abandonment of the children of foreigners and particularly by foreigners from lands where abortions are not legal,* and *handicapped children,* who *demand high financial means* for their healthcare.
>
> **Source:** Ministry of Healthcare (2005).

This quotation otherises not only the babybox itself, but also the 'foreign' child in it. The babybox is pictured as 'a tunnel' used to extract Czech funds for foreigners.

Another tactic of otherisation constitutes the babybox as a place of moral decay and social pathology. It pictures babyboxes as a space which enables 'irresponsible', 'pathological', and 'criminal' behaviour by parents:

Extract 7

Nevertheless, *to make it possible to leave children in a babybox* and furthermore to propagate it, opens the door to further and further use or rather misuse of this possibility and *leads to a larger scale of this criminal activity*, which would in this way be legalized. Giving away a child is most *certainly an unacceptable social phenomenon, it is a socially pathological phenomenon*, and it should not be supported by society as a whole. The already *low level of responsibility of parents would grow even weaker*, and the *moral evolution of society would be influenced in a negative way*. It would be sad if a public institution with as good a reputation in society as the General University Hospital took part in these activities.

Source: Schneiberg (2005a)

This quotation connects the moralising discourse with the strategies of criminalisation and pathologisation of babyboxes. Here the Ministry of Health is presented as the patron of 'healthy' society and population. The state defends children from the irresponsible behaviour of their parents, while the establishment of babyboxes would mean enabling parents to behave irresponsibly. All actors who make alliances with this 'criminal' project therefore risk their reputation. It is interesting to note the relationship between the 'low level of morality in society' and the hospital with an allegedly excellent moral reputation. The hospital is represented here not as a public space which serves people as they are, but rather as an educator and moral authority which should not accept immoral behaviour in society in any way.

The users of babyboxes are represented as pathological and immoral. For example, Alena Plšková, the officer from the police board who gave the order to investigate mothers who left their children in babyboxes, explained her decision in the following manner. In her interview for Czech TV she connected babyboxes with drug addicts and alcoholics and said that the police would attempt to investigate the mothers of abandoned children. The reason for this was the intention of the police to learn about the health conditions of the mothers. 'There may be children whose parents were drug addicts or alcoholics. These children are born with the syndrome of addiction.'[6] In other texts there appears a connection with Roma women and prostitutes, groups that are both said to endanger society. In this way we come to the racist discursive construction of babyboxes as a certain micro-space of *'Untermensch'*. It is seen as a place which allows the penetration of contaminated and uncontrolled populations from outside macro-spaces (from foreign countries), and from the 'underclass' of drug addicts and prostitutes.

Yet another strategy of otherisation is to constitute babyboxes as dirty and unhygienic spaces:

Extract 8

How will the babybox be treated? Will they disinfect the box after each child, whose epidemiological situation might be in a different critical stage; will the linen be changed, etc? (...) What if somebody put a dead dog or cat into the babybox??? Or even a dead child??? (An actual experience from recent months in Germany).

Source: Schneiberg (2005a)

Here the the babybox is described as a space of possible hygienic threat. In this way the dominant discourse legitimises the practices of purification and medicalisation of the social space of childhood. The 'Declaration of the Ministry of Healthcare' is a good example of the 'purification of space' strategy, used to maintain state control over possibly 'uncertain' and uncontrolled space on behalf of the state bureaucracy.

Extract 9

From the hygienic-epidemiological point of view, *'babyboxes' as healthcare devices should fulfill the technical parameters of incubators.* The producers of these healthcare devices *must fulfill the legal regulations* which are *valid for the sphere of healthcare devices,* that is law 123/2000, concerning healthcare devices and about changes to related laws, such as law 22/1997, about the technical requirements for the products in their valid form, further to government decision 336/2004, in which the technical requirements for healthcare devices were defined, law 102/2001, about the general security of the products.

Source: Ministry of Healthcare (2005)

4.5 The discursive strategy of negative temporalisation

As Fairclough claims, constructions of space are closely interconnected with time, so that it is often difficult to separate them (2003, p. 151). The discursive connection of certain times with certain spaces serves the dominant discourse as a strategy of exclusion. In the following extract, the babybox as a space is constructed into a particular chronology:

> **Extract 10**
>
> The *abandonment of children in this way [via babybox] was certainly normal in the Middle Ages,* when it was the only possibility for an unhappy mother to get rid of an unwanted child. She defended herself first of all in this way, her bare existence and her social status; possibly she escaped shame and contempt. *It was not the child's interests that were important at that time.* Children did not have rights at that time, especially extramarital children, girls etc. *In modern times a similar practice was known in France, and may be explained exactly by the circumstance that children had no rights there.* Napoleon declared all abandoned children to be the children of France. That meant that the children belonged to 'the state', and they could be trained to be soldiers. *The fact that the babybox functioned in Cuba in 1952 confirms the former statement.*
>
> *Today in the twenty-first century, a woman does not have to give away her child because of social contempt;* a single mother may claim higher social monetary support than a married woman. The rights of children are repeatedly declared and accented, and everybody is obliged to defend the interests of the child. *Now this kind of abandonment and solution to the situation is certainly an anachronism* and would resemble the situation if *we turned back* to treatment with cups, or use carriages with horses for transport.
>
> **Source:** Schneiberg (2005a)

Time is not a neutral category for the medical expert here, but a progressive sequence. Here history is constructed as the progress of rationalisation. The historical space-time here develops progressively from the 'dark past' (Middle Ages) of social prejudice, through the time of injustice in periods of wars and revolutions (Napoleon's France, Cuba 1952), to the rationality and justice of the paternalistic social state in the present. In this construction of time-space relations, the babybox is placed in the past, which is full of social prejudices and the absence of rights.

The babybox is thus excluded as an 'anachronism' and 'turning back'. It is excluded from the rationalised modernity of the post-communist Czech Republic, in which the state is again presented as the protector of children's rights and the patron of mothers (especially of single mothers) and where the social grounds for babyboxes are lacking. By this discursive practice NGO activities are excluded from the sphere of childcare and total state control is legitimised.

5 Counter-discourse

5.1 The discursive strategy of emotionalisation

In contrast to the former group of texts, the counter-discourse represents babyboxes as a secure place. This is done with the help of the discursive strategy of *emotionalisation,* which empathically and emotionally pictures the contemporary situation of mothers in crisis. The mothers of abandoned children are presented as 'unhappy mothers'. The text of Marie Vodičková, the chairwoman of The Foundation for Children at Risk, may serve as a telling example. This document was written as a complaint against the initiative of Alena Plšková, who ordered the police to investigate mothers who left their babies in babyboxes.

> **Extract 11**
>
> I suppose that the task of the Czech police is to look for criminals and missing persons, and not for *unhappy mothers who leave their babies in babyboxes* and not in a *rubbish bin.* Her declaration in the media may lead to a situation where mothers would feel endangered to use babyboxes, because they will not feel sure that their identity will remain undetected, and they will attempt to get rid of their babies in a way that would not allow them to be detected. That is, they will leave their babies *far from their living places, in rubbish dumps, in dustbins, in the forest and other places* where *the corpses of newborns* are usually found.
>
> **Source:** Vodičková, M. (2006) 'Complaint and Application for the Criminal Persecution of Police Detective Alena Plšková'

This discursive strategy attempts to evoke sympathy and understanding not only for mothers but also for their children, whose lives are at stake and whose only hope is the babybox. The babybox is constructed here as a safe place, and is contrasted with 'rubbish containers', 'the forest', 'dustbins', and other places where 'the corpses of newborns' are usually found.

The dominant discourse does not talk about death and unhappiness; this theme does not suit the optimism of state-socialist ideology. On the contrary, however, the counter-discourse dwells on this theme. In this answer to a proposed ban on babyboxes, saving children's' lives is presented as a sanctified rescue activity which is poorly suited to bureaucratic obstacles and limitations:

Extract 12

Furthermore, without a doubt real life brings such situations and the number of abandoned or killed babies does not decrease. Criminality experts maintain that the number of children found is only the tip of an iceberg and the real number is many times higher... *We realize that the right to life is a sanctified mission that is much more important than philosophical and legal considerations or material obstacles and that it is the supreme task.* One can solve the question how the life of the child will be arranged only after its life is saved. There is no reason to consider further life arrangements when the child is found in a dustbin or rubbish container.

Source: Foundation for Abandoned Children STATIM (2005) 'The Answer of the Foundation for Abandoned Children STATIM to the Declaration of the Ministry of Healthcare.'

The babybox is also constructed as a *blessed space* by using the biblical metaphor of a 'little Moses box'.[7] In this formulation, abandoned babies are not discursively constructed as (inheritably) ill bodies and a hygienic threat to the population, but as a gift like the biblical character of baby Moses from the rubbish container. An illustration of this discursive construction may be observed in an article written by journalist Tereza Šimůnková:

Extract 13

The little Moses box is a heated box. It is 70cm long, 50cm wide and 50cm deep. When you press a red button and turn the handle, the door will open and a baby may be put in. At the same time a bell rings in GynCentrum, and the pagers will beep for the nurse and doctor in service. *The personnel ready to help will come within one minute.*

Source: Šimůnková, T. (2005) 'Mojžíšové z popelnic' (Moses from Dustbins)

Here the space of babybox is described in terms which should evoke the feeling of safety; the box is suited to the size of a baby and designed to assure quick rescue. Thus by evoking sympathy and describing mothers, children and the babybox in an empathetic manner, this discourse includes them in the space of emotion-sensitivity as objects of social concern and aid.

5.2 The discursive strategy of pluralisation

Pluralisation is used to oppose attempts to homogenise and to bureaucratise aid for abandoned children as well as to counter accusations that NGO activists violated law No. 359/1999 regarding the social and legal protection of children. This strategy emphasises the multifaceted nature of society and life, which is richer and more complicated than legal regulation can ever be. It defends the rights of civic participants to provide aid to abandoned children in the following way:

Extract 14

Life is very multifaceted and therefore the *activities of citizens and institutions should not be limited in this sphere... and bound to authorization by the state.*

There happens to be phenomena and situations in life which are new and not regulated by law. *Reality is such that the law is always behind the multiformity of life.* This does not mean, however, that we should ignore them for the sole reason that the law does not define and prescribe their correction in exact terms.

Source: Foundation for Abandoned Children STATIM (2005)

Thus the discursive strategy of pluralisation constructs a macro-space for social action that includes as legal everything that is not defined by law as illegal. Therefore NGO activists also advocate Western liberal-democratic society as the model for a just and free society. A polemic against Ministry of Healthcare adviser Dr Schneiberg by a lawyer who collaborates with STATIM stated this explicitly. The macro-space of 'Western society' is discursively constructed in his text as a free space, where the rights of the individual are respected. This type of society is contrasted with the 'un-free' space of 'societies of the Eastern type':

Extract 15

The legal and philosophical consideration by which the author (Dr Schneiberg) grounds his conclusions testifies that the author does not understand some of the *grounding principles of modern society. The principle of freedom and the rights of the individual are most important for modern society which – in contrast to societies of the Eastern type* – limits the rights of the individual to an unavoidably necessary scale and only by law. Therefore the principle that allows everything which is not forbidden is not an expression of a nihilistic attitude towards the law. With respect to his statement about the law lagging behind morality concerning social tolerance in Germany, morality is not something unchangeable and valid in all civilizations. The aforementioned *social tolerance in Germany, where Babyklappe is tolerated, is an expression of high morals there.*

Source: STATIM (2005) 'Considerations of STATIM Concerning the Position of MUDr František Schneiberg.'

We can also see here the creation of a connection between macro-space and micro-space. The fact that babyboxes (*Babyklappe*) function in Germany is represented as testimony of the quality of this macro-space (modern Western society) as a space of freedom and individual rights. The babybox is represented as a manifestation of a free society. Thus the strategy of pluralisation constructs a space of multifaceted life in which the pluralist initiatives of aid are included as manifestations of freedom in society.

5.3 The discursive strategy of individualisation

Individualisation emphasises the roles of concrete persons as individual actors. Aid to abandoned children is presented as a personal engagement and an activity of self-realisation. Ludvík Hess, the founder of the project, announced the opening of the first babybox as the fulfillment of his greatest individual dream:

Extract 16

Today, on the morning of 5 May 2005, *my dream – the dream of a stubborn crazy man – was fulfilled.* With the help of *my friends, Zdeněk Meduna, František Hájek, Michal Čumpelík,* and under the surveillance of the registrar of GynCentrum, Petr Pícha and his cousin Bohouš Pícha, doctor Zdeněk Mayer and last but not least TV Nova, we installed the first babybox for abandoned children in Prague and in the Czech Republic. *If the Ministry of Health does not arrange my deportation to Siberia first, we will open the babybox in three weeks. I invite all sympathizers and opponents of the babybox to the opening celebration*. It will take place symbolically on 1 June 2005, on the international day for children. This date is also the thirteenth anniversary of the founding of GynCentrum. Let its honors and fame be acknowledged!

Source: Hess, L. (2005) 'Splněný sen' (The Dream Fulfilled).

The image of their opponent, the bureaucratic obstacles which the activist had to overcome, is characterised and slightly dramatised by the ironic remark about Siberia. Nevertheless, inviting both sympathisers and opponents to the opening celebration represents the liberality and open-mindedness of the happy victor (as opposed to the totalitarian image of the ministry). The celebration of the opening is thus constructed as a space of plurality.

Hess refers to his meeting with the fourth child found in the babybox in Prague in the following way:

Extract 17

Maruška Vodičková allowed me to drive her with little Kristýnka from *Fakultní nemocnice Bulovka* (the University Hospital Bulovka) to *Klokánek* [a non-state asylum for children at risk] in Štěrboholy. Today in the morning Kristýnka was released from the hospital, she is absolutely healthy and if I remember well, weighs 3100g. She needs to be nourished all around, the nurse told me that she just had a hundred [ml of milk]. Just imagine! When nobody was looking, I held Kristýnka in my arms and asked Jonáš, the photographer, to take a picture with my camera.

Source: Hess, L. (2006) 'Směl jsem si pochovat Kristýnku.' (I Might Keep Kristýnka in My Arms).

The discursive strategy of individualisation constructs children from babyboxes and the people who help them as people with concrete names, as human beings with individually depicted emotions and qualities. Positive attention to detail is paid while describing real events in the lives of the actors. Joy (as the sign of individual emotional engagement) is expressed for the health of the baby (in opposition to governmental concerns about abstract national health statistics and potentially ill children from babyboxes). The author also reveals his personal interest and engagement by his wish to have a unique souvenir: a picture from his own camera (despite the fact that the photographer mentioned also took pictures for the media). In this way, the space of abandoned children is personalised and humanised while every individual life saved is celebrated. Thus the babybox is constituted as a space for the celebration of individual human life.

6 Conclusions

1. The Babybox-Statim case provides new insight into the process of post-communist transformation in the fields of childhood, parenthood and civil society. The material I have analysed still belongs to the field of political transformation because it concerns changes in the politics of social care. These politics, however, do not appear as a state-supported process that runs according to the plan of 'catching up to European standards', 'building capitalism and democracy' or 'the restitution of civic society'. From the perspective of the micro-social level, this transformation appears rather as an ambivalent and heterogeneous process that might be characterised in Berdahl's terms as 'transition, construction, negotiation, restoration, subjectification, and contestation' (Berdahl, 2000). Although all the other parties in the Czech Parliament and Senate distance themselves from the communist minority, the dominant discourse of state politics is nonetheless still heavily embedded with the mentality of social-state governmentality. More than 15 years after the revolution it is not possible to state with any certainty that we've witnessed the end of oppressive supervision by state agencies nor the opening up of space for individual initiative. In fact it is visible that many spheres of Czech social life continue to be dominated by the patronage state and that many spheres of the post-communist system may still be accurately characterised by Perkin's definition of communism: 'The Communist system could be seen as the domination of public sector professionals pushed to the radical extreme and secured with the help of the coercive resources of the state' (cited by Bauman, 1992, p. 165). This seems to be the case in the sphere of childhood, and particularly abandoned childhood, while the impulse for transformation comes from the growing sphere of sub-politics. The micro-social perspective thus makes the conventional ideological and teleological discourse of existing transitology literature problematic.
2. The dominant discourse, which is typical for the texts from the state administration, uses several strategies in order to constitute 'normal' space for abandoned children as the space which is medically, nationally and bureaucratically controlled. The

discursive strategy of *medicalisation* constitutes space within the system of the state institutional care and nurturing as the only possible 'normal' space. While abandoned children are represented as primarily biological objects and metaphorically are constructed as 'ill bodies' (or potentially ill bodies), their world is subjugated to the space under medical surveillance and state control. The strategy of *nationalisation* constitutes the normal space as the one, which is congruent with the rules and goals of the Czech national health system. The strategy of *bureaucratisation* constitutes the necessity of absolute state control over the care of abandoned children. The dominant discourse also uses the strategies which exclude baby-box as 'other' and 'anachronistic'. The discursive strategy of *otherisation* excludes the babybox as an 'alien' space and the children in it as the children of foreigners and of immoral, pathological and irresponsible people. The discursive strategy of *negative temporalisation* excludes the space of babybox as one which allows an escape from the regulations of biopower of the post-socialist state as unsuitable for modern society. This analysis of the dominant discourse thus documents the attempts to restore 'socialist-state governmentality'.

3. The counter-discourse which constitutes itself against the biopolitical practices of the paternalistic state acts in the sphere of sub-politics. This counter-discourse uses the discursive strategies of *humanisation, emotionalisation* and *individualisation*. The counter-discourse produces a pluralised space for individualised aid, civic engagement and self-government. The fact that the babybox project was realised, despite the obstruction of the Ministry of Health and police, testifies that a new political culture has emerged in the process of transformation. Together with the expanding sphere of sub-politics, it may achieve partial victory against attempts to continue the overbearing practices of socialist-state governmentality.
4. Despite seeing certain similarities between the micro-transformation process, which I analysed here, and Beck's macro interpretation of political modernisation in reflexive society in liberal democratic civilisation ('neoliberal governmentality'), it is important to note an important difference in the post-communist experience. The dominant discourse of the executive power and state administration did not see the civic engagement and activities of the individual as a natural part of the political order and attempted to exclude it as an alien intruder to the realm of 'socialist-state governmentality'.

Notes

1. I wish to acknowledge the Ministry of Education, Youth and Physical Education of the Czech Republic (Ministerstvo školství, mládeže a tělovýchovy ČR), who funded the research project 'Reproduction and Integration of Society' ('Reprodukce a integrace společnosti'), project number MSM0021622408 on which this chapter is based, as well as Blair Taylor and my wife Halina for their help with the English version of the text.
2. The police of the Czech Republic find approximately three to four dead babies every year. It is difficult to estimate the real number of secretly killed children.
3. Source: 'Klaus varoval před dalšími baby-boxy', *Lidové noviny*, 13 April 2006.
4. See www.babybox.cz/English-resume.php for further information.
5. Which is visible not only in this case, but also in the policy, which promotes general genetic tests in pregnancy.
6. The declaration of Mrs Lena Plšková from the police board for Czech TV. Quoted from: 'Policie hledá anonymní matky z BabyBoxu' ('The police are looking for the mothers from BabyBox') *Žena-In*, internet magazine for women (30 March 2006).
7. Czech society is statistically the most atheistic in Europe and therefore the usage of religious connotations is rare indeed.

7

Critical Juncture: Church Slavonic and the Discourse of Cultural Preservation in Post-Soviet Russia

Brian P. Bennett

1 Religion and discourse

To date the subject of religion has been sorely neglected in the field of discourse studies. The encyclopedic 872-page *Handbook of Discourse Analysis* (Schiffrin et al., 2003), for example, manages to bypass the topic altogether. Yet of all the changes that have occurred in post-communist Europe, the most striking has arguably been in the realm of religion. Societies which had hitherto been predicated on communist ideologies and which had pursued programmes of anti-religious propaganda and repression have now 'got religion'. Of course, religion was never completely obliterated during the communist era. And different paths of religious transformation have obtained in post-communist Bulgaria, Poland, Hungary, Romania, the former East Germany, and so on, depending on a number of interlocking historical, socio-political and confessional (Protestant, Catholic, Orthodox) factors, as is evident from Sabrina Ramet's panoramic comparative study, *Nihil Obstat: Religion, Politics, and Social Change in East-Central Europe and Russia* (1998). Nevertheless, across the region the metamorphosis is undeniable and extraordinary.

In Russia the restoration of religion has been altogether remarkable. Once viewed as 'unutterable vileness' (Lenin), religion has figured very prominently in debates over the country's identity and its future path of development. The place of religion, especially Orthodoxy, within Russian society has been the focus of a profusion of discourse:

> In Russia alone, the relationship between the Church and society is discussed each year in hundreds of books, thousands of newspaper and journal articles, at dozens of conferences, and in a multitude of Internet publications. This issue is often brought up by Church officials, Orthodox clergy, theologians, sociologists, politicians, members of Orthodox social movements, physicians, artists, religion scholars, military leaders, popular singers, and members of many other vocations and walks of life (Chaplin, 2004, p. 31).

In fact, one could say that religiosity in Russia is *primarily* a matter of discourse. It is less about mass participation than mass media. In post-communist Russia, religion functions principally as an *'ideological construct*...relevant to general issues of identity, polity, national destiny' (Agadjanian, 2000, p. 277).

The profusion of religious discourse in post-communist Russia has been accompanied by changes in the conditions and circumstances of religion 'on the ground'. After 1991, missionaries from abroad started entering the country in noteworthy numbers. 'Cults' and New Religious Movements (NRMs) have sought establishment. Most significantly, the Russian Orthodox Church, vilified and disregarded for most of the Bolshevik era, has regained something of its pre-Revolutionary stature. Churches and monasteries have been reopened or rebuilt, sometimes rather spectacularly, as with the Cathedral of Christ the Saviour in Moscow. Polls consistently show the Russian Orthodox Church to be one of the most trusted institutions in society. Most Russians have a positive view of, and identify themselves to some degree with, Orthodoxy (even if they rarely attend church). Federal legislation has passed that favours the Church over competing faiths. Overall, the Russian Orthodox Church has attained a hegemonic position in the context of post-Soviet 'managed pluralism' (for example, see Warhola, 2004, p. 98).

The resurgence of Russian Orthodoxy in the post-communist period, however, has not gone unopposed by competing groups or even by members of the Church itself. Religion is no more monolithic than any other segment of society; it is always marked in varying degrees by internal or sectarian division. Speaking very schematically, the Russian Orthodox Church is divided into 'progressives' and 'conservatives' or – better –'reformists' and 'traditionalists' (Knox, 2005, p. 91). Each camp has its supporters inside and outside the Church, as well as its own organisations and publications, and each side attempts to impress its *imaginaire* of what constitutes authentic Orthodoxy on a shifting situation.

Since the collapse of the Soviet Union, the Russian Orthodox Church has been beset by a number of scandals and controversies. After decades of communist subjugation, the Church faced a challenge of staggering proportions. In attempting to respond to this monumental and multi-dimensional challenge, old fissures were exposed anew (ibid.). These fault lines primarily have to do with 'issues of Orthodoxy's accessibility, the Church's relations with other confessions, the place of Orthodoxy in national identity and the opportunities for alternative understandings of Orthodoxy to be expressed' (Knox, 2005, p. 10). In short, the cleavages have to do with *modernisation*, that is, with whether and/or how the Church should adapt to the modern, secular, democratic, pluralist world. Against any purportedly modernising agenda, however, there has been a strengthening in the post-communist period of 'preservationist tendencies', aimed at retaining elements such as the Julian calendar and the Church Slavonic language, which are deemed to constitute the indispensable infrastructure of the faith (Christiakov, 2005, p. 61).

The most divisive debate in the post-communist period has been over the basic question of which language to use in church services – the traditional Church Slavonic or modern Russian. Here is one characterisation of the language situation today:

> Religious services are conducted everywhere in medieval [Church] Slavonic, which is almost completely incomprehensible to churchgoers. The Slavonic language, while marvellous in itself, is analogous to the Catholic Latin; for the modern individual it is an obstacle to the path of religious enlightenment. It makes the long, Byzantine-style services inaccessible to most people, as they cannot understand what is being read and sung. Figuratively speaking, they cannot 'tune in to the spiritual channel' in which the service is being conducted (Christiakov, 2005, p. 54).

This formulation, by a Russian Orthodox cleric favourable to reform, sets up a number of oppositions. Slavonic is characterised as 'medieval,' 'Byzantine,' and 'incomprehensible'. It is likened to Latin – perhaps with the insinuation that the Roman Church has already dropped *its* incomprehensible language and that the Russian Church needs to play catch-up, as it were. Furthermore, Slavonic is depicted as an obstacle to the 'modern individual' who seeks not salvation (as we would expect in traditional Orthodox theology) but 'enlightenment'. The right 'spiritual channel' is 'inaccessible' to Russian churchgoers – as if they lack the latest in communication technology.

This passage highlights the importance in these debates of *discourse*, namely the concatenation of stories, statements, arguments, metaphors and the like that, as an ensemble, constructs a phenomenon. Second, this passage points to the way that discourse 'flows' in and out of different fields of action within a society. In the above quotation, the liturgical language issue is construed in terms of individualism, spirituality and technology. Such a discourse is patently reflective of the shifts in post-Soviet society whereby individuals are imagined to pursue personal goals in a kind of marketplace of spiritual outlets. Thus, external discourses can flow into and influence the religious sphere.

At the same time, religious discourses can flow outward into other fields of action such as the polity, the economy, the military and so on (Reisigl and Wodak, 2001, pp. 36–7). Indeed, in post-communist Russia a number of internal Church disputes crossed over into the public sphere and became the subject of debate in the national media. Examining *religious* discourses and debates can therefore contribute to a better overall understanding of social change and transformation in the post-communist era. As Irina Papkov (2004, p. 38) says: '...it is no longer possible to analyze Russia's trajectory without taking the religious question seriously.'

The purpose of this chapter is to show how the contestation over liturgical language became a *cause célèbre* when the 'preservationist' discourse of Orthodox traditionalists connected with a wider 'discourse of cultural preservation' (Bacon, 2002) circulating in post-Soviet Russia. The controversy passed beyond the church walls and entered the public domain, in the process drawing in some of Russia's leading writers and intellectuals, such as V. Rasputin and D. S. Likhachev, as well as émigrés and experts outside Russia, who debated the issue in the media. As the language of cultus *and* culture, liturgy *and* literature, Church Slavonic could serve as the 'airlock' leading from the strictly ecclesiastical to the broader socio-cultural controversy (see Kondrat'eva, 2002).

The analysis of this episode, which spanned the 1990s, must be sensitive to the post-communist milieu in Russia, which the discourses both reflect and react against. It must also be aware of the historical context of the controversy, and the ways that the past was repeatedly invoked and recontextualised in the most recent debate. Russian clerics have argued over the issue of liturgical language since the 19th century (Kravetskii and Pletneva, 2001). The situation was exacerbated when the Bolsheviks supported the so-called 'Renovationists', who tried to introduce vernacular Russian into the liturgy, ostensibly for the sake of the proletariat. 'The experience of the Renovationist schism caused deep trauma in the ROC [Russian Orthodox Church] and its spectre continues to haunt the hierarchy today' (Walters, 2004, p. 89). Although that spectre was certainly felt during the 1990s version of the debate – the reformists were consistently labelled by their opponents as 'Neo-Renovationists' – this aspect has been treated elsewhere (Bennett, forthcoming) and so is set aside in the present analysis.

2 Critical junctures

The concept of 'critical junctures' provides a useful lens for viewing the liturgical language debate that occurred in the post-communist Russian Church. Benjamin Forest and Juliet Johnson (2002) harness the concept to explain how contestations over various monuments in and around Moscow, including Victory Park, Lenin's Mausoleum and the Cathedral of Christ the Saviour, involved competing ideologies of the nation. The salient features of critical junctures are as follows:

- they occur at times of transition, when social, political – and, one could add, religious and linguistic – structures and practices are amenable to possibly far-reaching transformation;
- they are usually elite-driven;
- they normally occur in core cities, especially the capital;
- they trigger passionate debates between elites, who struggle for symbolic capital, over fundamental socio-political issues – in sum, they generate discourse;
- critical junctures are limited in time; they comprise a small window of opportunity;
- elite interventions during critical periods are not always successful; it may happen that afterwards practices and institutions end up being more entrenched than before (Forest and Johnson, 2002, p. 527).

To borrow a model used to analyse monuments and apply it to a language like Church Slavonic is perhaps not altogether unwarranted. For one thing, a number of the nationalists who weighed in on the debate had cut their teeth in *Pamiat'* [Memory], a pivotal right-wing cultural preservation movement of the Perestroika and early post-Soviet years. Moreover, monuments have a linguistic dimension to them, sometimes literally so, in the form of plaques and inscriptions. Figuratively, they may be read as 'texts' (Forest and Johnson, 2002, p. 526). The relationship is even clearer in Russian, where the term *pamiatnik* refers not only to monuments in the conventional sense of memorials, plinths and the like, but also to literary and linguistic 'monuments' (Hughes, 2004, p. 171), as in the book series *Pamiatniki Literaratury Drevnei Rusi* [Monuments of the Literature of Ancient Rus].

One element of the discourse about Church Slavonic will in fact be its identification with the great 'monuments' (*pamiatniki*) of Russian literary culture. A textbook expression of this predication may be found in the volume, *Russkaia dukhovnaia kul'tura* [Russian Spiritual Culture], put out by Moscow University. In the conclusion to the chapter on Church Slavonic, we read,

> Thus, during the course of eight centuries, Church Slavonic in its Russian recension was the literary language of Russians; instantiated in monuments [*pamiatnikakh*] of different genres, existing in a number of variants, it was an element of Russian culture, the language in which religious and secular thought was articulated in Rus (Remneva, 1995, p. 80).

It is this point, which links Church Slavonic not only with religion but with Russia's historic language and culture (the way that Latin could be identified not only with the Catholic Church but with Western civilisation more broadly), that enabled the 'in-house' debate to 'go public'.

3 Innovation and repercussion

The issue of Church Slavonic vs. Russian had actually begun to be debated again in the last years of the Soviet Union. But the controversy began in earnest in the early 1990s when one parish, headed by one Fr Georgii Kochetkov and located at a notable church in the capital of Moscow, began to introduce Russian into worship services, replacing or augmenting the traditional Church Slavonic (see Daniel, 2006, pp. 74–108, for a valuable summary of the episode). A pastor with reforming and missionary proclivities, Kochetkov was ostensibly interested in making the Orthodox faith fresh and relevant to people, especially new converts, in the new post-communist environment. He had built up a congregation of young and dedicated believers, including some notable members of the intelligentsia, such as S. S. Averintsev, a well-regarded member of the Academy of Sciences who helped prepare the new liturgical translations. Kochetkov also had connections with members of different denominations (for example, Baptists) and with church figures outside Russia – connections which would later be used against him by his opponents. It was in the early years of post-communist flux and transition that Kochetkov's parish started to make some innovations in the liturgy.

Once these innovations became known, they were denounced by traditionalists in the Church in the strongest terms possible as heresy and blasphemy. Xenophobic and ultranationalist elements got involved. At one point Kochetkov's parish was even surrounded by Cossacks, the stereotypical enforcers of Russian Orthodoxy, and by a paramilitary 'Black Hundred' group committed to storming the 'Kochetkovite stronghold' (Vasiliev, 2000). In 1994 the members of this parish were ousted from their accustomed place of worship, moved to a church that had been used as a Soviet naval museum, and replaced by a group of conservative monks headed by an abbot who is said to be Vladimir Putin's spiritual adviser. In 1997 some kind of altercation took place between a group of Kochetkov's parishioners and a priest who may have been placed at the parish by conservative forces as an *agent provocateur*. The priest was sent in an ambulance for psychiatric evaluation. He claimed to have been beaten and manhandled by the parishioners – an allegation they strongly deny. The facts are in dispute, but the end result was that Kochetkov was forbidden from conducting his priestly duties, while 12 of the parishioners were excommunicated. After several years of public appeals by those parties involved and their supporters, the injunctions were finally lifted.

On the one hand, the fracas over liturgical language is understandable. Russian Orthodoxy is pre-eminently a *liturgical* faith. Orthodoxy (Russian *Pravoslavie*) means 'right belief' but also 'right praise' or 'right worship'. Consequently, the slightest change in ritual can appear to threaten the faith itself (Borisov, 1994, p. 128). The major Schism (*Raskol*) of the 17th century was precipitated, on one level at least, by innovations introduced into the liturgy, a kind of 'doomsday scenario' sometimes invoked by the traditionalists opposed to Kochetkov's agenda.

On the other hand, the response to Kochetkov's liturgical language innovation seems disproportionate. After all, this appeared to be a limited and thoughtfully prepared experiment occurring at just one parish among the thousands that make up the Russian Orthodox Church. Moreover, it is usually understood that the policy of Orthodox

Christianity (at least in polemics with Catholicism) is to endorse the use of vernaculars in the liturgy (Borisov, 1994, pp. 128–9). What is more, the Orthodox Churches of Serbia and Bulgaria, as well as certain church bodies in America, have made at least a partial transition away form Church Slavonic without fatal consequences (Meyendorff, 1994). Yet Kochetkov's reforms triggered an intense and vitriolic debate. To the conservatives who opposed the change, the Russian Orthodox Church, and by extension the very nation, seemed to be endangered by Kochetkov's actions (see Parthé, 2004, p. 87). How, then, is one to explain the 'passionate emotional responses' and the 'depth of the antagonisms that Kochetkov's circle inspired' (Daniel, 2006, p. 88)?

In his insightful study of alphabet debates in post-Soviet Russia, Mark Sebba (2006, p. 115) remarks, '...issues within a society, which have in themselves nothing to do with language, can be displaced on to language, making it the apparent focus of disputes which in reality are over something else.' He goes on to say that: 'Where there is unease within a society about aspects of social change...people may use language as a scapegoat – or rather, as a symbolic battlefield' (ibid.). This is what happened with the language of Church Slavonic. In the 1990s it became a prime symbol in the quarrels and contestations over the rapid religious, linguistic and cultural changes taking place in post-Soviet Russian society. Interestingly, at least some of Kochetkov's opponents viewed the matter in just this way, noting that the issue of liturgical language constituted a kind of 'litmus test' (*lakmusovoi bumazhkoi*) revealing deeper tendencies at work (*Literaturnaia Rossiia*, 1994a).

As noted above, this debate goes back a long way in Russian Orthodoxy. The crucial issue has always been the question of intelligibility. In theory, at least, Orthodoxy promotes the use of living, not hieratic, languages in the liturgy. Reformists tend to argue that Church Slavonic is incomprehensible to ordinary Russian speakers – hence translation is not only possible but necessary; that post-communist Russia is desperately in need of true Orthodox spirituality; and that introducing the living language is fully congruent with the Orthodox and Cyrillomethodian traditions. Traditionalists advanced a number of counter-arguments: Church Slavonic is understood perfectly well by the *narod*, the common people, if not by neophytes; it is a sacred language given by God to the Slavic peoples through the intermediation of SS Cyril and Methodius; there is a millennium of prayer and piety behind it; doing away with it would sever the bonds uniting the

Orthodox Slavs and would likely cause another schism in the Russian Church.

But in addition to these well-rehearsed arguments, traditionalists also made a number of assertions that were very much 'of the moment'. For most traditionalists, introducing the vernacular into the Russian Orthodox Church would represent a catastrophic capitulation to the forces of Westernisation threatening Russia. One suggested that introducing the vernacular would be the equivalent of wearing jeans to the worship service, just as Western sectarians do (Tikhon and Kaverin, 1999, p. 270). Another compared the idea of combining Church Slavonic and Russian in the liturgy with a bishop's mitre emblazoned with an 'adidas' logo (Tikhon and Kaverin, 1999, p. 350). A third suggested that Russian Church will go the way of Catholicism: after it abandoned Latin, one is faced with the scandal of the rock-and-roll Mass (Tikhon and Kaverin, 1999, p. 206). Jeans, sports logos, rock music – these are obviously synecdochal symbols of the encroaching West. Such arguments, then, already point beyond the 'strictly religious discourse' (della Cava, 1996, p. 388) to the affairs of society and culture.

4 Preservation of Church and culture

The model of 'critical junctures' suggests that, at time of flux and transition, elite-driven changes in core cities trigger passionate debates over fundamental socio-political issues. The liturgical innovations associated with Kochetkov's parish generated debate inside and outside the Church. The main point being argued in this chapter is that the 'preservationist' discourse within Russian Orthodoxy intersected with a broader 'discourse of cultural preservation' circulating in post-communist Russia. Edwin Bacon (2002, p. 113) provides a helpful précis of this latter discourse:

> ... the West, wittingly or not, has carried out a policy of 'cultural imperialism' against Russia. The story has been told repeatedly since the collapse of the Soviet Union in 1991: Agatha Christie and Tom Clancy on the bookstalls in place of Tolstoy and Dostoevsky... Pepsi Cola instead of *kvas*, Marlboro instead of Kosmos cigarettes.

Note the way that *literature* is singled out in this discourse. Note, too, how a series of items which represent Russia or the West are set in binary opposition. On one side are Tolstoy, Dostoevsky, *kvas,* and Kosmos cigarettes; ranged against them are Agatha Christie, Tom Clancy, Pepsi and Marlboros. Bacon continues,

> This process is acknowledged by many Western observers with some sorrow. In Russia, nationalists vehemently attack the West on the same grounds –indeed, the term frequently used in Russian nationalist and communist circles in place of 'cultural imperialism' is 'cultural genocide'.

Thus, precisely at the moment Kochetkov was embarking on his 'modernising' liturgical reforms, debates were raging about the reputed ruination of Russian language and culture caused by the juggernaut of Westernisation.

Church Slavonic was hailed by traditionalists and nationalists as the *fons et origo* of Russia's rich 'spiritual culture' (*dukhovnaia kul'tura*), the antithesis of the tawdry capitalistic culture peddled by the West. During a television broadcast, Solzhenitsyn pleaded: 'We must save our Russian language, our national culture and spirituality' (quoted in Ryazanova-Clarke and Wade, 1999, p. 333). Its devotees viewed Church Slavonic as vital to the safeguarding of all three – not just Russian religion but also Russian language and Russian culture.

The end of the USSR saw dramatic changes in the Russian language. The language underwent a twofold process of de-Sovietisation and Westernisation (J. A. Dunn, 1999). Although religious vocabulary was rehabilitated and at last appeared in public media, the same was true for slang, criminal argot and obscenity. Moreover, some 10,000 foreign words, many of them from English, entered the lexis (Ustinova, 2005, p. 241), frequently in Latin letters. For many Russians '... the use of the Latin alphabet stresses the foreignness of the product in question and therefore its supposedly superior quality' (J. A. Dunn, 1999, p. 12). But to nationalists the foreignness was a sign of war, of occupation. As one critic declaimed: 'Do our cities not resemble cities subjugated by alien countries, their streets made gaudy by foreign language advertisements and signs, not infrequently, appearing in Latin letters?' (quoted in Gorham, 2000, p. 622). To some the language – hence the nation – was under siege.

It is not surprising that there were puristic reactions to these developments (see Thomas, 1991). There was great concern in some quarters over the matter of 'language ecology', and urgent pleadings to defend the national language from and cleanse it of harmful foreign elements.

For some the solution lay in the revivification of archaic and/or religious vocabulary. Solzhenitsyn published a dictionary of antiquated words in the hopes of expanding the lexis (Gorham 2000, pp. 620, 625). In a similar vein, some considered Church Slavonic the necessary tonic. Here is a rather typical example of this discourse:

> On the one hand, the teaching of Church Slavonic in schools of various kinds, the elevation of its status in society, the dissemination of texts in this language among the different strata of the populace along with the adequate understanding thereof, will promote the ecology of the Russian language, will counteract its getting clogged up [*zasoreniiu*] by unnecessary borrowings from Western European languages, its Americanization. On the other hand, [these actions] will promote the widening of Russian's lexical make-up, the resurrection of lofty words...; they will place a limit on the inordinate slangification [*slengizatsii*] of the literary language (which happens above all through the incorporation of criminal-argot phenomena into the language of belles-lettres), and they will have a noticeable effect on the linguistic culture of Russian society (Suprun, 1997, p. 45).

Some emphasised the need for Church Slavonic to be taught again in the public school system, as it was in Tsarist times. The benefits, they said, would be not only spiritual but cultural. In a booklet published with an episcopal blessing, the linguist V. K. Zhuravlev argued that it was Lenin who forbade the teaching of religion and Church Slavonic in the schools. This decree must now be reversed:

> The critical situation of the ecology of the Russian tongue and spiritual culture demands the need for a governmental law concerning the prohibition on teaching Slavonic in the Russian national school system. We need to resurrect it as an academic subject. [...] It can be said without exaggeration, that the spiritual regeneration of our people is tied in the closest manner to the fate of the Russian Orthodox Church and, in significant measure, to the fate of its language... (1994, pp. 3, 24).

An important element of the discourse of cultural preservation, then, is that Church Slavonic has long nourished the Russian literary language. At this point a roster of great cultural figures is often summoned. Church Slavonic is said to inform not only the canon of scripture but Russia's great canonical authors as well. Especially during the Soviet era but even afterwards, Russians considered themselves the best-read people in the world (Lovell, 2000). Russian identity was closely bound up with literature. According to Kathleen Parthé: 'One could say without exaggeration that well into the 1990s, many Russians saw themselves as a people whose character was largely defined by their greatest authors, among them Pushkin, Lermontov, Gogol, Tolstoy, Turgenev, Dostoevsky, Chekhov, and Akhmatova' (2004, p. 9). For many Russians, the activity of reading itself was consecrated, being viewed 'as an activity that is supposed to be pursued for spiritual self-improvement, and not for professional or social advancement' (Lovell 2000, p. 138). Reading the classics was the ritual *par excellence* of Russia's spiritual culture. In the post-communist era, however, kiosks and metro stalls proliferated, selling a jumble of detective novels, self-help manuals, and books on UFOs and fortune-telling. By the oppositional logic of the discourse, if Church Slavonic is equated with Russia's centuries-old high culture, then the street-vendor hodgepodge represents that which is debased, vernacular and foreign.

D. S. Likhachev was a world-famous scholar of medieval literature and an avuncular spokesman for Russian cultural and ecological preservation (see Devlin, 1999, p. 63). As a member of the Orthodox Church, he had theological and pastoral reasons why Church Slavonic should be retained. But Likhachev also made the case on linguistic and cultural grounds. It is worth quoting him at length:

> Nowadays, when we have fallen into a state of cultural indigence… we must preserve without fail our link with the past. We possess a magnificent written language and literature: the compositions of Metropolitan Ilarion, Kiril Turovskii, Serapion of Vladimir, Metropolitan Aleksii, Ermolai-Erasm, Nil Sorskii, Maksim Grek and hundreds others… [Here Likhachev mentions the *Pamiatniki* series.] Thanks to texts printed in parallel Old Russian and Contemporary Russian, we can appreciate the uncommon beauty of the language of the Church, the language of spiritual culture. If we relinquish the language which Lomonosov, Derzhavin, Pushkin, Lermontov, Tiutchev, Dostoevsky, Leskov, Tolstoy, Bunin, and many, many others knew so excellently and which they used in their works – the losses in our understanding of early Russian culture will be irreparable… [Church Slavonic] is the language of a noble culture: in it there are no vulgar words; in it is impossible to speak in a rude tone, to curse. It is a language which presupposes a certain level of moral culture… Repudiation

> of its use in the Church, of its study in school, leads to the further degradation of culture in Russia (1999, pp. 276–7).

The characterisation of the post-communist milieu as rude, vulgar and culturally degraded was shared by many members of the intelligentsia, even those (like Likhachev) who welcomed many of the new freedoms available.

Likhachev was a patriot but not a nationalist. He maintained that Russia's greatness came from its historic openness to other civilisations, including the West. Nationalists, however, emphasise the East-West divide. In the nationalist and 'red-brown' (communist-fascist) literature, Western culture is depicted as materialistic, decadent, vampirish, parasitical – the list goes on (see Devlin, 1999). What the West offers is the exact opposite of what is meant by the incantatory phrase 'spiritual culture', which is deep, authentic and numinous. The spread of meretricious Western culture onto Russian soil was linked and likened to the expansion of NATO and the bombing of Kosovo (see Bacon 2002, p. 109). It was viewed in ultra-conservative quarters as a grand conspiracy orchestrated by 'Jew-Masons'.

The national press played a crucial role in the articulation of this cultural-preservation discourse. The breakdown of what Stephen Lovell calls the 'Soviet cultural monophony' (2000, p. 149) resulted in the crystallisation of different socio-cultural 'interest groups', each with its own media. On the left were papers such as *Moskovskie Novosti* and *Nezavisimaia Gazeta*. On the right, *Den'*, *Nash Sovremennik*, *Molodaia Gvardiia*, and others (Knox, pp. 37–8). The ultra-right was particularly well represented, with some 30 newspapers of 'a fascist or anti-Semitic orientation' published in Moscow alone (Moskovich, 1999, p. 87). The connection between newspaper and readership, however, did not always match up in a predictable straight line (Lovell, 2000, p. 154), but might resemble instead a puzzling Möbius strip. For instance, the ultra-conservative *Rus' Pravoslavnaia* [Orthodox Rus] was published as an insert in the erstwhile anti-Christian *Sovetskaia Rossiia* [Soviet Russia].

There were a number of 'open letters' written supporting and denouncing Kochetkov and his parish. It is noteworthy that these were published in some of the newspapers mentioned above, not in little-known ecclesiastical journals. Two letters have been selected for discussion because they exemplify the intersection between the ecclesiastical 'preservationist' discourse and the broader 'cultural preservation' discourse. The analysis below offered is meant to be illustrative, not exhaustive.

5 Discourse and text: the open letter

Discourses are instantiated in texts. Discourse analysis must pay close attention not only to the genre of texts (Reisigl and Wodak, 2001, p. 36), but also to the relative 'weighting' of different genres within a given cultural system. Letter-writing – to the Politburo, the President, the Patriarch – has played a major role in Russian and Soviet society. 'Petitioning the authorities,' observes Stephen White, 'was a tradition that went back to medieval times, when a bucket was lowered from a window in the Old Kremlin Palace in which petitioners could place their grievances' (2000, p. 194). Russian citizens have long written to their leaders asking for information, assistance and accountability (ibid., pp. 194–203). According to Juliane Fürst, 'Letters have always been an important medium between rulers and subjects in the Soviet Union and Russia' (2006, p. 327). In the 1970s, some 60 to 70 million letters a year were written to the major Soviet newspapers, far more than to their Western counterparts. During the era of Perestroika, public letter-writing grew in quantity, audacity and diversity of subject matter, ranging across topics such as prostitution, hooliganism and the dark legacy of Stalinism (Riordan and Bridger, 1992). When leading writers or scientists – a Solzhenitsyn, a Sakharov or a Likhachev – put pen to paper in the form of an 'open letter', the impact was considerable.

An open letter to Patriarch Aleksii was published in the 4 March 1994 edition of *Literaturnaia Rossiia*, a conservative nationalist weekly ('Po povodu', 1994a; excerpts were translated in *The Current Digest of the Soviet Press* XLVI, no. 10 [1994].) The writers identity themselves as laymen of the Russian Orthodox Church and 'public figures in the fields of science and culture' (*deiateli nauki i kul'tury*). Among the petitioners is Valentin Rasputin, a luminary of the right-leaning 'Village Prose' movement, a conservative activist, and later a member of the presidential committee on the Russian Language (Parthé, 2004, pp. 90–2). It is also signed by Igor Shafarevich, a noted mathematician identified with promulgating the anti-semitic notion of 'Russophobia'. Another signatory, Vladimir Soloukhin, had written an exposé which blamed Jews for the murder of the writer Blok (Parthé, 2004, p. 118). In short, the letter is attributed to some of Russia's most well-known nationalists.

The authors of the letter argue that Church Slavonic is a pure source (*chistyi istochnik*), which has long sustained the Russian literary language. They contend that the language needs to be studied more and taught in school. That is the answer to the liturgical language crisis, not rationalised contemporary translations (*ratsionalizirovannymi sovremennymi perevodami*), whose quality and accuracy are dubious. They contend that the innovations emanating from Kochetkov's church, evidenced in linguistic modernism (*v iazykovom modernizme*), are 'widely supported by forces external to the Orthodox Church' (*shiroko podderzhivaetsia vneshnimi po otnosheniiu k Pravoslavnoi Tserkvi silami*), part of a 'war' (*bor'be*) being waged by groups 'inimical [or 'alien'] to ecclesiastical interests' (*chuzhdikh tserkovnym interesam*). They suggest that the temptation to reform church practice goes 'hand in hand with the historically unprecedented spiritual aggression of foreign faiths' (*nariadu s istoricheski bespretsedentnoi dukhovnoi agressiei inoslaviia*) besieging Russia and 'is associated heresies and schisms introduced into Russia from outside' (*assotsiruetsia ... s privnosimymi v Rossiiu isvne eresiami i raskolami*). The rhetorical culmination is an *a fortiori* argument: the innovations carried on at the Moscow church 'appear to us to be all the more dangerous because they destroy church life not from without but from within' (*Oni-to i iavliaiutsia, po nashemu rasumeniiu, naibolee opasnymi, ibo nesut rasrushenie tserkovnoi zhizni ne isvne, no iznutri*).

As we have seen, the vocabulary of invasion, occupation and even genocide permeates the discourse of cultural preservation, especially in its ultranationalist versions. This martial aspect is most evident here. The liturgical innovations are explicitly labelled in terms of 'war' and 'aggression'. There is a pronounced us-vs.-them rhetoric. In addition to identifying themselves as members of the Church, the very act of writing to the Patriarch is an expression of group affirmation and participation (see Fürst, 2006, pp. 331–2). The authors also make reference to a liturgy celebrated by the Patriarch and attended by musicians, artists, scholars, and writers – a vision of unity between clerical and cultural elites. This in-group, as it were, is opposed to an out-group, which is subdivided into forces that are labelled 'foreign,' 'external' and 'inimical' (or 'alien'). Kochetkov and his parishioners are said to be acting in concert with these external agents. They are all the more dangerous because they are wreaking havoc *from the inside* [*ne isvne, no iznutri*]. Thus they are identified with quislings or traitors: they do the bidding of foreign powers, betraying Russia from within.

The next week (11 March 1994) another open letter to the Patriarch appeared in the same paper, *Literaturnaia Rossiia*; this one was signed by a coalition of Orthodox clerics, journalists and literary figures ('S pros'boi', 1994b). The letter begins by saying that the Church Slavonic liturgy was bequeathed to all the Slavic brethren by Cyril and Methodius. Kochetkov's translation represents an anti-Orthodox modernism (*antipravoslavnyi modernizm*) which shatters these historic bonds and could lead to a new schism. It is an 'encroachment' (*posiagatel'stva*) on the Church Slavonic language, a 'deliberate profanation' (*narochituiu profanatsiiu*) of the liturgy and an 'insult' (*oskorblenie*) to the religious sensibilities of the faithful. According to the authors, the fact that Kochetkov et al. repudiate the Cyrillomethodian legacy and substitute their own so-called 'translations' is an act of 'monstrous vandalism' (*chudovishchnyi vandalizm*) against the sacred liturgical texts (*sviatye bogosluzhebnye teksty*).

The vocabulary of corruption and degradation constitutes another aspect of the discourse of cultural reservation: the Russian language is clogged by obscenities and vulgarisms; bookstores are stocked with Western pulp fiction instead of the Russian classics; and so on. The letter from Rasputin et al. begins by describing Church Slavonic as a 'pure source' for the Russian literary language, but it is really this second letter which articulates this theme more fully. Here the threat from Kochetkov is construed not so much in terms of war and treachery, but as 'profanation' and 'insult'. Interestingly, it castigates Kochetkov's modernist *translations* as an act of vandalism against the Cyrillomethodian liturgical books, a metaphor which brings us back to the understanding of Church Slavonic as the language of Russia's spiritual and literary monuments.

6 The consequences of failure

The liturgical language debate of the 1990s generated considerable controversy inside and outside the Russian Orthodox Church. The model of 'critical junctures' can help shed light on certain key features of this debate. During a period of crisis and instability, Church reformists took advantage of a window of opportunity to initiate a kind of modernising programme. This took place in the political capital, which in this case is also the religious capital, insofar as the Patriarchate is headquartered there. The question of preserving Church Slavonic became one symbolic battlefield in post-communist Russia. Kochetkov's strategy reactivated an old debate and polarised the Church between reformists and traditionalists.

Responding to the types of criticisms from traditionalists and nationalists found in the two letters discussed above, and hoping to prevent a schism in a Church reeling from division and controversy (see Knox, 2005, pp. 163–79), Patriarch Aleskii quashed any attempts to move from medieval Slavonic to modern Russian in the liturgy. The window of opportunity was closed – or perhaps we could say was slammed shut, given the vehemence of the opposition. The failure may have actually strengthened the antecedent practice. Although the Russian Church may pursue a limited programme of 'Russification' with regard to its liturgical books, this will be carried out by individuals authorised by the ecclesiastical hierarchy. A wholesale translation into Russian is impossible, according to an article in *Belgorodskaia Pravda* by Metropolitan Kirill (2007), the church's spokesperson ('Molit'sia budem po-russki', 30 July). That is a significant outcome, given the fact that the Russian Orthodox Church is one of the biggest ecclesiastical bodies in the world, with a membership that exceeds the population of many European countries.

Moreover, this particular debate was no mere 'in-house' squabble played out in musty church journals. Its significance can also be measured in the way that it dovetailed with the wider discourse of cultural preservation, the one reinforcing the other; and in the way that the debate became a *cause célèbre,* drawing in high-profile elites such as Rasputin, Shafarevich, Averinstev, and Likhachev – there are no bigger names in recent Russian cultural affairs.

As this case study hopefully demonstrates, then, religious debates and discourses are not always cloistered affairs. They have the potential to reverberate and ramify throughout society. Accordingly, they deserve serious attention in post-communist and discourse studies.

8
Narrating Transition in East German Company Histories

Helen Kelly-Holmes

The tale of Sleeping Beauty is a familiar one, and the allegorical application of this particular narrative to the case of the former German Democratic Republic, for example by German writer Peter Schneider (1990), seems particularly appropriate: Sleeping Beauty is the defenceless Eastern occupation zone; the wicked fairy the Soviet occupation authority, the Soviet Union and ultimately 'communist' ideology; her castle is the East German economy, sleeping, by Western standards, for 40 years; and her handsome prince is of course West Germany and its particular brand of market economics. The awakening and renewal are the economic transition to a viable, market-driven economy.

This is, of course, not the only narrative to be written about the rescue of the East by the West, of socialism or communism by the market. Indeed, the Sleeping Beauty narrative is positively modest in comparison to Francis Fukuyama's (1992) grand narrative to end all narratives, his claim that the story has been told, that it not only had a beginning and a middle but also a very definite end, in the 'triumphal incantation of capitalism' as Jacques Derrida (1994) has called it.

Of course, the East German state itself was no stranger to writing and rewriting grand narratives. Most notable, perhaps, was the 'New Economic System', which, in 1966, told the story that actually existing socialism was not in fact a period of transition, a step on the way to fully fledged communism, the ultimate happy ending, but was in fact a valid ending in itself.[1]

Narratives need metaphors to simplify and exemplify complex events.[2] In the case of Central and Eastern Europe, the metaphor of the path or 'triumphal march' to socialism has been replaced by the far less decisive metaphor of 'transition'. Transition is a term that tends never to be explained, because it is of course understood that this is a transition from the wrong way of doing things to the right way, the only way, as Fukuyama and others would have it. Transition implies something smooth and even easy, and, unlike the struggle and strife metaphors of socialism, it seems to require a simple and seamless adjustment, although the reality has of course been rather different. Burawoy and Verdery (1999), for example, point out that transition, rather than being understood as 'a process of connecting the past to the future' seems instead to be theorised as being 'committed to some pregiven future or rooted in an unyielding past' (p. 4). They point to the need to 'focus on the day-to-day reality of postsocialism' in an effort to uncover the 'ambiguous accounts' of transition and transformation (p. 6), and to show how the macro affects the micro, and, perhaps most importantly, how micro-level agents are 'refashioning themselves in opposition to what governments intend' (p. 9).

This chapter reports on one type of micro-level practice within the macro context of transition in the form of an analysis of 13 East German company histories. First of all, the discourse of East German economic transition is discussed, in order to give an overview of the context and process of 'transition' as well as the lexis and texts of that process. The company history is then positioned as a narrative document of transition, within this broader discourse, before the individual company histories are described and discussed in terms of a number of different narrative strategies they employ. The aim of the chapter is to analyse these company histories in order to see how they function as sub-narratives within the grand narrative of 'transition' outlined above, and to explore how they make sense of the process of transition, by framing it within a narrative framework. Also of interest is the commercial motivation of these texts and how this shapes the stories told about 'transition', since company histories are not just narratives, but also public relations and ultimately advertising documents that define and give coherence to the brand identity.

1 The discourse of transition

For East German companies, the period of transition probably encompasses the time from the fall of the Berlin Wall in November 1989 to the official winding up of the *Treuhandanstalt,* the East German privatisation agency, in December 1994. The original *Treuhand,* the THA, was set up the by Modrow government in March 1990. However, progress in turning East German combines and people's own enterprises into fully functioning, capitalised companies was slow and the de Maizière government replaced the original *Treuhand,* composed in the main of former government officials of the GDR, with a body that worked together with the West German authorities, in the run-up to unification in October of that year. Facilitating the transition to a market economy was the raison d'etre of the *Treuhand,* which was headed by West German businessman Detlev Rohwedder.[3] The legislation that brought the *Treuhand* into existence was designed to 'privatise and reorganise the people's own assets' (Treuhandgesetz, 1990).

The discourse of the *Treuhand* privatisation agency itself and its founding legislation both formalised and propagated the lexis of transition. For example, its nominalisation of processes of economic change such as *'Übertragung'* (transfer),[4] *'Umwandlung'* (transformation), *'Anpassung'* (adjustment), *'Sanierung'* (restructuring), *'Umstellung'* (conversion) and *'Übergang'* (transition), created a sense of inevitability about these processes and downplayed the role of individual agents and participants (Hodge and Kress, 1993; Fairclough, 2001b). The Act also made the direction and outcome of this transition explicit (a 'pregiven future' of 'textbook capitalism' as Burawoy and Verdery (1999) describe it) in its use of the adjectives and attributes of Western market discourse, drawing on the ideologies of this particular classification system (Fairclough, 2001a). Combines and people's own enterprises were to become *'marktfähig'* (capable of operating in a market economy), *'effizient'* (efficient), *'ertragsfähig'* (profitable), *'sanierungsfähig'* (capable of restructuring/salvageable) and *'wettbewerbsfähig'* (competitive). They would learn how to operate 'according to business/entrepreneurial standards' (*'nach unternehmerischen Grundsätzen'*), and 'in line with the principles of the social market economy' (*'nach den Prinzipien der sozialen Marktwirtschaft'*). These terms can be seen to function as surface-level buzzwords, framing the discussion of the future of East German companies, and ultimately of not only the entire East German, but also the united German economy, within a commonsense ideology of 'the market'. They index wider societal and economic processes and trends on regional, national and global levels, in which Derrida's triumphal incantation finds their resonance. In such a frame, the lexis of socialism is not only outmoded, but also incompatible.

The discourse of the *Treuhand* privatisation agency also marked down an economic *'Stunde Null'* or year zero for these enterprises. They were to be metaphorically reborn in the market system, and entered anew as registered companies with a new opening balance sheet and other 'founding' documents. Their GDR life died with a 'closing balance of the economic unit' (*'Schlußbilanz der Wirtschaftseinheit'*) and their market life began with an 'opening balance sheet on their day of transformation' (*'Eröffnungsbilanz zum Stichtag der Umwandlung'*). This type of lexis mirrors very much Burawoy and Verdery's (1999) characterisation of the neoliberal transition theory as exploiting and reinforcing a genesis myth. The transitional nature of these enterprises was attested to by the fact that they had to describe themselves in the interim as limited companies *'im Aufbau'* – literally, under construction.

In reality, however, only very few East German companies and brands survived this transition. The vast majority were taken over by West German companies or were simply closed down and liquidated by the *Treuhand*. Similarly, although there were a number of management buy-outs, the majority of these transitions involved management 'buy-ins', with very few East Germans actually being involved in or benefiting from the privatisation process. In the period following the fall of the Berlin Wall, and also in the initial years of unification with the West, East German products and brands became one of the victims of transition and transformation. Having been denied the forbidden fruits of the West for so long, citizens in the GDR were eager to purchase and experience Western products. This led to a huge demand for Western products and a correspondingly large decline in the sale of Eastern products. In addition, not only did products not survive the transition to fully fledged Western brands, but in practical terms many of the manufacturing facilities were not equipped to survive the transition to Western-style economic and management practices.[5]

It did not take long, however, for disillusionment with West German products to set in. As early as 1995, only five years post-unification, 45 per cent of East Germans surveyed claimed to buy East German products intentionally if at all possible, with only two per cent reporting that they intentionally chose brands from West Germany (*Der Spiegel*, 1995). Gradually, the brands and companies of actually existing socialism began to find a voice again, as, for example, in *Berliner Kosmetik's* re-launch slogan aimed at consumers in other transition economies such as the Czech Republic, Slovakia and Poland, as well as Eastern Germany: 'What was good yesterday doesn't have to be bad today' (see Kelly-Holmes, 1999).

The company histories of East German survivor brands not only form part of the narrative of transition, they also recreate and revalorise the 'life-historical capital' of the GDR (see Habermas, 1993). The film *Goodbye Lenin!* (2003) illustrated this with its depiction of the hero, Alex, desperately roaming the aisles of East Berlin shops looking for GDR brands, without success. It is interesting that in order for him to recreate the GDR in his sick mother's room, the visual, aural and verbal presence of these everyday names was as essential as the television programmes, folk festivals, uniforms and street signs. Their continued presence in the market contributes to a continuing presence of the GDR, its nomenclature and its 'lifeworld' (Habermas, 1993), something that has been turned into a market opportunity by the many websites now specialising in East German brands (for example, www.Kaufhalle-des-Ostens.de; www.ostkost.de; and www.ostprodukte.de) which use the survivor myth in their slogans, for example: 'They're still here: the good products from the GDR' (www.ostprodukte.de).

2 Company histories as narratives

Company histories (see www.firmengeschichte.de or www.geschichteburo.de for details) can be seen to fall within the scope of non-fictional, historical narratives, in much the same way as general histories and biographies, which in Barthes's words '... ceaselessly substitute meaning for the straightforward copy of the events recounted' (1977, p. 79). Furthermore, individual company histories also comprise notional chapters in a national economic and industrial history, and as such may have wider resonance and societal importance, providing a substantial contribution to understanding our society and culture.

However, the company history is not just a narrative, it is also a commodity, or, in marketing terms, a 'unique selling proposition', something that differentiates the company, brand or product from competitors. Thus, this market-driven function can be seen to have an impact on the way in which the company history is written: for example, how it constructs a chronology of events; the emphasis it puts on certain events rather than others; how the company or brand's internal history is constructed in the wider context of external events; and what identity is created for the brand or product in relation to these historical events. It is 'through telling stories we say who we are and who we are not' (Thornborrow and Coates, 2005, p. 7), and the notion of the particular, personalised and individual story seems important not just for the company's sense of itself, its identity, but also for customers', competitors' and others' sense of it.

This latter point has particular resonance for the company history genre, since, as noted above, this type of text is not only a non-fictional, historical narrative, a text in which the '... desire for the imaginary, the possible, must contest with the imperatives of the real, the actual' (White, 1996, p. 276), it is also – and primarily – a public relations- or marketing-driven text. It is biography with a market-driven purpose and an important marketing instrument.

The company histories included in the study can all be characterised as narratives using Toolan's (2001) definition: they each have a high degree of 'constructedness', and 'sequence, emphasis and pace' in these texts are planned; they exhibit a good deal of prefabrication and intertextuality, creating a familiarity in both manifest and constitutive terms (see Fairclough, 1992) for the reader, not only in relation to other company histories, general histories and biographies, but also to the 'public narratives and collective memories about German history, such as the Cold War, the GDR and the FRG period, and national unification' (Armbruster and Meinhof, 2005, p. 44); they follow a typical trajectory – they go where the reader expects them to go; they have a narrator, in this case the anthropomorphised brand or company; and they exploit linguistic features to recall events that are distanced in space or time from both the reader and narrator (Toolan, 2001, pp. 4–6). The chronicling function, which is seen as a key distinguishing feature of the narrative (De Fina, 2003), is very prominent in these accounts, sometimes even to the extent that this is graphically represented in the form of a timeline. These company histories are also the 'little stories', in Lyotard's (1984) terms, that represent the micro-level experience of the 'grand narrative' (Lyotard, 1984) of transition: as such they both draw on this grand or public narrative and at the same time contribute to it, in much the same way as personal narratives of transition on the East-West German border (see Armbruster and Meinhof, 2005; Meinhof and Galasiński, 2005).

3 The study

With these assumptions in mind, the company histories of 13 GDR brands[6] that still exist 17 years after the fall of the Berlin Wall were examined, in an attempt to address the following questions: How do these companies and brands 'organise their experiences' of transition into a sequence of events? How are historical periods separated and sequenced and what emphasis is given to particular periods? And, to what extent do the stories these companies and brands tell show, on the one hand, their attempt to reason or to make sense of the process of transition, and, on the other, to represent themselves as being in or finished with this process? Finally, how do they construct themselves, and what kinds of identities do they create for themselves, in relation to the GDR and the transition?

I selected the websites from the www.ostprodukte.de and www.ost-kost.de sites and looked up company histories on these various websites. Some brands did not have any histories and instead only had minimal product-ordering information available on their websites. Obviously, the method of selecting the brands, using an internet site and then using only those brands and companies that, in turn, had an internet site with a company/brand history, does limit the scope of the study and its universality. After all, not all products and brands have websites or want to be presented in a forum like ostprodukte.de or ost-kost.de. Another factor is representativeness. These Ostalgie and GDR-produce websites tend to bias food products and everyday household items, thus excluding the very significant industrial sector.

What is discussed below then is simply the way in which 13 GDR brands tell their stories of 'actually existing socialism' as it was called and of the transition to a market economy, and how these particular 'memory stories' and 'self-narratives categorise and plot historical experience' (Armbruster and Meinhof, 2005, p. 41) The brands in question are: Zetti chocolates; Berggold pralines; Ur-Krostitzer pils; Halloren sweets; Florena skincare products; Born Senf mustard; Fit washing-up liquid; Rügenfisch fish products; Pfeffi sweets; Grabower confectionary; Kathi soups and sauces; Vita Cola; and Röstfein coffee. The first eight brands (Zetti, Berggold, Ur-Krostitzer, Halloren, Florena, Born Senf, Grabower and Röstfein) pre-date the GDR, while the latter five (Fit, Rügenfisch, Pfeffi, Kathi, and Vita Cola) were all founded during the time of the GDR.

Based on the analysis of the histories, in terms of their organisation and chronology of events, the time periods and how they were covered, and the language used to describe these events, four main narrative trends emerge, namely continuity, survivor, restitution/justice and mainstreaming. These narrative approaches will now be discussed in detail.

4 The continuity narrative

The continuity narrative is particularly strong in the company histories of brands that pre-date the GDR. This narrative scheme represents an attempt to present the brand and the company as bigger than the experience of the GDR and to position it as spanning the 19th and 20th centuries. Often, in this first trend, there is no explicit mention of the GDR and little or no reference to any events that took place in that time period, with the emphasis instead on the pre- and post-GDR periods, in an attempt to focus on continuity – the GDR being constructed (by its absence) as a historical blip or an unimportant period.

All of the brands and companies that adopt this approach were founded in the 1800s or early 1900s and so it seems reasonable that they might not pay too much attention to the time period of the GDR. Nonetheless, the disproportionate attention given to other periods, in particular the time since the fall of the Berlin Wall, does seem to suggest a strong desire to disassociate themselves from the GDR. For example, Halloren sweets provides a complete timeline chronicling the story of the company since its foundation in 1804. Eight entries inform the pre-transition narrative (186 years), while ten entries recount the events since unification in 1990 (16 years). There is only one entry from the time of the GDR, 1950, to do with the renaming of the company, but the GDR itself is never mentioned.

Even for those brands that do recognise and deal with the period of the GDR in a neutral if not quite positive way, there are certain gaps in the story told of actually existing socialism. The history of Florena creams and cosmetics is a good example here. The story is presented in a chronicle stretching from 1852 to the present day. There are entries for the 1950s and 1960s, but none between 1966 and 1990, a period of 24 years. In contrast, between 1990 and the current day, a 16-year period, there are 13 entries – compared with four for the 40 years of the GDR. Likewise, Berggold chocolates has a total of 14 entries spanning its history since 1876. Five of these 14 deal with the years since unification, and although there are three entries for the period of the GDR (1949, 1955, 1966), there is, again, nothing between 1966 and 1990. This period (from the introduction of the New Economic System in the mid-1960s to the *Wende*) seems to be the focus of the Sleeping Beauty myth in many of these company histories, conveying the impression that the GDR economy slept its way through the 1970s and 1980s.

The approach of trying to present the brand as bigger than its GDR existence is best exemplified in the history of Ur-Krostitzer pils. This is perhaps not surprising when the reader learns that the company history begins in 1534. What is particularly noteworthy here is the emphasis on the pre-20th-century period. Four pages in total detail events between 1534 and 1900, with only two pages dealing with the 20th century. And, given the pedantic detail paid to pre-20th-century events, it seems remarkable that there is no reference to the Second World War – the only entry between 1907 and 1949 is a company name change adding AG (or publicly listed company) in 1937. Nor is there any mention of the GDR. The major emphasis instead is on the brand's imperial past, summed up in the brand's slogan: 'A genuinely royal pleasure since Gustav-Adolf's time'.

The Ur-Krostitzer approach highlights another factor common to these pre-GDR continuity brands, namely the way in which they treat the period of Nazism and the Second World War. Halloren sweets has an entry for 1934 and one for 1943; the former deals with internal restructuring of the company and a reassurance that it was, at the time, involved in producing 'top-quality pralines'. The entry for 1943 neutrally tells the reader that the production of chocolate products was halted and that the company was instead involved in producing aircraft parts. These statements are constructed in purely factual terms and their only lexical slant is towards a type of marketing vocabulary, with the use of attributes such as 'top-quality'. There are no value judgements here, nor any perceived need for self-reflection or justification. There is an unwritten, implicit understanding between the company and the reader of the company history that they both know the context, and that in this type of mixed marketing/historical text, there is no need for explanation or apology.

5 The survivor narrative

The second narrative strategy, that of constructing the brand or company as a victim of transition, which has, against all odds, survived the Western economic takeover, is adopted exclusively by brands and companies that were founded during the period of the GDR. This is perhaps not surprising, since such brands and company names would have been seen, arguably more than the previous brands discussed, as part of the nomenclature of the GDR's 'lifeworld' and consequently would perhaps be expected to deal with the period of the GDR in a more detailed way. Furthermore, in contrast to the continuity strategy, they have continued to identify themselves as GDR brands, and for many this is the central part of their marketing strategy and message – their post-communist identity has become their 'unique selling proposition' in marketing terms.

A further difference between continuity and survivor narratives is in the treatment of the GDR. Unlike continuity narratives, the GDR is acknowledged and dealt with in these histories, and this treatment tends to be neutral or even mildly positive, rather than negative. Another common element in these survivor histories is the emphasis – in terms of headings, number of entries and quantity of text – on the post-transition period, rather than on any other historical period or event.

Vita Cola's history only begins in 1954 and is divided into three periods, each of which is given about the same amount of text, although these periods differ greatly in length: the first covers 35 years from 1954 to 1989; the second runs from 1990 to 2000, a ten-year period; and the final section covers 2001 to the present day. The first section, although entitled 1954–1989, actually deals extensively with the *'Gründerjahre'*, the first four years of the company's establishment, with the years afterwards being ignored. So, again, even though this is a GDR brand, the same type of Sleeping Beauty myth seems to prevail in relation to the 1960s, 1970s and 1980s as with the brands that pre-dated the GDR.

Vita Cola's discussion of the GDR era is a rather objective one. There is no attempt to disguise the context as anything other than that of 'actually existing socialism' and the nomenclature of the time is used in a matter-of-fact and uninhibited way: e.g. *DDR-Patentamt* (the GDR patent office), *Regierungskommission für Preise* (government pricing commission), *Zentralreferat Lebensmittelindustrie* (central organisation of the grocery industry). It is only when transition begins that the language becomes more subjective and less factual, and this is where what could best be described as the mythologising part of the narrative really begins, the brand being presented as a victim of fate, increased consumer choice, and the transition to the market economy:

> After the fall of the Wall, Vita Cola's fate seemed to be sealed, as consumers turned to those brands that they had been denied for an eternity. Vita Cola disappeared from the shelves.

This explicit referencing of greater historical processes (the fall of the Wall and the economic policies of the former GDR) also contrasts sharply with the continuity narrative approach, which leaves it up to the reader to situate company events within a wider historical context.

The narrative then moves on to the rescue by the handsome prince. Against all the odds, the brand is resurrected, rescued by the Thüringer Waldquell Mineralbrunnen GmbH company and lives to fight another day: 'The successful revitalisation of the brand has been remarkable.' Vita Cola's identity – and that of the other brands which exploit the survivor narrative – is not so much grounded in its narration of the GDR time as it is in its construction of itself as a survivor brand. Thus, the emphasis, in terms of quantity of text, is on the transition period, when the brand was threatened with extinction, and the post-transition period, when the brand rose from the ashes to success as an *Ostmarke* or

Eastern brand. Transition then is at the very heart of Vita Cola's identity.

This theme of resurrection also features in Pfeffi sweets' very brief company history on its website (www.pfeffi.de). Like Vita Cola, Pfeffi deliberately constructs itself as a GDR survivor brand. For example, as the website opens, the following slogan appears, accompanied by the iconic image of a Trabant car painted in peppermint green: 'Hurrah! Pfeffi is back' There is no actual company history in terms of a chronology on the site, and the brand instead relies heavily on the website visitor's knowledge of the context and vocabulary of the GDR, as the following extract demonstrates: 'The Pfeffi Story: The triumphal march (*Siegeszug*) of the sweet goes on'. Furthermore, the brand also acknowledges explicitly the current status of former GDR brands and their marketing niche by describing the product as 'the cult sweet of the former GDR'.

The resurrection metaphor contrasts sharply with the approaches taken by continuity brands. For example, Ur-Krostitzer pils, which, as discussed above, constructs itself as a continuity brand and shuns the 'Ostalgia' approach, details its 'rescue' in a very different way. The brand describes itself simply as 'belonging' to the Radeberger beer group, based in Frankfurt since 1990. For the reader with 'insider' knowledge of the *Wende* it is clear that Ur-Krostitzer was taken over by a West German concern. However, rather than being described as a takeover, or as a type of hero-rescue, the brand presents itself as an equal partner to, or at least desirable acquisition for Radeberger, rather than as a victim in need of rescue.

6 The restitution/justice narrative

The restitution narrative dominates in the company histories of family enterprises, which depict the period of actually existing socialism as something abnormal, an aberration. Unlike the continuity narratives, which ignore the GDR, in this narrative scheme, the GDR is a rogue state that disenfranchised and expropriated family firms.

Kathi cakes and confectionery is a GDR brand, tracing its history to 1951, when the company name was entered into the trade register of the GDR and, in common with VitaCola, Pfeffi sweets and others, the language and nomenclature of the GDR are present in its narrative: '*das westliche Ausland*' (the West), '*Endverbraucherpreis*' (final consumer price), etc. However, unlike Vita Cola, the history of the GDR is told in emotional and critical language; for example, the 1960s are described as a time of 'economic chaos'. Furthermore, Kathi, a family business, is presented as the victim of the GDR regime and economic system: 'In 1965 Kathi was banned from exporting to the West and was punished for the good quality of its products', and, 'On 1 April, 1972 the company was finally seized by the organs of the state from the owners'. Transition to a market economy is then presented as a restitution of normality, bringing justice to these companies and brands, rather than the threat of extinction. The title for the section on transition reads: 'A new beginning: In February 1990 the company was re-privatised'. The entries dealing with the current company all emphasise the family nature of the business, and the word 'family' is mentioned many times in these paragraphs; for example: 'Fundamental to Kathi's particular identity is a clear recognition of the enterpreneurial responsibility of family ownership'.

The Born Senf mustard company history also positions the brand as having a justice/restitution identity: 'In 1990 the family had what was rightfully theirs restored to them and embarked with energy on continuing the work of Margarete Born.' Again, here, as in many of the other accounts, the narrative relies on 'insider' or shared knowledge, since nowhere in the account is the reader told that the company was in fact ever expropriated, and, as stated earlier, the entire period of the GDR is lost in this narrative. So, apparently, for this company it is not about constructing itself in terms of the GDR or even in terms of transition to the market or relaunching itself in the free-market system, but instead it is an identity that centres around the restoration of normal relations for this family company, emphasised particularly in the use of the word 'continue'. In such a scheme, the unnamed period of the GDR is portrayed as an abnormal state of affairs.

Interestingly, in common with continuity narratives, Born Senf's restitution narrative only alludes to certain events in the wider historical context. The sole entry for the Nazi period reads as follows: 'In 1934 exports made up over 70 per cent of the business. Thanks to the farsightedness of Walter Krüger, the company secretary, who feared Germany's isolation, the company concentrated on extending its domestic business'. It is understood here that the reader knows the context of and reasons for Germany's 'isolation', and so there is, by implication, some reference to the external events of the Second World War. The account then jumps to 1946, when part of the factory was burned down, but the reader is not told how or why or by whom, and the next event recounted is in 1970, 24 years later. As with Halloren, these events are viewed purely through the telescope of the company itself and how it was affected in a very particular way, without any attempt to evaluate or excuse. Ironically, although this is a document of history, it is also a history-free document, in the sense that the wider historical context is explicitly ignored.

7 The mainstreaming narrative

A final trend in the company histories of GDR brands is the rejection of the survivor identity and the use of the company history document instead for the purposes of mainstreaming the brand as a regional or all-German player. Unlike Pfeffi and Vita Cola, Fit washing-up liquid, rather than explicitly identifying itself as a GDR or post-communist brand, instead concentrates on positioning itself as an Eastern brand: 'The best known washing up liquid in the East is 50! *"Fit"* is often used as a synonym for washing up liquid in the new federal states.' The choice of the more neutral, post-unification terms 'East' and 'new federal states' rather than 'former GDR' (as in the case of Pfeffi and others) is also noteworthy and seems to indicate a distancing from survivor narratives and a GDR/post-communist marketing identity. The brand's approach seems to be to carve out a niche for itself as a legitimate brand that has regional dominance/significance in the East, rather than positioning itself in the category of a survivor or cult brand, something which seems essential if it is to fulfil its ambition of becoming a mainstream, national brand, an ambition hinted at in the following extract: 'Now *Fit* is gradually being introduced into West German supermarkets.' The statement seems quite modest, in comparison with marketing speak in general, and almost has the tone of a rehabilitation or recovery process. Furthermore, despite the fact that the end of the GDR and the transition process are not referred to directly, the 'hero' motif is still present: 'In 1993 Dr. Wolfgang Groß, a chemist, took over the company and invested more than 60 million DM in it.'

Rügenfisch, a GDR fish-processing company founded in 1951, deals explicitly with transition in the entry for the year 1990: 'Since the economic and currency union, the company's main customers have been firms in the old federal states (West Germany).' This reference to economic and monetary union is the only allusion to external events in the entire chronicle. Even though the company's history is detailed throughout the period of the GDR, this could be the history of a company in the West, since the lexis, nomenclature and key events of the GDR are never mentioned. Neither does the company reflect the period in a negative way – the details are simply given matter-of-factly. This tone is continued in its account of the 1990 transition and, unlike many of the entries for other brands dealing with the same period, Rügenfisch does not construct itself as a victim of events. The account then goes on to detail the brand's success at breaking into the all-German market, seen as the ultimate symbol of success, and launching the brand on the export market. In other words, the process is seen very much as one of normalisation, not to a previous state of affairs (as in the case of family-owned enterprises such as Kathi and Born Senf), but more in the sense of 'mainstreaming', becoming a 'normal' brand in the sense of the market economy, a brand that could be West German, and one that is 'legitimate' and competitive in this new context.

8 Conclusions

In terms of their organisation of events in an attempt to represent the past, to have '...real events display the coherence, integrity, fullness, and closure' (White, 1996, p. 284) of a story, the company histories discussed display a number of common traits and structures. First of all, for the brands that were founded in the 19th century or in the early part of the 20th century, the Nazi era and the Second World War are a black hole. There could be many reasons for this; the company may, for instance, feel that the period does not need to be discussed or explained or it is deemed simply too difficult – both of which are interesting. So, we end up with, to play on Eric Hobsbawm's title, a very, very short 20th century. This lack of context means that it is assumed that the reader of the site knows why these businesses were expropriated and why there was this first transition to a planned socialist economy. Furthermore, external (macro) events and processes tend to be implied, whereas internal (micro) ones – involving the intersection of external and internal – are made explicit. It is up to the informed reader to glean the information about the implied external context from the highly detailed information about internal company dealings and events.

As regards the kinds of narrative that these companies and brands write in their chronicling of transition and the identities they have created for themselves in the process, a number of sub-narratives emerge within the wider public narrative or meta-narrative of 'transition'. First of all, there is the 'bigger than the GDR' approach to understanding and presenting the self. This is where companies pay very little attention to the 40 years of the GDR, sometimes not even mentioning it in their histories, while paying much more attention in quantitative and qualitative terms to the preceding era and/or the years since transition. In such a scheme, the economic transition to a market economy is presented in a matter-of-fact way as one of the many transitions that these brands and companies have gone through.

Secondly, there is the survivor narrative – the brand is the victim of transition, and celebrates itself and presents itself as a survivor of the GDR era. These brands tend to divide up their history into before and after the GDR period, with transition presented as something painful and far from smooth. The Prince Charming character tends to feature heavily in these particular narratives. The survivor narratives could, on the one hand, be seen to form part of a counter-narrative to the public narrative or grand narrative of transition. However, this is undermined somewhat by the fact that a number of these brands are now owned by West German parent companies – so it would seem that the survivor narrative is just a strategy utilised for marketing purposes. However, it could be argued that even where the narrative is employed as a marketing instrument by a West German parent to add local flavour to its Eastern subsidiary, the effect of the narrative and its possible contribution to a positive post-communist identity is hard to predict.

Thirdly, there is the 'restitution and justice' narrative, where the company is restored to its rightful owners, usually family businesses. Here transition is a process of normalisation, with the period of the GDR presented as a period of abnormality. For these companies, the family brand is the defining characteristic of their post-transition identity.

Two further identities emerge in what can best be described as a mainstreaming strategy: the first is that of a regional, Eastern brand. This is different to the GDR-survivor identity, in the sense that the brand defines itself primarily as having regional status and dominance in the new federal states, while at no time utilising a nostalgia strategy. The identity of these brands is mainstream rather than cult or niche, as it is in the case of GDR-survivor brands. The second, related identity is that of pan-German contender. Here the brand rejects or downplays its GDR and/or Eastern heritage in favour of a telling of its history that presents it as a serious, 'normal' German brand. Both the continuity and the mainstreaming narratives, more than the others examined, exemplify the use of narrative to present the company as 'typical' and 'culture-confirming' (Bruner, 2001) in relation to Western notions of markets and marketing.

A number of other noteworthy anecdotes emerge from this small study, for instance, the preponderance of food and drink products among the survivor brands. It could either be the case that these brands have a company structure and products that were most suited to surviving transition, or it may be a reflection of the role of food and drink products in society, which means that they are products that people are less likely to dispense with easily, and that by their very nature lend themselves more readily to a nostalgia-type marketing appeal.

The final thing which the histories have in common is their 'sleeping spell', reflecting the Sleeping Beauty narrative approach to telling the story of the GDR's existence from the late 1950s to the late 1980s. This seems to be about marketing and public relations on the one hand, and on the other, reinterpreting or reassessing the self from the other's point of view. In her study of the narratives which parents would pass on to their children about everyday life in the GDR, Beth Linklater (1999) commented on the overwhelmingly positive impressions of the GDR represented in these accounts. However, the market-driven function of the company history text means perhaps that the GDR has to be remembered in a particular way, one that shows, teleologically, that it was doomed to fail and to result in 'normalisation', that is, the return to a market economy. As Julian Preece has pointed out in relation to autobiographical accounts of the *Wende*, 'in the light of the end ... the previous years suddenly made sense or could be made to make sense very easily ... it became possible to say where history had been leading all along' (1996, p. 358). It is clear that very many things did happen in those years in all of the companies looked at. However, this time now belongs to the 'deep sleep' era of the GDR economy, particularly as viewed by the West; it also seems to have been adopted by these East German companies and brands in telling their story.

In his *Postcommunism* (1999), Richard Sakwa identifies one key characteristic of post-communist societies as the tendency to interpret the present in terms of the past. However, the narrative of the post-communist company history represents an interesting subversion of this hypothesis. In these marketing-driven histories, it is the present that dictates the interpretation of the past. In the contemporary context of the marketised economy, in Eastern Germany as well as in other post-communist societies, the period of actually existing socialism seems incompatible with legitimate 'market-capable', 'efficient' companies; instead it must be reinterpreted in its transformation into a marketing instrument, and the determining factor in how its story will be told is the identity and positioning desired by the brand today.

Notes

1. For a discussion of these issues see Dennis (1988, pp. 33ff) and Garvy (1966).
2. See Lakoff (1981) and Chilton (1981).
3. Birgit Breuel, at the time finance minister in Lower Saxony, took over following Rohwedder's assassination in 1991.
4. All translations are the author's.
5. For an overview of these issues see, for instance, Priewe and Hickel (1991).
6. See: www.berggold.de; www.born-feinkost.de; www.fit.de; www.flocke.de; www.florena.de; www.grabower.de; www.halloren.de; www.ost-kost.de; www.pfeffi.de; www.roestfein.de; www.ruegenfisch.de; www.ur-krostitzer.de; www.vita-cola.de.

Part III

Transformation(s) of the Semi-public/Semi-private and Private Spheres – Discourse and the Experience of Transformation

9

'Mea Culpa': The Social Production of Public Disclosure and Reconciliation with the Past

Cristian Tileagă

1 Introduction

It can be sensibly argued that transformations of social, political and moral frameworks for constructing personal and political subjectivities have been taking place in a variety of forms and with different effects across a range of Eastern European contexts. In order to understand and describe individual experiences of social change, researchers have usually engaged in documenting the nature of these particular transformations of social, political and moral frameworks for constructing personal and political subjectivities. Although this is a very important research goal in its own right, it may not tell the whole story. Questions still remain: How are these social, political and moral frameworks constructed by members of society through the use of various cultural and discursive resources to make sense of themselves and others? How are personal and political subjectivities actually constructed and reproduced, assumed or contested?

The transition from communism to democracy has been a period when possibilities of constructing and affirming (alternative) personal and political subjectivities/identities have been innumerable. At the same time, this period has also been one of re-evaluating and reaffirming personal/political biographies from under the sway of the communist and post-communist recent past. This chapter is an attempt to capture individual experiences of social change through an example of 're-acquisition of biography' (Miller, 1999) and reconciliation with the past.

In common with many other East European countries, the end of the communist era in Romania has seen the publication of documents which have been perceived as evidence of complicity between the Securitate (the communist secret police) and certain public figures. The process of releasing and making public documents of the Securitate has been very slow and riddled with controversy. Investigations of the released documents have led to a series of allegations of 'collaboration' with the Securitate which, in turn, has led to a number of public statements (which I will refer to as 'public disclosures') from the subjects of those allegations: politicians, public intellectuals, clerics and journalists, in a variety of forms (such as interviews with journalists and letters to newspapers). These texts can be seen as serving to account for their past actions and can be viewed through the lens of reconciliation with the past.

This chapter is concerned with the production and politics of public disclosure in relation to accounting for 'collaboration' with the Securitate. It examines, in detail, a 'confession' of 'being an informer' by a Romanian public intellectual in a letter sent to one of Romania's wide-circulation national newspapers. A discursive psychological approach (Edwards and Potter, 2001) is used to consider how disclosure and reconciliation with the past are accomplished in the letter, where issues such as subjectivity, remembering, public accountability and biography become relevant. My analytic topic is the description and treatment of public disclosure and reconciliation with the past *by members of society*, not its 'objectivity' for me as researcher (see Eglin and Hester, 2003).

The specific focus will be on several inter-related dimensions: a) considering such issues as action-oriented and participants' accomplishments; b) taking into consideration how the text itself is 'organized so as to potentially persuade readers towards a specified set of relevances' (Watson, 1997, p. 89); and c) accounting for the social management of morality and self-presentation as a complex, delicate and ambivalent operation. Whereas previously disclosure and reconciliation with the past has been seen as a case of reflecting on the personal, historical and political (Miller, 1999, 2003), here I wish to develop and suggest a conception of reconciliation with the past as a way of doing something towards its production.

2 Context and research

The context is that of the Romanian public sphere. There have been several attempts, mainly originating in Critical Discourse Analysis (CDA) (see Preoteasa, 2002; Ieţcu, 2006),[1] to consider, from a discursive perspective, the Romanian public sphere. These contributions have revealed some of the discursive and ideological dynamics of (democratic) dialogue in the Romanian public sphere (see also Fairclough, 2005b on the contribution of CDA to research on the process of 'transition' in Central and Eastern Europe, especially Romania).

Social change, transformation, narrative, auto/biography and memory have constituted recurrent themes in discursive/narrative approaches to social change and transition (for example, Andrews, 2000; Konopasek and Andrews, 2000). As Andrews has noted, 'members of societies in acute social change are not only (and perhaps not even) experiencing a liberation of their memory; they are scrambling to construct new and acceptable identities for themselves, ones which will be compatible with the changed world in which they now live' (2000, p. 181). It has been argued that the stories which people tell about 'themselves and their pasts are a product of the present, as well as the past' (p. 181). Other authors have drawn attention to the theme of guilt and complicity and the impact of totalitarianism in terms of memory's revision of the past (Passerini, 2005).

Biographical, narrative and life-story research have attempted to describe and explain the changes of individuals' biographies and identities brought about by disclosures and attempts at reconciliation. A relevant example is research conducted by Barbara Miller (1999). In her book on Stasi informers, she analyses 'narratives of guilt and compliance' in East Germany, attempting to construct a socio-psychological framework of 'reconciliation with the past'. Narratives of guilt and compliance are interpreted through the use of psychological categories and theories (such as cognitive dissonance and selective memory) and by developing explanations in terms of socialisation, double morality, double standards and the acceptance of political lies.

However, while valid within their own terms, such phenomena can be examined by seeing displays of disclosure and reconciliation and of regret or remorse as accomplishments of participants in the management of public accountability. What seems to be missing is a focus away from how participants retroactively 'interpret' their past and present their selves (Miller, 2003) towards how the past/present selves, the private/public and the personal/political unfold and become entangled in a space of public visibility and accountability.

3 Confession and the active text

1. 'He has got it off his chest'
2. 'I cannot quite pull myself together'
3. 'Now he is a free person'

4. 'Repentance does not have moral significance'
5. 'This action should be saluted'
6. 'I am amazed and aggrieved'
7. 'This case is another argument for condemning communism'[2]

These are just some of the press headlines summarising the public comments made by a range of Romanian public intellectuals as a reaction to a 'confession' by a fellow public intellectual (and friend) of being an 'informer' for the Securitate. Others have refused to comment. These statements constitute various ways to 'activate or animate' (Watson, 1997, p. 88) the confession as an 'active text' (Smith, 1990a; Watson, 1997), actively organising reconciliation with the past as a significant social action. The letter is inspected for how it 'actively makes sense' (p. 85) of confessing having been an informer for the Securitate.

The act of confessing can be seen as furnishing the visible display of public accountability through which an audience can assess the confessor's character (see Lynch and Bogen, 1996). It is a sort of 'obligatory act of speech which...breaks the bonds of discretion and forgetfulness' (Foucault, 1978, p. 62). What might be of interest to researchers of communism and post-communism, but also to psychologists, sociologists and ethnographers of transition, is the production of public disclosure and reconciliation with the past that is intimately linked to the 'hermeneutic of the self' (to use Foucault's terminology) and 'community' that it engenders.

The focus of this chapter is on illustrating the subtle ways in which disclosure and reconciliation with the past are exercised as publicly accountable practices in the management of self-presentation and moral character. The aim is to consider an example of public disclosure (a confession) and viewing it as a site where public accountability is being managed (Lynch and Bogen, 1996). It is not my aim to chart the 'subjective' psychological world of public disclosure. Rather, I seek to understand 'the constitutional work that accomplishes an event or object' – such as a confession – 'in the process of its textual inscription' (Smith, 1990b, p. 216).

In communist (but also post-communist) times, 'the individual was formed as a category of knowledge through the accumulated case records (the file) which documented individual life histories within a particular institutional nexus' (Featherstone, 2006, pp. 591–2). The Securitate was one of these institutions that not only constituted the individual as a category of knowledge through accumulated records, but did so in the service of a hegemonic political order, for the purposes of social control and oppression.[3] The production and control of the public record of politics, people and events by the Securitate has led to a kind of 'textually mediated' production of domination and coercion.

As Smith (1990b) has argued, 'the appearance of meaning as a text... detaches meaning from the lived processes of its transitory construction, made and remade at each moment of people's talk' (p. 210). It is worth noting that for diverse categories of researchers (historians of communism and post-communism, sociologists and psychologists of transition, ethnographers), textual materials have been seen as sources of information on something else (historical, political 'realities'), rather than as phenomena in their own right. As Watson (1997) argues,

> texts are placed in the service of the examination of 'other', separately conceived phenomena. From this standpoint, the text purportedly comprises a *resource* for accessing... phenomena existing 'beyond' the text... where the text operates as an essentially unexamined conduit, a kind of neutral 'window' or 'channel' to them (p. 81, italics in original).

Texts have not been treated 'as active social phenomena' (p. 84) and social products. But what happens when people turn themselves into 'socially organized biographical objects' (Plummer, 2001, p. 43)? One way to think about this is to see 'writing' (like 'saying') things as a way of doing something (see Watson, 1997). The question which then arises is what discursive resources do people use to 'do things' when they turn themselves into 'socially organized biographical objects'?

As Lepper puts it,

> writers and readers, no less than speakers and hearers, use categorical resources to debate, negotiate, conceal and impugn, and to act to gain the concurrence of other parties to the 'talk'. Through written, no less than through spoken interaction, the work of shared understanding is routinely accomplished according to observable procedures which can be formulated and verified (2000, p. 77).

4 Method

In common with discursive psychology (Edwards, 1997; Edwards and Potter, 2001), drawing on insights from membership categorisation analysis (Sacks, 1995) and ethnomethodology (Eglin and Hester, 2003; Lynch and Bogen, 1996; Smith, 1990a, 1990b) this chapter attempts to restore public disclosure and reconciliation to their situated, observable, visible nature, as accountable community practices. This involves a detailed examination of the situated means of their production. Whereas, in other approaches, disclosure and reconciliation are considered to be 'psychological', here I see them as public, 'practical-textual accomplishments' (Barthélémy, 2003). This entails treating instances of public disclosure (such as this confession letter) as performative and action-oriented, 'such that issues of sincerity, truth, honest confession, lies, errors, confabulations, and so on' (Edwards, 1997, p. 280) (as well as 'guilt', 'remorse' or 'regret') constitute matters that talk and text manage and accomplish 'in analyzable ways' (ibid.).

The question to ask is not why, but *how* a text 'is ... written in just this way' (Livingston, 1995, p. 21). In the context of 'telling the truth' about the self (and the past), one can read accounts as a kind of 'apologia for who and what one has been' (Freeman, 1993, p. 20, in Edwards, 1997). As Edwards suggests, it is for this particular reason that, as analysts,

> we have no business ... reading *through* them to the life beyond, any more that we can read through discourse of any kind, to recover the world it purports to represent. Rather, they have to be read reflexively, in the ethnomethodological sense, as part of, as moves in, and as constituting the lives they are ostensibly 'about' (1997, p. 271, italics in original).

Thus I will refrain from speculating about the 'the real truth' of the biographical or political account and instead will focus on the complex matter of the *produced* unfinished business (see Lynch and Bogen, 1996) of public disclosure and reconciliation investigated in their local-historical circumstances. The focus is on the constitutive properties of text that help reveal how public disclosure and reconciliation are *produced* as 'matters for members, and therefore discoverable in their orientations to and treatments of them' (Eglin and Hester, 2003, p. 4). In an attempt to go beyond a 'linguistic analysis of texts' (Fairclough, 2003), this chapter engages with the practical methods, and cultural and categorial resources through which public disclosure, moral justification, accountability, memory, apology and reconciliation are managed in text. The intention here is not to define an exclusive research endeavour, but to develop the capacity to investigate a series of phenomena that constitute (or might constitute) the concern of psychologists, sociologists, historians, ethnographers and anthropologists of communism and post-communism.

5 Analysis

The data for this chapter comes from the text of the confession itself as published in the online edition of a major central (wide-circulation) Romanian newspaper (see below for the excerpt from the original letter). It can be argued that what one is dealing with here is some sort of 'naturally-occurring life writing' (Stanley, 1993, p. 47) within a framework of public accountability. As Lynch and Bogen (1996) note, a pervasive feature of public avowals is that they are usually given 'for the record'. They can be summarised, quoted and 'recycled' in news reports, newspapers and so on.

The newspaper headline introduces the article which contains the letter under the wider editorial heading 'Current Affairs' (*Actualitate*) with the gist prefaced by the author's name: 'I have been an informer for the Securitate' (*Am turnat la Securitate*). The letter is described as a 'harrowing document' (*document cutremurător*). The two descriptions construct the account *as* an (unexpected) confession and predispose the reader towards a particular way of reading the account (see Lee, 1984, in Watson, 1997). Disclosure is tied to the moral categories of 'informer' and 'Securitate' as an observable matter of 'fact' for the record.

The offered 'title' of the letter: 'Political police or informed-on informer informed on-informed on' (Poliţie politică sau turnat-turnător turnat-turnat) can be seen as a way to generate a context of alternative categorisations and category work. 'Political police' is the (accusatory) label used by the National Council for the Study of the Securitate Archives (CNSAS) for people involved in 'political police activities'.[4] Note the 'twin' categories introduced in the title. The sequence of categorisation (turnat-turnător; turnat-turnat) signals the existence of an alternative set of categorisations that might be commonsensically attached to the notion of 'political police'. The membership category 'informer' is qualified through the introduction of a set of categories, implicative-relational pairs.

The letter is divided into two main sections. The 'Essence', the first part, is followed by the 'Existence'. The analysis in this chapter focuses on the 'Essence' and how this first part of the letter constitutes a set of 'reading' relevances.

Political police
Or
Informed on-informer informed on-informed on

The Essence

I have signed an engagement of collaboration with the Securitate on 29 March 1976, when I was a pupil in my last high-school year (I was born on 20 Aug 1957), as a result of about three weeks of pressures. Approximately between 1976 and 1982, with irregular intermittences, including one of over one year and a half, I provided the Securitate information notes under the conspirational name of 'Valentin'. I informed the Securitate in writing about some of [my] friends and some of my acquaintances, without warning them, without confessing to them *post-festum* until my writing of this text, without apologizing, without assuming publicly this shameful and painful past.

I informed on them sometimes, with death in my soul, but I never betrayed them: I have not been an agent provocateur; I have not received missions of any kind; I have not been promised and there have not been advantages created for me; none of my information notes has gone beyond generalities and information which I considered already known; during all this time, I remained hostile to the Securitate and the party-state; they responded likewise. Between 1974 and 1989, the Securitate received information on me from other informers, and at specific junctures they opened 'Information Surveillance Dossiers' (*dosare de urmărire informativă* – D.U.I).

So, for fifteen years, I went through the first and the last of the three situations in which a citizen of the RSR[5] could find himself in as far as the Securitate was concerned (if the individual was not a direct part of its apparatus): 1) informed on; 2) informer; 3) informer-informed on – this sketchy typology of the informer will be detailed as one goes along.

In these pages, I will briefly tell my story and I will reconstitute schematically several relevant episodes, relying on memory, personal notes from the time and of some archival documents hosted by the CNSAS and requested by me in August 2002.

Until the present moment, after the more recent reception by the CNSAS of an enormous quantity of dossiers, these are the only available documents regarding me.

Ethically and morally, confession and repentance are coming too late: to the gravity of my deeds from 25–30 years ago, one can add the indefensible gravity of silence, of life lived in lies and duplicity. Only psychologically and historically (from ego-history, through micro-history, to history) it is better *too* late than never.

The opening line of the letter goes to the heart of the matter: 'I have signed an engagement of collaboration with the Securitate'. The emphasis is on the actuality of the 'fact' of 'collaboration'. At this point, there is no mitigation. The account can be seen to stand 'on behalf of a reality which is separate from, and beyond the text itself' (Davies, 1993, p. 118). The reader is then provided with the date which is followed by an occupational stage-of-life category ('pupil'). At the same time, one gets a significant biographical detail (the date of birth) (lines 003–005). This is the first indication that this is to be read as a biographical account, as well as a confession of past 'wrongdoing'. At line 003–004, one can read a statement that deals with the implicit intentionality of the act: not *choosing* to collaborate with the Securitate, but doing so 'as a result of about three weeks of pressures'.

Lines 001–003 can be seen as an attempt to manage inferences about the moral identity, and the disposition of the teller-as-character to act in a particular way (cf. Lynch and Bogen, 1996, p. 283; see also Sacks, 1995). The opening lines of the letter set the background for constructions of 'moral self-assessment' (Edwards, 2006) and moral character.

The length of time of being an informer for the Securitate is given (line 004): 'approximately between 1976 and 1982'. It is emphasised that this has not been a continuous commitment; it included 'irregular intermittences, of which one of over one year and a half' (lines 005–006). Reporting the frequency or prevalence of a practice can work to propose and substantiate the implicit rightness and wrongness of those practices. The activity is mentioned: providing 'information notes' under the name of 'Valentin' (line 007).

The first two sentences (lines 001–005) can be seen as an attempt to inscribe factual and biographical information on the record and open the way for 'linking factual reality to psychological states, motives and dispositions' (Edwards, 2006, p. 477). One can see how the 'factual' (what happened and when) is tied to features of an organisational reality, that of the Securitate: the *conspirational name*, providing *information notes*. It is under this framework that accounts of actions, moral identity and accountability can be offered and defended (see Edwards, 2006). This also has relevance for what is already *on* the record (the Securitate 'file', the 'information notes', the public written accounts, the CNSAS investigations. etc.) and what is *becoming* the public record (see Lynch and Bogen, 1996). To have a 'record', to have 'collaborated', to have a 'file' with the Securitate can be said to be linked to 'an organisational accomplishment creating a special character for whoever is located in the records' (Smith, 1990b, p. 213).

Further details are given at lines 007–011: 'I informed the Securitate in writing about some of [my] friends and some of my acquaintances'. Moral accountability and moral character are managed through the invocation of the membership categories 'friends' and 'acquaintances' that can be said to imply a set of category-bound activities and a 'locus for rights and obligations' (Lepper, 2000, p. 196). The invocation of these categories makes relevant the absence of moral courses of action such as the ones listed: 'without warning them', 'without confessing', 'without apologizing', 'without assuming publicly this shameful and painful past'. What one may call 'guilt', 'regret' 'remorse' and 'shame' is produced as a feature of *discourse* through the invocation of moral categories. Confessing and expressing regret is not simply a matter of *admitting* having 'collaborated' with the Securitate, but displaying a repertoire of 'moral discourse' (Bergmann, 1998) that can constitute a 'resource for the construction of moral actors and courses of moral action' (p. 287).

Having 'collaborated' with the Securitate is not an issue of strict political accountability, but of public and moral accountability. Having been an 'informer' is, presumably, not necessarily linked to having supported an oppressive regime, but also to having been in a position to reveal the private details of the lives of others, 'friends' and 'acquaintances'. The letter is not only addressed to the public, to a larger audience, but also to 'friends', people who might know the 'author' well and would not have necessarily expected such news.

Note at lines (012–013), 'I informed on sometimes, with death in my soul, but I never betrayed them'. Through the use of 'sometimes', the metaphor '*cu moartea în suflet*' and the extreme case formulation 'never' one is provided with a formulation of general disposition to act in a particular way. 'Sometimes' serves to portray the 'relative' character of the state of affairs, as well as the frequency of the practice. As Pomerantz

(1986, p. 228) points out, 'proportional measures reporting the frequency or prevalence or practices are used to propose and substantiate the rightness and wrongness of those practices'. 'I never betrayed them' is a way of normalising actions and character (see Edwards, 2000, p. 348; see also Edwards, 1997). This is done through denying having been a member of morally reprehensible category (like 'betraying your friends'). This works to suggest that the particular categories and actions being denied are 'an instance of a general category of actions' that the person 'is not disposed to do' (Edwards, 2006, p. 485).

The avowal of 'being an informer' is based on a denial of other 'available character types and membership categories' (Lynch and Bogen, 1996, p. 317): 'agent provocateur' and receiving 'missions' (lines 013–016). This categorial deploying is used to 'generate, manage and interpret the social order as a moral order' (Lepper, 2000, p. 39). Membership or identity categories such as 'being an informer', 'agent provocateur', and so on, can lend themselves 'to characteriological formulations of persons – their tendencies, dispositions, moral nature, desires and intentions' (Edwards, 2006, p. 498). One can note that there is a relationship between the deployment and accomplishment of morality and the invocation of membership or identity categories.

One way to read the statement at lines 016–018, on the information given to the Securitate, is to see it as a move of 'relativisation' (see Miller, 1999) of past actions, in claiming that 'anything of consequence' (p. 108) has been reported. An alternative reading would see it as an attempt of constructing disposition and intention as a way to fend off possible implications of being seen as someone who would deliberately give information to the Securitate (note the extreme case formulation '*none of* my information notes...' and the direct avowal of having remained hostile to the Securitate and the party-state 'during all this time' – lines 017–018). This is an integral part of a move of managing 'moral self-assessment' (Edwards, 2006) and moral accountability, discursively producing disposition and moral character. One can see how issues such as public disclosure are intimately associated to moral self-assessment moves concerning what (type of person) one is and what (type of person) one was. The repeated use of 'I' can perhaps be seen as a persuasive way to communicate sincerity (Wilson, 1990) and accomplish credibility.

At lines 018–021, one can note a subtle category shift: from 'informer' to having 'Information Surveillance Dossiers'. The situated production of moral character can be said to rely on a 'struggle over the production and control of the public record' (Lynch and Bogen, 1996, p. 179) of collaboration with the Securitate. It has been argued that *records* 'define the human beings to whom they refer in specific and particular ways. In so doing they call upon and activate a series of... membership categorisation devices' (Prior, 2004, p. 380). Membership categories such as 'informer' (and 'under surveillance') are underlined by means of the Securitate 'record' and procedures. In some circumstances, as Atkinson and Coffey (1997) note, the 'written record' can take 'precedence over members' own recollections and intentions' (p. 57). The Securitate 'records' – the 'dossiers' – mediate the constitution of an organisational relation between the person and an organisational course of action (collecting information on certain people, or placing people under surveillance, and so on). The category shift from 'informer' to 'informed on' is bound to an organisational accomplishment of accountability. Categories such as 'informer' and 'under surveillance' 'depend as a condition of their meaning on organizational process' (Smith, 1990a, p. 137). Public disclosure is legitimated through establishing a relationship with an organisational accomplishment of accountability.

Lines 023–028 are a sort of conclusive summary of the biographical and factual details previously offered. The personal 'story' is presented as unexceptional, certainly typical for a Romanian living under communism. Placing personal history within the ordinariness of the situation in which 'a citizen of RSR could find himself' involves claiming membership in two out of the three categories mentioned: 'informed on' and 'informer informed on'. The previously used category, that of 'informer', is subverted and a 'new' implicative-relational category ('informer informed on) is proposed. The merging of the two categories, 'informer' (agent of the action 'providing information to Securitate' – active) and 'informed on' (recipient of the action 'providing information to Securitate' – passive) provides for the construction of a particular moral order and moral character. It also opens the way for particular accounts to be given that might justify moral character and conduct. The trajectory of the confession and (confessional) self is constituted and accounted for within the boundaries of these categories/identities.

At lines 029–035, the resources for telling the story ('my story') are mentioned: memory, personal notes and 'archival documents' from the CNSAS, personally requested. The reconstruction of the personal past is a process mediated by the 'textual traces' (Smith, 1990b, p. 220) contained in personal and 'official' records. As some authors have argued, 'archival and auto-archival work' (Lynch, 1999, p. 69) deeply influences the writing of personal history. There is also a sense that the 'official' archive is incomplete. As Lynch and Bogen note, 'implicit ownership of an order of contextual details', can provide the writer with 'a conventional right to corroborate or contest details of an event that may already be known by other means' (1996, p. 164).

The ending of the 'Essence' (lines 036–040) can be seen as an example of performative sincerity (Lynch and Bogen, 1996, p. 50) and a continuation of the production of moral accountability and moral character. One could argue that the last lines display a shared cultural understanding of the meaning of 'saying sorry' (Le Couteur, 2001) in relation to the timely nature of the confession. This is a way to get moral emotions and moral character (a sense of morality) 'publicly available and publicly explainable' (Sacks, 1995, p. 195) to anonymous and non-anonymous parties. With the benefit of hindsight, the writer manages to open up a 'textual space' and moral universe in which to enact a discourse on the nature of private and public accountability (see Erben, 1993, p. 15). It is important not to ignore that when one is 'confessing'; one is also expressing moral meanings, as 'it is the society's appreciation or disdain of an individual's (norm-conforming or norm-breaking) behaviour that may change [an] individual's moral standing' (Bergmann, 1998, p. 286).

6 Conclusion

Focusing on a public confession of 'collaboration' with the Securitate, this chapter has examined issues such as public disclosure and reconciliation with the past as action-oriented, and participants' accomplishments. It has also offered an account of the social management of morality and self-presentation as a complex, delicate and ambivalent operation. As one moves from the private to the public and from the personal to the political, the meaningfulness of public disclosure is not guaranteed by a possible identifiable essence (such as confession) nor is it achieved through a reliance on the description of a particular state of mind (guilt, regret, remorse, etc.).

This chapter has considered the constitutive properties of a confessional text. It is suggested that this particular textual construction constitutes a set of 'reading' relevances: 1) it precludes using 'guilt' or 'remorse' as the only interpretive procedure; the use of various membership categories and organisational knowledge 'inhibits' (Smith, 1990a, p. 142) the application of 'guilt' or 'remorse' as the sole interpretive schema; 2) it suggests an alternative interpretative schema: the temporal/biographical sequence of categorisation (informer, informed on) is intended as an alternative guide to 'reading'. Following this 'instruction', the reader is able to connect the avowal not only to the 'author' of the letter, but also to the wider context (political and ideological).

One is running the risk of misreading public disclosure and attempts at reconciliation with the past if one treats them as accounts of actual, underlying psychological processes. Public disclosure and reconciliation with the past have no essential (psychological) meaning in themselves. Rather, their meaningfulness, as a matter for members of society, depends on them being seen as an integral part of a range of public, *accountable* practices, whether those of the individual or of the media. Arguably, there is no need to separate the 'private' from the 'public', or the 'personal' from the 'political', in order to understand public disclosure and reconciliation (with the communist past). The 'personal' can be said to be 'inextricably intertwined with the "public" and the "political"' (Davies, 1993, p. 118) in constituting an ideological space for the affirmation of struggles of 're-acquisition of biography' (Miller, 1999). The writer is 'using oneself as an ethnographic exemplar' (Gergen and Gergen, 2002, p. 14) in order to accomplish an auto-ethnography of the private/public, personal/political. As Edles (2002) has noted, '"the auto-ethnographer" is *doubly* privileged ... ethnographic authority rests on both being an "Insider" *and* being the "Ethnographer"' (p. 157, emphasis in original; see also Plummer, 2001).

If personal/political 'history' can be said to be mediated by the 'archival', 'textual refiguring' (Featherstone, 2006) of the past, then public disclosure and reconciliation with the past can be seen as engagements in a struggle to recapture, repossess and reclaim 'archontic' power (Derrida, 1997) – to exercise some degree of control over the authorship, collection and interpretation of a body of writings on the self. This could be seen as a move from the 'official', political archontic power (that of the Securitate primarily, in this context) to a 'personal' (nonetheless political) one.

The moral accountability of public disclosure is rendered observable in the situated act of its production. Instead of considering disclosure and reconciliation as having something to do with the inner psychology of the individual, it is worth emphasising their character as intertwined social practices that define a community. Their production (and consumption) is 'done in ways that are characteristic of a community', and their 'occurrence is part of what binds the community together and helps to constitute it as a community' (Lemke, 1995, p. 9). It is hoped that this chapter will help promote a different perception and practice of reconciliation with the past in the (Romanian) public sphere which will rely less on the internal psychology of the individuals and more on the resources that members of society use to make sense of their and others' practices.

These are not only issues of scholarly interest. It is contended that it is precisely issues such as the ongoing management of subjectivity and morality and the intricate nature of the 'textual' mediation of personal/ public history that need to be understood by people actively engaged in the public accounting and framing of 'coming to terms' with the communist past (for example, journalists, politicians, historians, political scientists). If it is true that the production and consumption of disclosure and reconciliation in the public arena enlists an 'interpretive community', then it may be worth paying attention to the various ways in which members of society display and treat the morality, sincerity and 'character' of one another. The interest should be on how such psychological features are made public and available for everyone else to see.

By illustrating the subtle ways in which disclosure and reconciliation are exercised as publicly accountable practices, this chapter has hopefully provided a range of analytic insights that could be used to encourage both academic and non-academic parties to be more reflective about possibilities of studying social transformation, social change and transition.

Notes

1. The studies mentioned here focus on public intellectuals. After the 1989 Revolution one has witnessed the evolution and affirmation of a critical mass of intellectuals (most of them grouped around the Group of Social Dialogue (GDS) and the cultural magazine *22*) who were very influential in shaping cultural, societal and even political concerns.
2. 1) 'A scăpat de piatra din suflet'
   2) 'Nu-mi prea vin în fire'
   3) 'Acum e un om liber'
   4) 'Pocăinţa nu are semnificaţie morală'
   5) 'Gestul ar trebui salutat'
   6) 'Sunt uluit şi îndurerat'
   7) 'Cazul e un argument în plus pentru condamnarea comunismului'
   (source: *Cotidianul*, online edition – www.cotidianul.ro – 6 September 2006).
3. For more details on the Securitate see Deletant (1996) and Oprea (2002).
4. According to the National Council for the Study of the Securitate Archives, 'political police' refers to all of the structures and activities of the Securitate, created for the instauration and maintenance of communist-totalitarian power, as well as for the suppression or restriction of fundamental human rights and liberties.
5. Romanian Socialist Republic.

10

Small Stories Fight Back: Narratives of Polish Economic Migration on an Internet Forum[1]

Aleksandra Galasińska

1 Introduction

A long and distinctive history of Polish emigration (see Iglicka-Okólska, 1997; Slany, 1997; Iglicka, 2001; Cyrus, 2006) has left its mark on the cultural tradition of Poland. Both literature and film discuss this phenomenon widely and the media feed returns to the topic frequently. The recent outflow from Poland after the EU enlargement of 2004 added a new dimension to the existing discussion about migration in both the public and private spheres as well as in academia. Having such a long tradition of migration, it is not surprising then that consecutive waves of Polish migrants have had to deal emotionally with the existence of a grand narrative of migration and position themselves in relation to it. That means they have to produce or indeed reproduce their own versions of a migrant story. Moreover, they have to negotiate their stories with several groups of challenging 'others', that is, a local community in the home country, a local community in the host country, as well as existing Polish communities in the country of destination. This chapter discusses one such issue: the changing form and function of a grand narrative of migration among Polish migrants to the UK. I shall focus on stories of migrants as mediated and discussed on an internet forum.

There were two main strands of modern Polish migration to the West, which produced competing narratives. The first strand of political emigration, associated with a romantic narrative of exile and loss of homeland, is highly contextualised in the political history of 19th and 20th-century Europe, in particular the Polish struggle for independence as well as the change in the political system after the Second World War (see Sword, 1996; Hładkiewicz, 1997; Iglicka, 2000; Burrell, 2006). Political emigration, for all intents and purposes, ended in 1989 with the collapse of communism. The second strand of Polish migrants was the one associated with the economic exodus which began at the end of the 19th and the beginning of the 20th century (Morawska, 1989), mainly to the United States but also to Germany, Belgium, the Netherlands and France. This strand's grand narrative is the one of penniless Poles who succeeded in the West, and is contextualised in the economic development of modern Western societies as opposed to Central and Eastern European 'backwardness'. In this study I shall concentrate on narratives of the Polish economic migrants in the post-enlargement period. I shall analyse what constitutes their narrative of migration, how this narrative is created and how it is used as a form of resistance against the historically bounded grand narrative of migration. In doing so I hope to shed light on new translocal discourses of Polish social and economic transformation in the context of the EU expansion after 2004.

2 Assumptions

2.1 Polish economic migration and the myth of the West

My point of departure is the Cold War and the Iron Curtain dividing Europe into two sides of ideological conflict, with the West seen in the official discourses as the arch-enemy and the abode of evil. But the simplicity of the historic-political context is somewhat complicated by the economic one. Bauman (1992) argued that communism and capitalism in Europe were the two faces of modernism; both were based on economic production. And it is precisely economic production that was the main battleground between the two systems for the 'ordinary people'. As recipients and consumers of the economic goods produced in communism, they quickly discovered that products which penetrated their life from the West were of much better quality, and aesthetic value. The 'Western' goods people were sent and brought home from travels or short-term migration were obvious evidence that life was better 'over there' (see Morawska, 2001; Stola, 2001; Duvell; 2006; Sowiński, 2006). Paradoxically, and contrary to the political messages sent to citizens, the state reinforced this belief by establishing a chain of special shops where people could purchase Western goods paying only in hard currency. The battle between intellectual and lived ideologies of communism (Billig et al., 1988) was won 'hands down' by the latter.

Of course, these Western products became symbols of not only economic but also cultural capital in the same way, as Pine (2002a) observed, since money earned in the West had a different symbolic value. Material objects in conjunction with stories about life in the West made the West a mythical symbol of prosperity, wealth and a comfortable lifestyle with no problems. In other ways, the West was always mythologised (Samuel and Thompson, 1990). As Bauman (1992) put it, people in the GDR destroyed the Berlin Wall not because they did not love Erich Honecker (the communist leader of the GDR, much ridiculed in Poland), but because they did not love their Trabants and wanted to drive VWs and Audis.

In an earlier study Galasiński and Galasińska (2007) demonstrated how Polish economic emigrants to the UK positioned the mythical West not only as the coveted Promised Land, but also a destination, the road to which is hard and full of obstacles. Getting to the West was, in the case of their informants, an achievement in its own right and it should be rewarded, be it in the form of a good life there or back in Poland. This is very clearly in tune with representations of departure from communist Poland to the West as 'escaping'. Up until 1989 passports to leave the Eastern bloc were strictly rationed, with people going to extremes to leave the country, not to mention the fact that in the 1950s and 1960s one risked imprisonment when caught or even death in the attempt. These historical, economic and political contexts influenced a grand narrative of Polish economic migration.

2.2 The narrative of Polish economic migration

The recent narrative turn in the social sciences shows that narratives are the most important part of our constructions of self (see Linde, 1993; Bruner, 1991; Bamberg, 2000; Wortham, 2001; Brockmeier and Carbaugh, 2001; Thornborrow and Coates, 2005), but it is precisely in the case of migrants that narratives are particularly rich in elements of social and cultural identity (De Fina, 2003; Baynham and De Fina, 2005). Moreover, narrative is not an autonomous event (see Ochs and Capps, 2001; Georgakopoulou, 2006), interwoven with the socio-cultural and political-historical, as well as spatio-temporal, context. If the individual narrative is repeated by many tellers in the same or similar canonical form, then it becomes a grand narrative – a blueprint for all stories – that, as Andrews puts it, 'offer[s] a way of identifying what is assumed to be a normative experience' (Andrews, 2004, p. 2). Baynham (2003; 2005) called it a hegemonic migrant's narrative, stressing its gendered character, as it is usually associated with a male economic migration. In Galasińki and Galasińska (2007) we described the Polish hegemonic narrative of migration as that of

> a penniless Pole (usually a man) [who] emigrates and makes his success work in the host country where he settles down. This is the Polish version of the American Dream, except that America can be anywhere, as long as the economic system lets the individual prove his ability to 'make it', using his resourcefulness and industriousness, which, previously, were stifled in the home country. Alternatively the potential migrant brings all this money back to Poland where he is set up for life (p. 51).

It is worth stressing that this grand narrative of economic migration focuses exclusively upon *what* could be achieved by a migrant, leaving the aspect of *how* it could be achieved untouched or silenced. The only details related to the *how* question were those described by leaving Poland; in other words, once you are able to get out of the country (see the context of 'closed' borders and rationalised passports), and get to the West (see the context of restricted visas and work permits) you are in good shape. It is not surprising then, that stories of migration before 2004 were focused on the detailed construction of departure from Poland (see Galasińska and Kozłowska, forthcoming).

Another aspect of *how* is related to the concept of class/education and economic migration from Poland. The context of the political division of the European continent and the economic discrepancy between East and West, reinforced with the clandestine character of migrant outflow, quite frequently allowed Poles to 'forget' their class background and perform jobs below their qualifications. Stories of Polish graduates or engineers working as cleaners, agricultural workers, builders and manual workers penetrated private spheres back in the home country, and were more often approved than condemned in private discourses. In other words, in Poland, for years, it wasn't important how you earned your money in the West, as long as you succeeded. The hegemonic migration of success hid, or at least mitigated, the part of the story about the 'undignified' working and living conditions of migrants.

Last but not least, I shall point to a relationship between grand narrative and stereotypes. Wodak argues that 'stereotypes and prejudicial beliefs are (thus) enforced and manifested *inter alia* by metaphors, analogies, insinuations as well as *stories* [my emphasis]' (2006, p. 185). As my research shows, some parts of the grand narrative of Polish economic migration became recontextualised in the era of economic transformation, drawing on culturally embedded stereotypes of Polish migrants.

2.3 Migration and political and economic transformation

Polish economic migration after 1989 has to be contextualised not only in the processes of both social and political post-communist transformation and the enlargement of the EU, but also in terms of Central and Eastern European countries' historical reality of closed borders. As I mentioned earlier, until 1989 passports to leave the Eastern bloc were strictly rationed, with people going to extremes to leave the country. Getting to the long-mythologised West was an achievement in its own right. At the same time, visas and work-permit restrictions in the West for citizens from CEECs were strictly implemented, 'symmetrically', making borders difficult to penetrate. Democratic reforms in the late 1980s enabled ordinary people in the East to get their passports and presented the possibility of unrestricted travel. However, these restrictions were waived from one side of the border only, leaving landing in the Promised Land still a matter of pure luck. Fortress Europe quite often did not like visitors from behind the former Iron Curtain.

This situation changed dramatically almost overnight when, after several years of negotiations, eight CEE counties, with Poland being the largest of them, entered the EU in May 2004, followed by Bulgaria and Romania in January 2007. The United Kingdom was one of the first countries from Europe 15 to open its labour market for 'new' Europeans after that date. While post-1989 migrants usually repeated the historically grounded patterns of clandestine economic migration from Poland, usually based on existing networks of fellow Poles (see Morawska, 2001; Triandafyllidou, 2006), post-2004 arrivals gradually changed these patterns, moving, travelling and looking for jobs more independently. As Garapich argues 'temporary, circular, unpredictable, open-ended, strategically adaptive migration activities have flourished after full liberalization of migration regime' (2006, p. 15), and suddenly Polish migrants became 'well-adapted trans-national actors, using – or at least trying to – the best of both worlds, keeping feet in both places and building their class identities in both settings with stronger emphasis on individual achievement, human agency, self-determination and flexibility' (p. 4). In this chapter I shall investigate discursively constructed bottom-up views of transformation as transnational process, focusing on the micro level of personal experience of migrants who became trans-national actors of global changes.

3 Data

The data for this chapter come from an internet discussion forum attached to the influential Polish daily *Gazeta Wyborcza*. As a trigger for a particular discussion, I chose two highly commented-upon articles[2] related to the success of Polish post-2004 transnational income-seekers in the UK. Both articles were published in summer 2005, over a year after hundreds of thousands of Poles legally entered the UK labour market, triggering articles that were different in style. The first one was written in an informative mode, 'objectively' informed about highly qualified office workers and professionals from Poland, successfully employed by various British employers, quoting statistical data, showing diagrams and avoiding commentary from editors. The second article, by contrast, showed mediated versions of new migrants' personal stories since their arrival in the UK, focusing on their successful social, economic and emotional adaptation to their new, chosen domicile. In these media texts, the omitted part of Polish grand narrative of economic migration – not what you achieved working abroad, but rather how you achieved it – became salient and important.

The articles attracted more than 300 comments on a readers' forum. The discussions triggered were very similar in topic and focused almost exclusively upon the issue of whether Poles, as trans-national migrants, could be successful, not by bringing money home, but also, more importantly, while working and living in the country of destination. As this forum is open to anyone (with an internet connection), discussants were drawn from both groups – those who live in Poland, and those who had decided to leave the country. In presenting their opinions, people used different styles of entry ranging from argumentative discourses, short comments, anecdotes and jokes, as well as narratives.

In this chapter I focus on personal stories, which were presented on the *Gazeta Wyborcza* forum as a means to illustrate the discussant's point. By doing so I follow Georgakopoulou's (2006) postulate on stretching narrative research in linguistics by analysing less-often researched stories told outside the research interview. Such a choice of data avoids the co-authoring and co-construction of stories elicited by the researcher during interviews and asymmetrical power relations during an interview process. Moreover, it allows looking at stories' 'embeddedness in discourse surroundings' and 'the way in which stories transposed, (re)shaped and recycled across time and space' (2006, p. 252). Georgakopoulou's dynamic and dialogical approach to narrative demonstrated that interactional data, such as computer- mediated communication, became a rich source of what she called *narratives-in-interaction.* Focusing on this type of story in my research, I present the role of personal narrative in argumentative discussion (Ochs and Capps, 2001) on migration and its experience. I will also discuss the relationship between personal narrative and a culturally embedded grand narrative in the broader context of post-communist transformation, and in particular the EU extension.

4 Analysis

As I stated above, the overall topic of discussion in the data at hand focused on the possibilities for Poles to succeed abroad. The main argument of those who argued against success lay in the historically collective knowledge of Poles, based on a 'hidden' part of a grand narrative described above. They argued that Polish workers abroad are unable to get professional, satisfying, well-paid jobs leading to promotion. In their opinion this is the result of historically established patterns of economic migration from Poland, which in turn prevents climbing a social ladder in a host country; thus their claim that Poles who arrived in Britain after May 2004 cannot have a normal life and achieve contentment. Such a discourse is the effect of a recontextualisation of discourses on migration from before 1989 but also before 2004 (see Triandaffylidou, 2006).

In response to that, discussants from the UK posted their personal stories to counter the above claims. I consider them as a specific version of counter-narratives, which are defined as 'stories which people tell and live which offer resistance, either implicitly or explicitly (our case), to dominant cultural narratives' (Andrews, 2004, p. 1). Presenting these stories on a forum was a specific way of discursively addressing a discussed problem using forms usually not chosen in discussion. In a similar vein, Harris (2005) observed a hybridised form of court trials discourse, when stories were used as evidence. There is a striking resemblance in the data at hand regarding a form and contents of collected narratives which I shall discuss below. Two aspects, which are still the core of narrative investigation, are a) what was said and b) how it was said; these represent two different approaches, that of psychology and that of linguistic/discourse analysis, respectively. Both aspects do not have to be mutually exclusive, if narrative is understood, as Johnstone (2001, p. 644) proposes, as 'a way of constructing "events" and giving them meaning'. Thus in what follows, in line with 'the second wave of narrative analysis' (Georgakopoulou, 2007, p. 146) which is understood as the study of narrative-in-context, I focus on what it is narrators *do* while narrating (Bamberg, 2007), and in particular how narrators are engaged in the activity of narrating as resisting. While identifying certain content-related arguments (see Reisigl and Wodak, 2001; Wagner and Wodak, 2006) and their textual realisation in analysed narratives, I offer, at the same time, a broader macro interpretation of bottom-up discourses of migration in the era of transition.

4.1 Short stories as small stories

To begin with, there is the compactness of the stories, a feature already observed by those who have analysed interactional narratives (see Bamberg, 2004; and also Bamberg and Georgakopoulou, 2005). *Small stories,* as they are called, are claimed not to be disadvantaged in terms of their quality, but rather remain 'an antidote to the modernist concept of grand narratives' (Georgakopoulou, 2006, p. 239). Consider the following examples in which discussants describe their way of getting a job in the UK.

Example 1

came two years ago. After a year I found a good job in an office. After two years I have the courage to set up my own company. I tell everyone who is going to come here: great, a good idea, but learn the language. The better knowledge of the language one has, the better job one could get. No graduate's diplomas but the English language is important here.

Example 2

I was seven months without a job, I was sending my CV to many companies and agencies day after day, I was constantly going for interviews and nothing. Nothing, nothing, nothing, I was rejected all the time, too little experience, and so on, and so forth. I felt awful. But I did not give up!!! I've got a job I wanted thanks to my persistence! Three years ago I was on the lowest level, after less then a year I've got promoted (twice).

I would like to draw the reader's attention to the fact that the members of both forums narrate a considerably long time in their life in an extremely compact way. In Example 1, a man uses three moves relating to two years in his migrant's life; while a woman, in Example 2, narrates an almost four-year span only marginally longer than in Example 1. I would argue that the condensed qualities of the analysed narratives are multifunctional; on the one hand their stories are short due to the mediated interactional character of discussion. On an internet forum, a long post could easily be ignored, perceived as boring and time-consuming by both discussants and readers. Keeping their story short, tellers do not risk immediate rejection but increase their chance of being heard/read/commented upon. Short forms reflect the temporal qualities of interaction and thus become an interactional feature of narratives-in-interaction.

On the other hand, in line with Bamberg and Georgakopoulou's (2005) argument about celebrating small in opposition to grand, a compact form of personal account serves also as a perfect way of resisting arguments based on the grand narrative of migrants being socially 'handicapped'. Telling small stories of their personal success, they not only stress resistance to the contents of a grand narrative, but they also use a linguistic form (short against the long, developed Labovian model) while resisting. It is as if they would like to say, 'you could use all these bold, stereotypical pictures of Poles abroad, living in terrible conditions, below a poverty line, working in low jobs, badly paid, long hours, abused by employers and fellow migrants, etc. but look, here I am, in the office, happy and successful. I am a living proof that you are wrong. End of story'. In that way, tellers celebrate the micro versus the macro, using personal and private versus collective and public.

4.2 Listen to my story

It is worth pointing out the omnipresence of the use of 'I' in the stories presented. Again this not only stresses the micro versus macro character of collected data, but also shows how the grammatical form of the first person is used as a contrast to, and rejection of, presenting Poles working abroad as an unanimous group, as it was in the case of grand narrative. Consider these further examples, when the 'I' form is played against different groups of people:

Example 3

One can get a middle management job easily and straightforwardly in the UK and I don't have in mind 'an office manager' (a secretary/PA) or 'a mop manager' (a cleaner) job. Believe me, I am pretty happy with a middle management job, without a prospect of becoming a chairman, but in a serious and well managed company in the UK instead and some how I don't miss the mess and corrupted arrangements which I left in the one country on the continent...

Example 4

I work as a specialist/professional, as I already wrote about, I didn't think for a minute to look for a job other than in my specialisation...to find a job took me four weeks in total, and the only 'question' about my nationality was that whether I needed a job permit...

Example 5

I am just sitting in England, at my desk, in a 'white collar' and I am writing this post. Maybe I am not a manager, but I am at the same position as many Englishmen and my boss is Portuguese. It is possible if someone does something instead of moaning.

All these three examples show a professional 'I' connected with vocabulary relating to middle management, professional and white collar. However, I would like to highlight the fact that this professional 'I' is contrasted with different particular others. The woman in Example 3 takes against people engaged in certain negative social practices in her home country; by doing so she distances herself from Poles who are not engaged in migration. In another vein, the man from Example 4 positioned himself against those who seek jobs below their qualification, which we could guess is a stereotypical Polish migrant from the grand narrative. This is achieved *inter alia* by mentioning work permits, a main obstacle for Poles looking for legal employment in Britain before 2004. Finally, the discussant in Example 5 distances himself/herself from both groups mentioned above. On the one hand, this person stresses his equal work status in the office with British as well as other 'European' colleagues, which is against stereotypical perceptions of migrants. On the other hand, there is an implicitly salient group of 'moaners', probably situated in Poland, who do nothing, against whom the teller positions himself/herself as well.

Analysing counter-narratives, Andrews (2005) observed that they are usually told from an out-group point of view, or with a consciousness of being a member of an outside group. In the data presented, the latter is a very salient practice, although achieved involuntarily by the forum's participant. Despite using the grammatical 'I', and stressing a personal experience, those who presented their stories participate in common social practice (participating in an internet forum discussion). This in turn influenced their discursive practice (formulating forum entries) and thus it is not a coincidence that all such stories resemble each other. In that way participants resemble multiple co-tellers (see Ochs and Caps, 2001) of 'the same story'. If one combines this fact with the sheer mass of post-enlargement Polish migration to the UK, as well as with statistical data about the age of these migrants (approximately 85 per cent are below 35 years of age; Osipovic, 2007), one could claim that the narratives presented reflected generational experience, which quite simply is turned into a generational memory of migration during the transformation process (for detailed discussion about the relationship between memory and experience see Misztal, 2003). In that way small stories start to have a big impact and stand even more strongly against the grand narrative.

4.3 But I never...

There is another linguistic feature of the personal stories on this forum, which is quite often represented across the sample. I have in mind the extreme-case formulation *never*, which can be observed in the following examples.

> **Example 6**
>
> Of course you have to have proper qualifications, better higher than local people, and you have to be able to communicate. It is not a problem then. I do work like that here and I never worked in a bar or a factory.
>
> **Example 7**
>
> I left because I knew that I would manage also here. I work on my dissertation and I am OK. I never had to brew coffee because it happened that I know the language perfectly and I didn't have to. I've got a fantastic job just three weeks after my arrival and a few months later the university gave me a scholarship and a additionally it employed me part time (that I would not brew anything anywhere and could concentrate on my study). It sounds easy but before that I spent almost all my life learning vocabulary, grammar and pronunciation and some other things which are mentally challenging, so I worked my way.

What is interesting in these examples, as well as in Example 4 (*'nawet przez minutę nie myślałem o tym, żeby szukać innej pracy, niż w zawodzie'*... 'I didn't think for a minute to look for a job other than in my specialisation...'), is not the fact that the temporal (*nigdy*) and spatial (*nigdzie*) *never* is linked with manual labour or jobs below qualification. In my opinion, more interesting is the fact that by using the same formulation, many discussants co-construct their stories. This in turn further reinforces my argument from a previous section that the set of personal narratives becomes a group narrative, interactionally co-constructed and co-written on a public discussion forum. This point, however, does not mitigate or minimalise the resisting aspect of these narratives against a grand narrative.

4.4 Listen how I earned my money

Continuing to look at different aspects of resisting a grand narrative, I have to return to this hidden, omitted and silenced part of it: namely, the means of earning money abroad. As I mentioned before, this part was not included in the grand narrative. We have learned in great detail how people travelled abroad and crossed borders (see Galasińska and Kozłowska, forthcoming), but little is known about how they actually worked and lived there. Economic assets were more important than the ways they achieved them. However, it is also argued that the omitted parts of the stories are signally important for the coherence of narrative (see Blommaert 2005; and also Galasiński and Galasińska, 2005). In the examples presented below, discussants on an internet forum are actually telling what was previously not found in the grand narrative of economic migration of Poles:

Example 8

On one not so pretty day I decided that I had enough of this shambles in Poland, I looked at adverts in the UK, I noticed that with my qualifications an average salary is 35K per year, so I packed and came to London...for two weeks I 'become acclimatized' ;-) later I 'put' my CV on internet job sites and I replied for 'some' ads, one hundred in total within two weeks, I attended six interviews and 'negotiated' further twice...after three weeks (for a week I had to go to Poland because of 'family' business) of 'negotiations' I had a signed contract, salary as stated in the ad that means as on the 'market', full 'social' allowance, and so on...so it is possible if one can do something.

Example 9

I am in the UK because in an interview I was better than Englishmen. I work as IT specialist and my salary is 32K GBP per year + bonuses + private pension scheme paid by an employer. An average salary on this level is 27K per year. I am the only Pole in this company. I don't regret my departure for the UK, I sold the flat (paying 10 per cent to the taxman) and moved out from smelly Krakow.

A particularly interesting aspect of these stories is how the economic details of the stories (such as salary, job packages, bonuses) parallel accounts of how money is actually earned. Not only '*what* or how much I get' but also '*how* I achieved it' became equal parts of these small stories and the two topics coexist happily in them. Both the former and latter are constructed using a significant vocabulary, pointing at a discursive change called by Fairclough (1992) a commodification of discourse. A lexicon of concepts related to globalisation and marketisation, such as *work, job interview, company, negotiations,* are stable elements of the forums' participants' discourses. Their accounts are clearly underpinned by the context of a new political order of Europe 25, which resulted in new economic possibilities for 'the New Europeans' outside their homeland and not by the context of 'impossible'-to-get work permits.

4.5 Stretching time and place, stretching tellership

I would like to highlight one more quality of the personal narratives under investigation. Again this differs significantly from the hegemonic grand narrative I used as a point of departure for this chapter. Here I would like to focus on the time and space management of these small stories, pointing to their dynamic and outward-looking characteristics. My argument is that a demonstrated personal success in the UK has its roots earlier, in Poland. The grand narrative, anchored in mythologisation of the West, was allowed to succeed only when one crossed the border and arrived at that place where everything was possible. In other words, only then and there could one prove to be successful, earning hard currency no matter how. In that sense, the time and the space of the grand narrative are static and of a deterministic quality.

In contrast, in the data analysed, the spatial and temporal dimensions of being successful are more dynamic, stretched and quite often open-ended, although the UK is presented more frequently as a destination point. In Example 8 the man mentioned his qualification in the context of looking for a good job in Britain while still living in Poland.

This implied that his success (defined as qualification/experience) was performed there and by moving to the UK he only continues to be successful. In other words, time in Poland is, in this narrative, a necessary component of his further achievements in the UK. The man in Example 6 constructs his story in a similar vein, even using the same vocabulary (*kwalifikacje* – qualifications). The female discussant in Example 7 frames her story in the opening and closing by linguistically extending her time/space for success. She started in a very minimalist way – just by using *also* (see '*Wyjechałam, bo wiedziałam, że poradzę sobie i tutaj*' – 'I left because I knew that I would manage also in here.'). She finishes her story in what could be evaluation in the Labovian (1972) sense and, at the same time, a retrospection to her life back in Poland (see '*Brzmi to lekko ale przedtem spędziłam całe prawie życie wkuwając słówka, gramatykę i ćwicząc wymowę i inne takie wymagające wysiłku umysłowego, więc sporo się napracowałam.*' – 'It sounds easy but before that I spent almost all my life learning vocabulary, grammar and pronunciation and some other things which are mentally challenging, so I worked my way.'). However, in doing this, she clearly identified the beginning of her success as being in Poland, as was the case with the man from Example 8.

Finally, the dynamism of the stories is extended to a dynamism of tellership. I have already elaborated on the interactional character of the data presented, which is dynamic in its nature. I also pointed out the fact that these stories are dynamic as private and public texts at the same time, being posted on a widely accessed internet forum (only technical obstacles and lack of knowledge of Polish language prevent others from reading these stories). Moreover, I demonstrated their dynamism as achieved by their short form, which implied the need for a quick response from discussants. There is, however, one more element of dynamisation in my data, especially in the context of resisting grand narrative. As I mentioned earlier, referring to Baynham's work, the hegemony of a grand narrative lies *inter alia* in its gendered qualities, as an almost exclusively male story. The narratives analysed here are told by both men and women and, more importantly, their stories are similar in form and content. It could be argued that it is a form of democratisation (Fairclough, 1992) of these stories, as women join men in co-construction of a new narrative of Polish economic migration. I would like to take this argument further though, namely by reversing it. Researchers of discourse and gender observe that male and female discourse users traditionally apply different genres or modes of expressions (see, for example, Wodak, 1986). It has to be said that while women prefer narrative, men express themselves in argument, demonstrating a non-personalised mode, in reports and the like. In this view there are men who join women in co-constructing a new narrative of migration by using the same form of expression traditionally prescribed to women. However, either way, both genders join forces to present a united front against a dominant cultural script. Could one perhaps not link these findings with a broader concept of a social solidarity which is historically embedded in the Polish struggle for social change?

5 Conclusions

In this chapter I focused on an experience of migration in the era of post-communist transformation as discussed and narrated in a computer-mediated internet forum. In my analysis I identified certain characteristics of the narratives presented, such as 1) short form; 2) exclusive use of first-person singular, in contrast to other social actors, mainly those who stayed in Poland as well as other less successful Polish migrants; 3) repetitive use of the extreme-case formulation *never* linked with content-related reporting on manual work or work below one's qualification; 4) detailed descriptions of getting and performing satisfying, well-paid jobs, narrated with market-oriented vocabulary; 5) dynamically stretched spatial, as well as temporal, aspects of narratives and also dynamism of genderless tellership. Moreover, I stressed the co-tellership of what appeared, at first glance, as exclusively personal stories, pointing to elements of a generational experience in the data presented.

In my interpretation of these qualities, I showed how personal narratives of post-enlargement migration were used as an argumentative tool against historically bounded hegemonic discourses of Polish economic migration, contextualised in the era of pre-1989 closed borders. In doing so, I empirically explored the theoretical claims of many researchers of post-communism, who argue that transformation can only be understood in relation to what existed before (see Sakwa, 1999; Burawoy and Verdery, 1999; and also Kelly-Holmes, Chapter 8 in this volume; Krzyżanowski and Wodak, Chapter 1 in this volume). Focusing on the role of personal stories, I showed how post-communist transformation penetrated discourses, not only at the macro but also at the micro level of lived experience. Presenting narratives of economic post-enlargement migrations, I extended the issue at the translocal level, showing an additional horizontal aspect of transformation. New translocal discourses of Polish social and economic transformation in the context of the EU expansion after 2004 seem to have proved that however vertical and horizontal the process itself is seen (see Krzyżanowski and Wodak, ibid.), we have to get to the level of personal experiences and personal discourses in order to avoid generalisation and to demonstrate the full picture of it. Thus, it is up to the individual agency of many to perform, as well as indeed narrate, transformation as a social process.

Notes

1. I would like to thank Alexandra Georgakopoulou and Anna Triandafyllidou for their valuable comments on an earlier version of this paper, as well as Brian Bennett for his help with the English version of the text.
2. W. Nowak, 'Z Polską na Czysto'. *Gazeta Wyborcza*, 5 September 2005: http://forum.gazeta.pl/forum/72,2.html?f=521&w=28636640&s=0 'Polacy Pracują w Anglii też w Białych Kołnierzykach'. *Gazeta Wyborcza*, 29 July 2005: http://forum.gazeta.pl/forum/72,2.html?f=23&w=27078484&a=27078484

11
Narratives of Disenfranchised Self in the Polish Post-Communist Reality

Dariusz Galasiński

1 Postcommunism and Identities

Since the events of 1989–91 in Central and Eastern Europe, the comfortable political certainties and official ideologies of the Cold War were called into question on both sides of the former Iron Curtain. The introduction of liberalised ideologies, both at the official level and in most of the freed media also had to be translated into most of the countries' systems. New laws and new textbooks which would accommodate the new social and political realities had to be written. Political parties had to espouse new ways of communicating with voters. Finally, new official national narrative had to be found. But what are mostly discursive changes have been coupled with those which, although semiotised and ideologised, can be seen as deep changes in the social fabric of the communities. State budgets could not cope with just about any significant expenditure, and health and social security systems needed immediate and deep reform. Most importantly, the collapse of heavy nationalised industry meant that jobs were no longer secure and unemployment rose at a frightening rate.

What initially was a monolith of the anti-communist opposition (almost a third of Polish population belonged to the first, 1980–1, Solidarity movement!) very quickly fragmented into more and more groups, with different views on Poland's political, social and economic way forward, on settling accounts with communism and communists, and on the role of the powerful Catholic Church (see also Outhwaite and Ray, 2005). This fragmentation was coupled with the ever more acute uncertainty as to the direction, shape and the result of the transformations (see, for example, Sakwa, 1999). Bauman (1992a, p. 130) who sees post-communism in terms of cultural liminality, puts it aptly as the period in which 'everything can happen, but little can be done'.

There is little doubt that the post-1989 changes put enormous pressure upon those who were subject to them. Giddens' (1991) question of 'how to live' became ever more acute. Finding oneself within the ever-changing political, social and even historical scene became ever more difficult and posed considerably more questions than solutions. The 'individual' struggles over the emerging sharp differences both in the public as well as private spheres inevitably meant struggles over one's identities (Chouliaraki and Fairclough, 1999).

Indeed, claims that the post-communist transformations have had a profound impact upon people's subjectivities are quite ubiquitous in the literature. For example, while Baron (1997) argues that the end of communism signified the collapse of the collective memories of the communist period, Outhwaite and Ray (2005) take the argument further and relate it to the relationship of such memories and group identities and the need to reconfigure them (see also De Soto, 2000). The ideological changes, and particularly emergence of heated abortion debates, resulted in the reconfiguration of gender politics and thus gender identities (Gal and Kligman, 2000a; 2000b). Pine (2002b) also suggests that gender identities have been under stress from the changes in the labour market resulting in the disenfranchisement particularly of certain groups of women (see also Kaneff, 2002). The transformations are claimed to have had an impact upon people's national (Koczanowicz and Kołodziejska, 1999; Kuzio, 2001; Rausing, 2002) as well as transnational identities (Buchowski, 2001) with a significant rise of nationalism in the region and the need to re-evaluate and reposition the Other (see Salecl, 1994). This is coupled with the claims that Eastern Europeans want to be normal, to be who they really are, and that they want unproblematic identities (Kennedy, 1994). In other words, the pressure on identities comes from the need to position oneself in relation to the transformations themselves, what they stand for and, significantly, what they are a break from. Sakwa (1999) notes that evaluation of the communist past is at the heart of post-communist societies; moreover, as E. Dunn (1999) points out, communist practices and experiences are used in making sense of the current situation.

Two significant shortcomings can be mentioned in relation to the claims mentioned above. First, even if intuitively accurate, the claims must be taken as, at the very best, approximations of the relationship between macro-scale transformations and micro-scale identities.

Second, while the micro-scale ethnographic studies escape this reservation, they, on the other hand, stop well short of offering in-depth insight into the actual local identity configurations as they are enacted in the discourses of the informants.

There has so far been practically no research on the actual discursive configurations of identities in 'private' discourses of people who bear the brunt of the transformations (for exceptions see Meinhof and Galasiński, 2005; Galasińska et al., 2002). In this chapter I aim to answer the questions raised by the relationship between the system transformations in Poland and the identities of those who live through them. In other words, I am interested in uncovering the ways in which the self is positioned with regard to the transformations, where in the transformations the informants see themselves, and how they respond to them and live in them.

More generally, I am attempting to explore the relationship between economic, political and social macro-context and the individual experiences which occur in it. How do the happenings in the public macrosphere permeate and underpin the 'private' discourses of the self. I am therefore not only asking questions of the possibility of a 'post-communist' identity, but, importantly, I am asking questions of the politicisation of the self at the lowest level of lived experience.

It is commonly accepted now that identity is a context-bound discursive enterprise. It is a discursive construct, rather than a fixed inner sense or essence of self to be discovered. It is a discourse of (not) belonging, similarity and difference, which is continually negotiated and renegotiated within a localised social context – a continual process of becoming. Always provisional and subject to change, it also incorporates, especially at the level of conscious identification, the relatively stable macro-narratives and images of who and what belongs to *us* (especially when it comes to such constructs as nation) and who and what belongs to *them*, the domain of the Other (see Barker and Galasiński, 2001; also Meinhof and Galasiński, 2005). Thus, while constantly provisional, identity-discourse also has a tendency to freeze the macronarratives of the (our) nation as well as the nation(s) of the Other.

2 The data and methodology

The data I am drawing upon here were collected as parts of four separate studies. Primarily, I refer to the Polish sections of two studies into the construction of identities in border communities, funded firstly by the British ESRC and, later, by the EC's Fifth Framework Programme.

The other two were pilot studies into experiences of post-communism among people living in large-scale blocks of flats, a generation of young adults who had experienced communism as young children and who entered adulthood in the new political and economic reality.

The interviews in the first two projects from which the data are taken were triggered by photography. Thus, instead of the interview being set up by a number of questions that the interviewer asks and to an extent reveals their interest, we showed symbolically charged photographs clearly showing the times before the Second World War, after the war and, finally, from the post-1989 period. We asked informants to tell us about them, attempting to allow the interviewees to set the interview's agenda, in that they were able to choose what they said on all levels of discourse – from the topic and general content to the linguistic form with which they expressed it (see Meinhof and Galasiński, 2005). In the latter two projects, we used semi-structured interview techniques. In all cases I note the generation the informant belongs to.

Methodologically, the paper is anchored in the constructionist view of discourse underpinned by the assumptions of critically oriented discourse analysis. Thus I assume that social reality is constructed through and within language. Language, as a social phenomenon, is both a product and a reflection of the values and beliefs of the society which produces it and, in turn, represents and reinforces them (Billig et al., 1988). Every language use designed to represent reality necessarily entails decisions as to which aspects of that reality to include, and decisions as to how to arrange them. Each of these selections, both in content and in lexico-grammatical form, made in the construction of a message carries its share of these ingrained values, so that the reality represented is ideologically constructed (Hodge and Kress, 1993, p. 5). It is also through discourse (that is, practices of language use) that language users constitute social realities: their knowledge of social situations, the interpersonal roles they play, and their identities and relations with other interacting social groups (van Leeuwen and Wodak, 1999).

The necessarily selective character of representation entails that it is through discourse that ideologies (systems of social representations shared by members of a group) are formulated, reproduced and reinforced (van Dijk, 1998; Billig et al., 1988; Fowler, 1985). I agree with Chouliaraki and Fairclough (1999) who propose that ideologies form perspectives capable of 'ironing out' the contradictions, dilemmas and antagonisms of practices in ways which accord with the interests and projects of power (see also Hall, 1996b, p. 26). Language use is therefore necessarily ideological, inevitably constructing reality from a particular point of view.

In my analysis I shall be focusing, therefore, on both the content and the form of the message, trying to relate it to the larger political context in which they are made. Each act of analysis, moreover, carries with it a decision as to which of the aspects of the message to focus upon as the most relevant in constructing the realities under consideration. Using both systemic-linguistic analysis (Halliday, 1985) as well as a hermeneutic-like interpretation of discourses in terms of the context in which they were submerged (see Titscher et al., 2000), I will attempt to reach the ideological underpinnings of the informants' experiences.

In the analysis below I focus upon on one of the macro-topics of the interviews: the discussions of how the informants experienced, coped and dealt with the system transformation. Entire interviews were trawled through for fragments in which the informants took up the topic, which were extracted for in-depth analysis. In the text below, I show typical extracts, that is, those which are 'representative' (I am not using the term commonsensically; rather I am making claims to the representativeness of these representations).

3 Stories of the disenfranchised self

The discourses we were offered were ones of alienation and oppression. The new reality, even though at times represented as a new historical era, was usually positioned alongside the communist period, and when contrasted, the current period was either 'as bad' or 'even worse' than the previous one. The promise of the new beginning, so clear in the discourses of the non-communist governments after 1989, has not borne fruit.

3.1 Self and the hard new reality

First, I would like to discuss a few examples in which the informants position themselves in the new post-communist reality.

Example 1: LK, female, middle generation

(a) LK: the work, exactly the work. It wouldn't be so bad if it weren't for the work.
I: the work?
LK: because there used to be so much work but one didn't have the money to buy and there weren't the goods, that's the truth. The shelves were empty. Pasta and matches, nothing else.
I: and vinegar.

LK: one queued for a piece of meat at night.
I: and the coupons.
LK: yes.
I: 25 on the bone.
LK: now we have full shelves, but so what if factories are falling apart, it's obvious. The wages we had three four years ago, we have half of it now.

[...]

(b) LK: someone must keep the factory going. They are not going to do it, but we...
I: right.
LK: that's why we have what we have.
I: oh God.
LK: but
I: but?
LK: but one lives on.

[...]

(c) LK: you know what? I'll tell you something. I suspect something. I know I used to do these kind of things and who knows whether it has had some effect on my child. For one, in the meantime the private firms came in. It was like the parents are out the whole day. And that's the truth. When s/he [gender unspecified] goes out, as I went for 6 o'clock, so I went out ten to five when I worked at the Moda. Or then for this businessman in Dimo. How many times I phoned for my mother to go, to look after R., because I can't, because there is an outgoing shipment for a deadline and I must. I could slave the whole day, the night and the following day in the morning till two o'clock. I came home and do you think I went to bed? Because of this tiredness I could not fall asleep.
I: I see.
LK: and to work in the morning. One day off and again the whole marathon. And I am not surprised that some children, some parents prefer to give money instead of looking after the children. That the parents think that if they give the children money the matter is sorted. They have too little contact with the children. This is how I see it.

The first aspect of what LK says that I would like to comment on is the constructed contrast between the shortage of goods in communist times and their abundance in post-communist Poland. Yet, interestingly, in both cases the goods are as inaccessible, because after 1989, LK and others cannot afford them. Linguistically, it is rendered by two generic statements. But, it is the generic statement about what is going on now that is constructed much closer to her experience.

When she speaks of pre-1989 Poland ('there used to be so much work but one didn't have the money to buy and there weren't the goods'), she uses the expression *człowiek* (literally 'man', 'human being', rendered here as 'one'); alternatively, in post-1989 Poland she uses the verb in the first person plural ('we have full shelves...'). While *człowiek* can be seen as distancing the speaker from the general experience, the first person plural here is an attempt to construct the speaker on a par with a number of others in the same situation. LK is constructing herself as a member of a group that is worse off: they cannot buy goods, they have lower salaries. Interestingly, she continues with the impersonal rendering of the queuing experience in communism (*stało się*, 'one queued', lit. 'one stood').

The experience of post-communism is rendered more personally, as something that touches the informant more. She, together with those like her, is worse off. But she does switch to the impersonal form 'one lives on'. This time, however, the expression is almost formulaic – the use of the verb *żyć* ('to live') in first person plural to convey the same meaning would be awkward in Polish, and it would not carry the connotations of a hard life.

Not only is life seen as hard in the account, but people are also seen to be doomed. LK constructs state oppression and the inevitability of people's fate, augmented by the opposition of the group of private owners (pejoratively, *prywaciarze*). The expression *żyje się* ('one lives on') shows daily existence as independent of the living person – life goes on and I have very little part in shaping it. The reflexive form (through the use of *się*) of the verb shows the process of living as occurring in its own right, without anyone interfering (incidentally, the proverbially bad working practices in communist Poland were rendered by the expression *robi się* ('one works', 'it works itself'). But LK also constructs herself and those like her as having to keep the factory going (Polish *trzeba*, which can be roughly rendered in English as 'one needs to', 'there is a need'). Being on the receiving end of some external and unnamed forces, they 'have what they have'. And indeed, they have a quarter of what they earned. Despite the default possessiveness of the verb, this time it is used more as the English 'get'. There is no opportunity, no chance of changing what comes their way.

In extract (c), LK shows herself as part of a system that she has no control over. Her account of the working day is finished by the phrase *opiat'* – 'again the marathon'. The repetitiveness of the situation is rendered by three words in a five-word clause. *Opiat'*, Russian for 'again', is underscored by Polish *znowu* ('again'). The two are introduced by the conjunction *i* ('and') one of whose meanings indicates continuation.

Life is constructed as constant struggle in which the self is more than likely to lose.

Example 2: ER, female, middle

ER: It's hard to get a job, and once you have it, you either fight to keep it or there are redundancies, or you try to get it again, and one says what kind of contacts one has, and when an element that you have to support yourself on your own appeared, that you have to earn money and so on, but it is so hard to get work and it is so unstable.

Example 3: LZ, male, young

I: just generally, how is life?
LZ: you know, it's hard.
I: mmm
LZ: it's hard, because it's like being on rockers, as I said, all, just all, time is passing, that you are simply so rushed that you don't know the day or the time, and it's simply, it's hard, hard.

In contrast to LK, ER constructs subjectivity more in agentive terms, but all the same, it is never individual. She constructs experience of the new reality in terms of a group of people to which, it is implied, she belongs. ER is part of these powerless individuals, who need to fight for survival. Moreover, agency ascribed to the people she talked about is quite negative; it is not agency of unfettered actors who choose to act. Rather their actions are invariably reactions to the demands of their situation, whether the informant is talking about the situation in generic terms (note the use of *trzeba*, 'one needs to'), or talks about particular situations (note references to redundancies and the need to earn money by oneself). But even the ultimate resolution of the fight for survival, getting a job, does not bring relief – the fight goes on, this time to keep the job, in case there are redundancies or others have connections.

ER finds herself in a reality in which she constantly must respond to forces which she is in opposition to, in a situation in which any action might be cancelled out by the situation's instability. This instability of life is also reflected in LZ's account. He also is at the mercy of forces around him, the reality which passes by, running him down.

3.2 Self and new politics

But the new reality is not only rejected because it means a hard life in which one is pushed to find oneself. The informants also constructed themselves as losers in the political sphere; they are outside the group of people who benefit and those people are local politicians.

> **Example 4: KG, male, middle generation**
>
> KG: ... now he says what do you want, the commune? What do you want from Solidarity? I say, you do see what is going on? Do you see what's going on? My sister also goes after my father. And I firmly say. And what? What of it that you have? For Solidarity, yes, I put up the posters myself at night. I had a night pass and I sometimes ran away. It was so enthusiastic, and timely, I knew what it was all about. I was married etc., but somehow when I look in the perspective of the time, then
> I: I see.
> KG: I remember that period as somehow
> I: and one's getting sad.
> KG: mmm. That's why I am saying that I would leave [emigrate]. For this psychological peace that, chill out, I know I have to do it, but now, one doesn't know what? It's a mess, an extraordinary mess. And the parents tell me that it's good. And I say, what is good? You go to see a doctor and you can't get to the doctor? That's good? Or, I say, OK. ... and the salaries of these people. I don't mind that anyone is earning money, and I don't mean the private, but the state jobs. And the councillors here in Zgorzelec. Is it in Zgorzelec or in stupid Warsaw? I never knew, I always thought that in these big cities, everywhere there are so many councillors. Are there 800 councillors there?

There is a striking difference between KG's account of the communist and post-communist realities. While in the case of the former, he positions himself as an actor, someone positively doing things, be it putting up posters, or simply knowing what was going on. He constructs a clear role for himself in that reality, including a personal role of a husband. Life in communism was simple, including the fact that you also knew whom to blame for things going wrong (elsewhere in interview, unquoted here). This is contrasted with a reality in which he positions himself as someone who has lost this clear orientation in the world. There is not a single action in which he is positioned as an agent. The chaos he speaks of is reflected in his narrative. There is no clear agency, no clearly defined groups of people he refers to. The reality is a muddle, which is introduced by his initial statement of not knowing what to do.

The chaos the informant constructs is underscored by the reference to the councillors. They are not part of any political process, they are simply a group of people, who, it is implied, are councillors only for the money, with not even an implicit structure to their activities.

His story is that of a person who has been let down by the new reality. It is one of helplessness, and lack of structure or direction. His role, if anything, is one of simply enduring the reality, as he shows himself, with others like him, by not managing to get to see his doctor. Interestingly, the contrast between the new systems is dramatised by his reference to his argument with his parents. Not only does he not ascribe to the new reality, he actually argues that the change from communism is a change for the worse. The dramatisation makes his narrative more powerful.

The next two fragments construct a group of people who benefit from the new system, leaving the average citizen on its own.

Example 5: EJ, female, youngest generation

EJ: For example, when I read Zgorzelec newspapers or listen to the radio about what kind of things go on, it's just beyond me. What those people do. They want to make a quick buck, as much money as possible. Build a house quickly while I am the mayor or a councillor of sorts. And they don't give a shit about the people, I beg your pardon, or Zgorzelec as a town. To make things better, I don't know. New pavements or streets or benches. Just for themselves.
I: Just for themselves?
EJ: Thieves.

Example 6: BJ, TJ, females, middle generation, AJ, male, oldest generation

AJ: one worked so many years in People's Poland and I have shit.
TJ: that's just it.
BJ: that's what the lady is asking, dad.

BJ: and this one – these mayors, they take one hundred thousand zlotys and I have seven hundred fifty zlotys.
TJ: and no one is interested in how you live, are they?
BJ: exactly. You know I just can't understand that
AJ: to hell with them all.
BJ: I mean, when I worked they would pop in for a coffee. I saw how they behaved, what kind of milieu they were in, that they were as grey as I was. Such sheep, but who allowed them, and pushed them that they got in and that they apparently [had] this so-called
TJ: they had support.

Only hinted at in KG's account of the new reality, the two informants above explicitly construct a reality in which only the elites are the winners. The 'offending' group of local politicians is contrasted with the 'people', 'the man in the street', the group to which both informants belong. Moreover, in Extract 6, there is not even a hint of an awareness that the people are in power because of the due democratic process. So there is, in fact, a simple answer to the question of who pushed them: it was the voters, the electorate and, potentially, also the three informants above. Interestingly the popular support the councillors enjoyed is undermined and getting office becomes not much more than a claim of those who got power – it seems it has little to do with the votes that put the councillors in their seats.

3.3 The communist view of post-communist reality

Consider, finally, the following extract, in which the informant takes on the entire period of communism and tries to balance out its provisions of social security with the political repression.

Extract 7: BL, female, oldest generation

BL: The times of the People's Republic of Poland had their advantages and if we wanted to go deep, it was true, into the concentration camps and the beginning it certainly was dreadful, but later we got used to the greyness. But there was certainty of work. Small salaries, everybody with little, but they lived somehow. You paid very little for your flat, electricity, tram, bus, railway so, let's say, I don't know whether if you put it on the scales of justice, whether these good things would outweigh, perhaps not over the people who – certainly not – suffered, were evicted, arrested later, right? It was all cruel. But if you take it now, it's colourful, fairy-tale like. We have wonderful shops, there is everything, but there is no work, no money, is there?

Communism seems to be a time of both political repression and job security, and the decision is just about too difficult to make for the informant. Her account is still accessing new perspectives in which to view the period, with the final support for communism coming in the form of rejecting the current situation – one in which there is no work – with the benefits of the communist social security system seemingly outweighing its cruelty to individual people.

Moreover, it is communism which appears more real; the narrative, as the others above do, offers access to the detail of life. The queues, the prices, the flats. People are not merely workers or consumers, they are also citizens. We see the fabric of the society's life, its concerns and dilemmas. Nothing of the sort happens when the stories touch upon the new reality. They construct the soundbites and television clips with momentary glimpses of an imaginary reality, a reality of the advertisement. It's a reality of full and colourful, but also inaccessible, shops. The informants seem to know them only from outside, from window shopping. They are as inaccessible as the fairy tale BL refers to. Real life is the life in communism. New reality – free Poland, if you like – has not provided the informants with such life. It's a life of constant struggle – whether unemployed or in work – and lack of engagement with the reality surrounding them.

4 The experience of post-communism

Komuno wróć! – 'Communism, come back!'. This is one of the slogans forged in the times of post-communism, expressing the nostalgia of the times of job security, of life with barely any decisions to make. But what I would like to argue is that while thrown away as a political system, as a dominant intellectual ideology of the power group, communism is alive and well in our informants' discourse. To put it briefly – communism, its discourses and the discourses about it, still provide the framework within which the discourses of new reality are created. It is in contrast and in opposition to communism that the new reality is assessed and constructed.

But I have carried out this argument through the perspective of subjectivity. I have argued that speaking of the new reality after the collapse of communism, the informants constructed themselves as disenfranchised from the reality. In a free Poland, they do not position themselves as free, unfettered agents, going about their business in a system that requires success. Rather they are oppressed by the forces around them, helpless in the face of the challenges that free and capitalist Poland poses for them.

It would be tempting, then, to position the argument of the disenfranchised self as an argument of a post-communist identity. If identity is a 'discourse of belonging' (Barker and Galasiński, 2001), then I have shown above a very clear construction of a group of people the informants position themselves among. They are the disenfranchised – those who do not get paid enough to go into the fairy-tale shops. They have a discourse of belonging in which to construct themselves.

The problem might be that such an identity does not have a particular label; there are no post-communists in the same way as there are Poles, men or women, or old or young people. The sense of jointedness in the informants' words does not translate into an explicit discursive space which creates a particular group. But then they do position themselves as, for lack of a better word, 'helpless' in a variety of social situations. They all would probably describe their lives by *żyje się* ('one lives on') – life live itself, so to speak.

But what of the lack of label? The lack of label, I would like to argue, is significant but not in terms of whether or not there is a post-communist identity. It is significant in terms of there being an obvious place for a label to be filled. In other words, because there is a lack of identity label there is a need for anchorage, for pinning down.

And indeed, the political scene in Poland over the last 15 years has been a good example how this 'post-communist identity', this 'discourse of helplessness' can and has been tapped into by political organisations. The last five years in particular can be characterised to a considerable extent by the rise of populist movements; the extraordinary success of Stanisław Tymiński, a completely unknown presidential candidate in 1990, the more recent success of the populist Samoobrona and its leader Andrzej Lepper (who recently made it to the office of Deputy Prime Minister of Poland), and Prawo i Sprawiedliwość show clearly how on the one hand, the post-communist discourse is used for political purposes and, on the other, how political organisations attempt to define those who share in it. The lack of label, then, is in fact a political opportunity for those whose political ambitions are fulfilled by pandering to the disenfranchised and reinforcing their narrative of the new reality.

5 The man from Eltra

In about 1990, just after the commencement of the vast political changes in Eastern Europe, I listened to an interview with a foreman at Eltra, an electronics factory which was about to go bust. This man, in a very dramatic way, explained that he could not understand why people did not want to buy the radios the factory produced any more. The bulky radio 'Julia', as the star product of the factory was called, was the coveted trophy of many a Pole (including my father, who received it for his 55th birthday as a *very* special present from someone who had *access* to the radios). The foreman was no longer in possession of his symbolic capital of someone who could 'arrange' to get his many friends one of these radios. For the foreman, the decision not buy the radios he and his fellow workers manufactured was very much a personal tragedy. The world as he knew it collapsed, most importantly because his many friends, and friends' friends, and their friends too, did not need him any more. They didn't, needless to say, because the newly opened market in Poland was slowly beginning to saturate with cheaper, and far superior, radios from the Far East. Moreover, the market economy also meant that there was no 'arranging' to be done. One could actually buy the radios in the shops, where the shop assistants began to learn to bend over backwards to sell their goods.

The inevitable was coming – there was no more space in which to store the Julia radios, and the company had no more money to pay its workforce. The fiftysomething foreman was about to be made redundant with, in his own words, no chance of finding new employment. I remember this story because it put such a damper on the success of 1989. Communists were out, Poland was free and independent, I could vote for whomever I wanted. The world took a turn for the better. But I realised to my surprise that in fact it hadn't. At least not for the foreman in the radio factory.

This paper is very much about this man and the many like him. It is about experiences of people who have and still do find the new reality too much to cope with. The extracts I have quoted here, typical of a number of others in the two corpora, show Poles who do not speak of the new reality they have to live in terms of Polish independence, nor in terms of their right to vote or of getting rid of Soviet domination. They speak of their experience of being disengaged from the new reality, of their disillusion, of being left on the margins, and of not counting in the bigger picture of society.

Bibliography

Abélès, M. (2000) 'Virtual Europe', in I. Bellier and T. M. Wilson (eds) *An Anthropology of the European Union: Building, Imaging and Experiencing the New Europe* (Oxford: Berg), pp. 31–50.

Adrey, J-B. (2005) 'Minority Language Rights Before and After the 2004 EU Enlargement: The Copenhagen Criteria in the Baltic States', in 'Language and Social Processes in the Baltic Republics Surrounding EU Accession'. *Journal of Multilingual and Multicultural Development* 26/5, Special Issue (G. Hogan-Brun, guest editor), pp. 453–68.

Agadjanian, A. (2000) 'Russian Religion in Media Discourse – Entropy Interlude in *Ideocratic* Tradition', in M. Kotiranta (ed.) *Religious Transition in Russia* (Helsinki: Kilmora), pp. 251–88.

Aligica, P. D. (2003) 'Neoclassical Economics and the Challenge of Transition: Lessons and Implications of the Eastern-European Economic Reform Experience', IWM Working Paper 3 (Vienna: IWM).

Andrews, M. (2000) 'Texts in a Changing Context: Reconstructing Lives in East Germany'. In P. Chamberlayne, J. Bornat and T. Wengraf (eds) *The Turn to Biographical Methods in Social Science: Comparative Issues and Examples* (London: Routledge), pp. 181–95.

Andrews, M. (2004) 'Counter-narratives and the Power to Oppose', in M. Bamberg and M. Andrews (eds) *Considering Counter-Narratives. Narrating, Resisting, Making Sense* (Amsterdam and Philadelphia: John Benjamins), pp. 1–6.

Appelbaum, R. P. (1970) *Theories of Social Change* (Chicago: Markham Publishing).

Archer, M. (1995) *Realist Social Theory: The Morphogenetic Approach* (Cambridge: Cambridge University Press).

Archer, M. (2003) *Structure, Agency and the Internal Conversation* (Cambridge: Cambridge University Press).

Arjomand, S. A. (2001) *Rethinking Civilisational Analysis*. Special Issue of *International Sociology*, 16 (3).

Armbruster, H. and U. H. Meinhof (2005) 'Storying East-German Pasts: Memory Discourses and Narratives of Readjustment on the German/Polish and Former German/German Border', in J. Thornborrow and J. Coates (eds) *The Sociolinguistics of Narrative* (Amsterdam and Philadelphia: John Benjamins) pp. 41–66.

Artis, M., A. Banerjee and M. Marcellino (eds) (2006) *The Central and Eastern European Countries and the EU Enlargement* (Cambridge: Cambridge University Press).

Ashwin, S. (ed.) (2000) *Gender, State and Society in Soviet and Post-Soviet Russia* (London and New York: Routledge).

Atkinson, P. and A. Coffey (1997) 'Analysing Documentary Realities', in D. Silverman (ed.) *Qualitative Research: Theory, Method and Practice* (London: Sage), pp. 45–62.

Bacon, E. (2002) 'Church and State in Contemporary Russia: Conflicting Discourses', in R. Fawn and S. White (eds) *Russia after Communism* (London, Portland: Frank Cass), pp. 97–116.

Bakhtin, M. (1981) *The Dialogic Imagination* (Austin: University of Texas Press).

Bakhtin, M. (1984) *The Dialogical Principle* (Manchester: Manchester University Press).

Balcerowicz, L. (2000) 'Poland's Transformation', *Finance and Development*, 37 (3), (www.imf.org/external/pubs/ft/fandd/2000/09/balcerow.htm).

Balibar, E. (2002) *Politics and the Other Scene* (London, New York: Verso).

Balibar, E. (2004) *We, the People of Europe? Reflection on Transnational Citizenship* (Princeton: Princeton University Press).

Bamberg, M. (ed.) (2000) Theme Issue on Narrative Identity, *Narrative Inquiry*, 10 (1).

Bamberg, M. (2004) 'Talk, Small Stories, and Adolescent Identities', *Human Development*, 47, pp. 331–53.

Bamberg, M. (2007) 'Stories: Big or Small-Why Do We Care?, in M. Bamberg (ed.) *Narrative – State of the Art* (Amsterdam and Philadelphia: John Benjamins), pp. 165–74.

Bamberg, M. and A. Georgakopoulou (2005) 'Small is Beautiful: Small Stories as a New Perspective in Narrative Analysis.' Paper presented to the 9th International Pragmatics Association Conference, 10–15 July 2005, Riva del Garda, Italy.

Barker, C. and D. Galasiński (2001) *Cultural Studies and Discourse Analysis: A Dialogue on Language and Identity* (London: Sage).

Baron, N. (1997) 'Perestroika, Politicians and Pandora's Box: The Collective Memory of Stalinism during Soviet Reform', *European Review of History*, 97 (4), (1997), pp. 73–91.

Barthes, R. (1977) *Image, Music, Text* (London: Fontana).

Barthélémy, M. (2003) 'Temporal Perspectives in the Practical-Textual Handling of a European Public Problem', *Social Science Information*, 42 (3), pp. 403–30.

Bauman, Z. (1992a) *Intimations of Postmodernity* (London: Routledge).

Bauman, Z. (1992b) 'The Polish Predicament. A Model in Search of Class Interests', *Telos*, 25 (2), pp. 113–30.

Bauman, Z. (2000) *Globalizacja* (Warsaw: PIW).

Baynham, M. (2003) 'Narrative in Space and Time: Beyond "Backdrop" Accounts of Narrative Orientation', *Narrative Inquiry*, 13 (2), pp. 347–66.

Baynham, M. (2005) 'Network and Agency in the Migration Stories of Moroccan Women', in M. Baynham and A. De Fina (eds) *Dislocation/Relocation. Narratives of Displacement* (Manchester, UK and Northampton MA: St Jerome Publishing), pp. 11–35.

Baynham, M. and A. De Fina (eds) (2005) *Dislocation/Relocation. Narratives of Displacement* (Manchester, UK and Northampton MA: St Jerome Publishing).

Beck, U. (1992) *Risk Society: Towards a New Modernity* (London and New York: Routledge).

Beck, U. (1997) *The Reinvention of Politics: Rethinking Modernity in the Global Social Order* (Cambridge: Polity Press).

Beck, U., A. Giddens and S. Lash (1994) *Reflexive Modernization: Politics, Tradition and Aesthetics in the Modern Social Order* (Cambridge: Polity Press).

Bennett, B. P. (forthcoming) 'On the Politics of Church Slavonic in Post-Soviet Russia'. In L. R. N. Ashley and W. H. Finke (eds) *Proceedings of the International Conference on Language and Politics* (New York: American Society of Geolinguistics).

Berdahl, D. (2000) 'Introduction: An Anthropology of Postsocialism', in D. Berdahl, M. Bunzl and M. Lampland (eds) *Altering States. Ethnographies of Transition in Eastern Europe and the Former Soviet Union* (Ann Arbor: University of Michigan Press), pp. 1–13.

Berdahl, D., M. Bunzl and M. Lampland (eds) (2000) *Altering States. Ethnographies of Transition in Eastern Europe and the Former Soviet Union* (Ann Arbor: University of Michigan Press).

Beresford-Hill, P. (ed.) (1997) *Education and Privatisation in Eastern Europe and the Baltic Republics*, Oxford Studies in Comparative Education (London: Symposium).

Berger, P. L. and T. Luckmann (1966) *The Social Construction of Reality: A Treatise in the Sociology of Knowledge* (Garden City NY: Anchor Books).

Bergmann, J. R. (1998) 'Introduction: Morality in Discourse', *Research on Language and Social Interaction*, 31 (3–4), pp. 279–94.

Billig, M., S. Condor, D. Edwards, M. Gane, D. Middleton and A. Radley (1988) *Ideological Dilemmas. A Social Psychology of Everyday Thinking* (London: Sage).

Blokker, P. (2005) 'Post-Communist Modernization, Transition Studies and Diversity in Europe', *European Journal of Social Theory*, 8 (4), pp. 503–25.

Blommaert, J. (ed.) (1999) *Language Ideological Debates* (Berlin: Mouton de Gruyter).

Blommaert, J. (2005) *Discourse. A Critical Introduction* (Cambridge: Cambridge University Press).

Blommaert, J. and J. Verschueren (1994) *Antiracisme* (Antwerp: Hadewijch).

Blommaert, J. and J. Verschueren (1998) *Debating Diversity* (London: Routledge).

Borisov, A. (1994) *Pobelevshie Nivy: Razmyshleniia o Russkoi Pravoslavnoi Tserkvi* (Moskva: Put').

Boudon, R. (1986) *Theories of Social Change* (Berkeley: University of California Press).

Bourdieu, P. (1973) 'Cultural Reproduction and Social Reproduction', in R. Brown (ed.) *Knowledge, Education and Cultural Change: Papers in the Sociology of Education* (London: Tavistock), pp. 71–112.

Bourdieu, P. (1982) *Ce que parler veut dire. L'économie des échanges linguistiques* (Paris: Fayard).

Bourdieu, P. (1993) *Outline of a Theory of Practice* (Cambridge: Cambridge University Press).

Bourdieu, P. (1994) 'Doxa and Common Life: an Interview', in S. Žižek (ed.) *Mapping Ideology* (London: Verso) pp. 265–77.

Bourdieu, P. (1998) *On Television* (New York: New Press).

Bönker, F., K. Müller and A. Pickel (2002) *Postcommunist Transformation and the Social Sciences. Cross-Disciplinary Approaches* (Oxford: Rowman and Littlefield).

Brockmeier, J. and D. Carbaugh (eds) (2001) *Narrative and Identity: Studies in Autobiography, Self and Culture* (Amsterdam: John Benjamins, 2001).

Brubaker, R. and F. Cooper (2000) 'Beyond "Identity"', *Theory and Society*, 29, pp. 1–47.

Bruner, J. (1991) 'The Narrative Construction of Reality', *Critical Inquiry*, 18, pp. 1–21.

Brysk, A. and G. Shafir (eds) (2004) *People Out of Place. Globalisation, Human Rights and the Citizenship Gap* (New York and London: Routledge).

Buchowski, M. (2001) *Rethinking Transformation. An Anthropological Perspective on Postsocialism* (Poznań: Wydawnictwo Humaniora).

Buckley, M. (ed.) (1997) *Post-Soviet Women: From the Baltic to Central Asia* (Cambridge: Cambridge University Press).

Bugarski, R. (1995) *Jezik od Mira do Rata* (Belgrade: Slovograph, 1995).

Bugarski, R. (2004) 'Language and Boundaries in the Yugoslav Context', in B. Busch and H. Kelly-Holmes (eds) *Language, Discourse and Borders* (Clevedon, Buffalo, Toronto, Sydney: Multilingual Matters), pp. 21–38.

Burawoy, M. and K. Verdery (eds) (1999) *Uncertain Transition: Ethnographies of Change in the Postsocialist World* (Lanham: Rowman and Littlefield).

Burawoy, M. and Verdery, K. 'Introduction', in M. Burawoy and K. Verdery (eds) *Uncertain Transition: Ethnographies of Change in the Postsocialist World* (Lanham: Rowman and Littlefield, 1999), pp. 1–18.

Burrell, K. (2006) *Moving Lives* (Aldershot: Ashgate).

Busch, B. (2004) *Sprachen im Disput. Medien und Öffentlichkeit in multilingualen Gesellschaften* (Klagenfurt: Drava).

Busch, B. and M. Krzyżanowski (2007) 'Inside/Outside the European Union: Enlargement, Migration Policy and the Search for Europe's Identity', in J. Anderson and W. Armstrong (eds) *The Geopolitics of European Union Enlargement* (London: Routledge), pp. 107–24.

Caldas-Coulthard, C. R. (2003) 'Cross-cultural Representation of "Otherness" in Media Discourse', in G. Weiss and R. Wodak (eds) *Critical Discourse Analysis. Theory and Interdisciplinarity* (Basingstoke: Palgrave Macmillan), pp. 272–96.

Calhoun, C. (ed.) (1994) *Social Theory and the Politics of Identity* (Oxford: Blackwell).

Carabine, J. (2001) 'Unmarried Motherhood 1830–1990: A Genealogical Analysis', in M. Wetherell, S. Taylor and S. J. Yates, *Discourse as Data* (London: Sage, in association with The Open University), pp. 267–310.

Chaplin, V. (2004) 'Orthodoxy and the Societal Ideal', in C. Marsh (ed.) *Burden or Blessing? Russian Orthodoxy and the Construction of Civil Society and Democracy* (Boston: Institute on Culture, Religion and World Affairs, Boston University), pp. 1–6.

Chilton, P. (1981) *Security Metaphors: Cold War Discourse from Containment to Common House* (Bern and New York: Peter Lang).

Chouliaraki, L. and N. Fairclough (1999) *Discourse in the Late Modernity. Rethinking Critical Discourse Analysis* (Edinburgh: Edinburgh University Press).

Christiakov, Father G. (2005) 'In Search of the "Russian Idea": A View from Inside the Russian Orthodox Church', in J. Johnson, M. Stepaniants and B. Forest (eds) *Religion and Identity in Modern Russia: the Revival of Orthodoxy and Islam* (Aldershot and Burlington VT: Ashgate), pp. 51–64.

Clark, I. (1997) *Globalization and Fragmentation* (Oxford: Oxford University Press).

Clark, T. D. (2002) *Beyond Post-Communist Studies: Political Science and the New Democracies of Europe* (New York and London: M. E. Sharpe).

Cohen, S. (2006) *Deportation is Freedom! The Orwellian World of Immigration Controls* (London and Philadelphia: Jessica Kingsley Publishers).

Cox, T. and B. Mason (1999) *Social and Economic Transformation in East Central Europe* (Cheltenham: Edward Elgar).

Cyrus, N. (2006) 'Polish Emigration: Permanent and Temporary Patterns', in A. Triandafyllidou (ed.) *Contemporary Polish Migration in Europe. Complex Patterns of Movements and Settlement* (Lewinston, Queenston, Lempeter: The Edwin Mellen Press) pp. 25–46.

Daniel, W. (2006) *The Orthodox Church and Civil Society in Russia* (College Station: Texas A&M University Press).

Davies, M. (1993) 'Healing Sylvia: Accounting for the Textual "Discovery" of Unconscious Knowledge', *Sociology,* 27 (1), pp. 110–20.

De Fina, A. (2003) *Identity in Narrative: A Study of Immigrant Discourse* (Amsterdam: John Benjamins).

de Smaele, H. (1999) 'The Applicability of Western Models on the Russian Media System', *European Journal of Communication,* 14, pp. 173–89.

De Soto, H. G. (2000) 'Contested Environments: Reconstructing Environment and Memory in Postsocialist Saxony-Anhalt', in D. Berdahl, M. Bunzl and M. Lampland (eds) *Altering States. Ethnographies of Transition in Eastern Europe and the Former Soviet Union* (Ann Arbor: University of Michigan Press), pp. 97–113.

Deletant, D. (1996) *Ceauşescu and the Securitate: Coercion and Dissent in Romania, 1965–89* (London: Hurst & Co).

della Cava, R. (1997) 'Reviving Orthodoxy in Russia. An Overview of the Factions in the Russian Orthodox Church in the Spring of 1996', *Cahiers du Monde russe,* 38 (3), pp. 387–414.

della Porta, D. and Caiani, M. (2006) 'The Europeanisation of Public Discourse in Italy. A Top-Down Process?', *European Union Politics,* 7 (1), pp. 77–112.

Dennis, M. (1988) *The German Democratic Republic* (London: Pinter).

Derrida, J. (1994) 'The Spectre of Marx', *New Left Review,* 205 (May/June), pp. 31–58.

Derrida, J. (1997) *Archive Fever* (Chicago: University of Chicago Press).

Der Spiegel (1995) 'Spiegel-Umfrage: Viele Ostdeutsche trauern den alten Zeiten nach'. No 27, pp. 40–7.

Devlin, J. (1999) *Slavophiles and Commissars: Enemies of Democracy in Modern Russia* (New York: St Martin's Press).

Doupona, M., J. Verschueren and I. Ž. Žagar. 'The Pragmatics of Legitimation: The Rhetoric of Refugee Policies in Slovenia', *Belgian Journal of Linguistics,* 11, pp. 183–216.

Dunn, E. (1999) 'Slick Salesmen and Simple People. Negotiated Capitalism in a Privatised Polish Firm', in M. Burawoy and K. Verdery (eds) *Uncertain Transition. Ethnographies of Change in the Postsocialist World* (Lanham: Rowman and Littlefield), pp. 125–50.

Dunn, J. A. (1999) 'The Transformation of Russian from a Language of the Soviet Type to a Language of the Western Type', in J. A. Dunn. (ed.) *Language and Society in Post-communist Europe: Selected Papers from the Fifth World Congress of Central and East European Studies, Warsaw, 1995* (Basingstoke: Macmillan Press; New York: St. Martin's Press), pp. 3–22.

Duvell, F. (ed.) (2006) 'Polish Immigrants in the United Kingdom', in A. Triandafyllidou (ed.) *Contemporary Polish Migration in Europe. Complex Patterns of Movements and Settlement* (Lewinston, Queenston, Lempeter: The Edwin Mellen Press, 2006), pp. 47–90.

Edles, L. (2002) *Cultural Sociology in Practice* (London: Blackwell).

Edwards, D. (1997) *Discourse and Cognition* (London: Sage).

Edwards, D. (2000) 'Extreme Case Formulations: Softeners, Investment and Doing Nonliteral', *Research on Language and Social Interaction*, 23 (4), pp. 347–73.

Edwards, D. (2006) 'Facts, Norms and Dispositions: Practical Uses of the Modal Verb *Would* in Police Interrogations', *Discourse Studies*, 8 (4), pp. 475–501.

Edwards, D. and Potter, J. (2001) 'Discursive Psychology', in A. McHoul and M. Rapley (eds) *How to Analyse Talk in Institutional Settings* (New York: Continuum), pp. 12–24.

Eglin, P. and S. Hester (2003) *The Montreal Massacre: A Story of Membership Categorisation Analysis* (Waterloo: Wilfrid Laurier University Press).

Eisenstadt, S. N. (ed.) (1987) *Kulturen der Achsenzeit: Ihre Ursprünge und Ihre Vielfalt*, 2 vols (Frankfurt am Main: Suhrkamp).

Eisenstadt, S. N. (ed.) (1992) *Kulturen der Achsenzeit II: Ihre institutionelle und kulturelle Dynamik*, 3 vols (Frankfurt am Main: Suhrkamp).

Eisenstadt, S. N. (1998) 'The Construction of Collective Identities. Some Analytical and Comparative Indications', *European Journal of Social Theory*, 1 (2), pp. 229–54.

Eisenstadt, S. N. and B. Giesen (1991) 'Die konstruktion Nationaler Identitat in vergleichender Perpsektive', in B. Giesen (ed.) *Nationale und Kulturelle Identitaet. Studien zur Entwicklung des kollektiven Bewustseins in der Neuzeit* (Frankfurt am Main: Suhrkamp), pp. 21–38.

Eisenstadt, S. N. and B. Giesen (1995) 'The Construction of Collective Identity', *European Journal of Sociology*, 36, pp. 72–102.

Erben, M. (1993) 'The Problem of Other Lives: Social Perspectives on Written Biography', *Sociology*, 27 (1), pp. 15–25.

Etzioni, A. and E. Etzioni-Halevy (1973) *Social Change: Sources, Patterns and Consequences* (New York: Basic Books).

Fairclough, N. (1992) *Discourse and Social Change* (Cambridge: Polity Press).

Fairclough, N. (1995) *Critical Discourse Analysis* (Boston: Addison Wesley).

Fairclough, N. (1996) 'Technologisation of Discourse', in C-R. Caldas-Coulthard and M. Coulthard (eds) *Texts and Practices: Readings in Critical Discourse Analysis* (London: Routledge), pp. 92–106.

Fairclough, N. (2001a) 'Critical Discourse Analysis as a Method of Social-Scientific Research', in R. Wodak and M. Meyer (eds) *Methods of Critical Discourse Analysis* (London: Sage), pp. 121–38.

Fairclough, N. (2001b) *Language and Power* (2nd edition) (Harlow: Longman).

Fairclough, N. (2001c) 'The Discourse of New Labour: Critical Discourse Analysis', in M. Wetherell, S. Taylor and S. J. Yates, *Discourse as Data* (London: Sage, in association with The Open University), pp. 229–66.

Fairclough, N. (2003) *Analysing Discourse: Textual Analysis for Social Research* (London: Routledge).

Fairclough, N. (2005a) 'Critical Discourse Analysis', *Marges Linguistiques*, 9 (www.marges-linguistiques.com).

Fairclough, N. (2005b) 'Critical Discourse Analysis as a Resource in Researching "Transition": the Romanian Presidential Election of 2004'. Paper presented at the Dilemmas of Post-Communist Condition Conference, Wolverhampton, UK.

Fairclough, N. (2005c) 'Critical Discourse Analysis in Trans-Disciplinary Research on Social Change: Transition, Re-Scaling, Poverty and Social Inclusion', *Lodz Papers in Pragmatics,* 1, pp. 37–58.

Fairclough, N. (2005d) 'Discourse in Processes of Social Change: "Transition" in Central and Eastern Europe', *British and American Studies,* 11, pp. 9–34.

Fairclough, N. (2007) 'The Contribution of Discourse Analysis to Research on Social Change', in N. Fairclough, P. Cortese and P. Ardizzone (eds) *Discourse in Contemporary Social Change* (Frankfurt am Main: Peter Lang), pp. 25–49.

Fairclough, N., R. Jessop and A. Sayer (2004) 'Critical Realism and Semiosis', in J. Joseph and J. Roberts (eds) *Realism, Discourse and Deconstruction* (London: Routledge), pp. 23–42.

Fairclough, N. and R. Wodak (1997) 'Critical Discourse Analysis', in T. A. van Dijk (ed.) *Discourse as Social Interaction* (London: Sage), pp. 259–84.

Fairclough, N and Wodak, R. (2008) 'The Bologna Process and the Knowledge-Based Economy: a Critical Discourse Analysis Approach', in N. Fairclough, B. Jessop and R. Wodak (eds) *Education and the Knowledge-based Economy in Europe* (Amsterdam: Sense Publishers).

Featherstone, K. (2004) 'Introduction: In the Name of Europe?', in K. Featherstone and C. Radaelli (eds) *The Politics of Europeanisation* (Oxford: Oxford University Press), pp. 3–26.

Featherstone, M. (2006) 'Archive', *Theory, Culture & Society,* 23 (2–3), pp. 591–6.

Flowerdew, J. (2002) 'Rhetorical Strategies and Identity Politics in the Discourse of Colonial Withdrawal', *Journal of Language and Politics,* 1 (1), pp. 149–80.

Forest, B. and J. Johnson (2002) 'Unraveling the Threads of History: Soviet-Era Monuments and Post-Soviet National Identity in Moscow', *Annals of the Association of American Geographers,* 92 (3), pp. 524–47.

Foucault, M. (1975) *Surveille et punir: naissance de la prison* (Paris: Gallimard).

Foucault, M. (1976) *La volonté de savoir. Historie de la sexualité, tome I* (Paris: Gallimard).

Foucault, M. (1978) *The History of Sexuality, Vol. 1* (Harmondsworth: Penguin).

Foucault, M. (1984 [1970]) 'The Order of Discourse', in M. J. Shapiro (ed.) *Language and Politics* (Oxford: Basil Blackwell), pp. 108–38.

Foucault, M. (1997) *Il faut défendre la sociéte. Course au Collège de France 1976* (Paris: Gallimard/Seuil).

Foucault, M. (2002) *The Archeology of Knowledge* (London and New York: Routledge).

Foundation for Abandoned Children STATIM (2005) 'The Answer of the Foundation for Abandoned Children STATIM to the Declaration of the Ministry of Healthcare', *Aktuality STATIM* , 23 April, available at www.statim.cz

Fowler, R. (1985) 'Power', in T. A. van Dijk (ed.) *Handbook of Discourse Analysis, Vol. IV* (London: Academic Press).

Freeman, M. (1993) *Rewriting the Self: History, Memory, Narrative* (London: Routledge).

Friedman, J. (1999) 'Indigenous Struggles and the Discreet Charm of the Bourgeoisie'. *Journal of World-Systems Research,* V (2), pp. 391–411.

Friedman, J. (2000) 'Globalization, Class and Culture in Global Systems', *Journal of World-Systems Research,* VI (3), pp. 636–56.

Fukuyama, F. (1992) *The End of History and the Last Man* (London: Penguin).

Funk N. and M. Mueller (eds) (1993) *Gender Politics and Post-communism: Reflections from Eastern Europe and the Former Soviet Union* (New York: Routledge).

Fürst, J. (2006) 'In Search of Soviet Salvation: Young People Write to the Stalinist Authorities', *Contemporary European History,* 15 (3), pp. 327–45.

Gal, S. and G. Kligman (eds) (2000a) *Reproducing Gender. Politics, Publics, and Everyday Life after Socialism* (Chichester: Princeton University Press).

Gal, S. and G. Kligman (2000b) *The Politics of Gender after Socialism: A Comparative-historical Essay* (Princeton: Princeton University Press).

Galasińska, A. (2006) 'Border Ethnography and Post-communist Discourses of Nationality in Poland', *Discourse and Society,* 17 (5), pp. 609–28.

Galasińska, A. and D. Galasiński (2007) 'Rejecting an Identity. Discourses of Europe in Polish Border Communities', in S. Millar and J. Wilson (eds) *The Discourse of Europe: Talk and Text in Everyday Life* (Amsterdam: John Benjamins), pp. 97–113.

Galasińska, A. and O. Kozłowska (forthcoming) '"Either" and "Both" – the Changing Concept of Living Space among Polish Post-communist Migrants to the United Kingdom', in M. Baynham, J. Collins and S. Slembrouck (eds) *Globalization and Language Contact: Spatiotemporal Scales, Migration Flows, and Communicative Practices.* (London and New York: Continuum, Advances in Applied Linguistics series).

Galasińska, A., C. Rollo, and U. H. Meinhof (2002) 'Urban Space and the Construction of Identity on the German-Polish Border', in U. H. Meinhof (ed.) *Living (with) Borders: Identity Discourses on East-West Borders in Europe* (Aldershot: Ashgate), pp. 119–39.

Galasiński, D. and A. Galasińska (2005) 'Untold Stories and the Construction of Identity in Narratives of Ethnic Conflict on the Polish-German Border', *Multilingua,* 24 (1–2), pp. 101–20.

Galasiński, D. and A. Galasińska (2007) 'Lost in Communism, Lost in Migration: Narratives of post-1989 Polish Migrant Experience', *Journal of Multicultural Discourses,* 2 (1), pp. 47–62.

Galbreath, D. J. (2005) *Nation-Building and Minority Politics in Post-Socialist States* (Stuttgart: Ibidem Verlag).

Galbreath, D. J. and M. E. Galvin (2005) 'The Titularization of Latvian Secondary Schools: The Historical Legacy of Soviet Policy Implementation?' *Journal of Baltic Studies,* 36 (3), pp. 449–66.

Garapich, M. (2006) 'De-localizing Class and Transnationalizing Super-diversity: Polish Migrants in London.' Paper presented to the 9th EASA Biennial Conference, 18–21 September, Bristol, UK.

Garvy, G. (1966) *Money, Credit and Banking in Eastern Europe* (New York: Federal Reserve Bank of New York).

Georgakopoulou, A. (2006) 'The Other Side of the Story: Towards a Narrative Analysis of Narrative-in-Interaction', *Discourse Studies,* 8 (2), pp. 265–87.

Georgakopoulou, A. (2007) 'Thinking Big with Small Stories in Narrative and Identity Analysis', in M. Bamberg (ed.) *Narrative – State of the Art* (Amsterdam and Philadelphia: John Benjamins), pp. 145–54.

Gergen, M. and K. Gergen (2002) 'Ethnographic Representation as Relationship', in A. Bochner and C. Ellis (eds) *Ethnographically Speaking* (Lanham: AltaMira Press), pp. 11–33.

Gerner, K. and S. Hedlund (1993) *The Baltic States at the End of the Soviet Empire* (London: Routledge).
Giddens, A. (1984) *The Constitution of Society: Outline of the Theory of Structuration* (Berkeley: University of California Press).
Giddens, A. (1991) *Modernity and Self-identity* (Cambridge: Polity).
Giesen, B. (1993) *Die Intelektuellen und die Nation* (Frankfurt am Main: Suhrkamp).
Giesen, B. (1999) 'Europa als Konstruktion der Intelektuellen', in R. Viehoff and R. T. Segers (eds) *Kultur, Identität, Europa* (Frankfurt am Main: Suhrkamp), pp. 130–47.
Girnth, H. (1996) 'Texte im politischen Diskurs. Ein Vorschlag zur diskursorientierten Beschreibung von Textsorten', *Mutterspache,* 1, pp. 66–80.
Gorham, M. S. (2000) '*Natsiia ili Snierizatsiia*? Identity and Pervation in Language Debates of Late and Post-Soviet Russia', *The Russian Review,* 59 (4), pp. 614–29.
Grabbe, H. (2001) 'How Does Europeanisation Affect CEE Governance? Conditionality, Diffusion and Diversity', *Journal of European Public Policy,* 8 (6), pp. 1013–31.
Grancelli, B. (ed.) (1995) *Social Change and Modernisation* (Berlin: Walter de Gruyter).
Green-Cowles, M., J. Caporaso and T. Risse (eds) (2001) *Transforming Europe: Europeanisation and Domestic Change* (Ithaca: Cornell University Press).
Grice, P. (1989) *Studies in the Way of Words* (Cambridge MA and London: Harvard University Press).
Gruber, H. and F. Menz (2004) 'Introduction: Language and Political Change: Micro- and Macro-Aspects of a Contested Relationship?', *Journal of Language and Politics,* 3 (2), pp. 175–89.
Gwiazda, A. (2002) 'Europeanisation in Candidate Countries from Central and Eastern Europe.' Paper delivered at the EPIC Workshop, Florence, 19 September.
Habermas, J. (1990) *Strukturwandel der Öffentlichkeit* (First published 1962) (Frankfurt/Main: Suhrkamp).
Habermas, J. (1993) 'The Second Life Fiction of the Federal Republic: We Have Become "Normal" Again', *New Left Review,* 197 (Jan./Feb), pp. 58–66.
Hall, S. (1996a) 'Introduction: Who Needs 'Identity'?', in S. Hall and P. du Gay (eds) *Questions of Cultural Identity* (London: Sage), pp. 1–17.
Hall, S. (1996b) 'The Problem of Ideology: Marxism without Guarantees', in D. Morley and D-K. Chen (eds) *Stuart Hall: Critical Dialogues in Cultural Studies* (London: Routledge).
Halliday, M. A. K. (1985) *Introduction to Functional Grammar* (London: Edward Arnold).
Hann C. M. (ed.) (2002) *Postsocialism: Ideals, Ideologies, and Practices in Eurasia* (London and New York: Routledge).
Harris, S. (2005) 'Telling Stories and Giving Evidence: The Hybridisation of Narrative and Non-narrative Modes of Discourse in a Sexual Assault Trial', in J. Thornborrow and J. Coates (eds) *The Sociolinguistics of Narrative: Theory, Context and Culture in Oral Story-telling* (Amsterdam and Philadelphia: John Benjamins), pp. 215–38.
Hausendorf, H. (2000) *Zugehörigkeit durch Sprache. Eine linguistische Studie am Beispiel der deutschen Wiedervereinigung* (Tübingen: Niemeyer).

Hausendorf, H. and A. Bora (eds) (2006) *Analysing Citizenship Talk* (Amsterdam: John Benjamins).
Hess, L. (2005) 'Splněný sen' [The Dream Fulfilled], *Aktuality STATIM* , 5 May, available at www.statim.cz
Hess, L. (2006) 'Směl jsem si pochovat Kristýnku.' [I Might Keep Kristýnka in My Arms] *LUDVÍK HESS – Aktuality*, 18 April, available at www.hess.cz
Hiden, J. and P. Salmon (1991) *The Baltic Nations and Europe. Estonia, Latvia and Lithuania in the 21st Century* (London and New York: Longman).
Hładkiewicz, W. (1997) 'Bilans i Perspektywy Emigracji Polskiej w Wielkiej Brytanii', *Przegląd Polonijny*, 23 (2), pp. 53–64.
Hodge, R. and G. Kress (1993) *Language as Ideology*, 2nd edition (London: Routledge).
Hogan-Brun, G. (2003) 'Baltic National Minorities in Transition', in G. Hogan-Brun and S. Wolff (eds) *Minority Languages in Europe: Status – Frameworks – Prospects* (Basingstoke and New York: Palgrave Macmillan), pp. 120–37.
Hogan-Brun, G. (2005a) 'Baltic Sociolinguistic Review', *Journal of Baltic Studies*, XXXV (1/3), Special Issue (G. Hogan-Brun, guest editor).
Hogan-Brun, G. (2005b) 'Language and Social Processes in the Baltic Republics Surrounding EU Accession', *Journal of Multilingual and Multicultural Development*, 25 (6), Special Issue (G. Hogan-Brun, guest editor).
Hogan-Brun, G. (2005c) 'The Baltic Republics and Language Ideological Debates Surrounding EU Accession', in 'Language and Social Processes in the Baltic Republics Surrounding EU Accession'. *Journal of Multilingual and Multicultural Development*, 26 (5), Special Issue (G. Hogan-Brun, guest editor), pp. 367–77.
Hogan-Brun, G. (2006) 'At the Interface of Language Ideology and Practice: The Public Discourse Surrounding the 2004 Education Reform in Latvia', *Language Policy*, 5 (3), pp. 315–35.
Hogan-Brun, G. (2007) 'Language-in-Education across the Baltic: Policies, Practices Challenges', *Comparative Education*, 43 (4), pp. 553–70.
Hogan-Brun, G., U. Ozolins, M. Ramonienė and M. Rannut (2007) *Language Policies and Practices in the Baltic States*. Polity series of 'Current Issues in Language Planning', 8 (4). (Clevedon: Multilingual Matters).
Hogan-Brun, G. and M. Ramonienė (2003) 'Emerging Language and Education Policies in Lithuania', *Language Policy*, 2, pp. 27–45.
Hogan-Brun, G. and M. Ramonienė (2004) 'Changing Levels of Bilingualism across the Baltic', *International Journal of Bilingual Education and Bilingualis*, 7 (1), pp. 62–77.
Holmes, L. (1997) *Post-communism: an Introduction* (Durham NC: Duke University Press).
Hughes, L. (2004) 'Monuments and Identity', in S. Franklin and E. Widdis (eds) *National Identity in Russian Culture: an Introduction* (Cambridge; New York: Cambridge University Press), pp. 171–96.
Ieţcu, I. (2006) 'Argumentation, Dialogue and Conflicting Moral Economies in Post-1989 Romania: An Argument Against the Trade Union Movement', *Discourse & Society*, 17 (5), pp. 627–50.
Iglicka, K. (2000) 'Mechanisms of Migration from Poland before and during the Transition Period', *Journal of Ethnic and Migration Studies*, 26 (1), pp. 61–73.
Iglicka, K. (2001) *Poland's Post-War Dynamic of Migration* (Aldershot: Ashgate).

Iglicka-Okólska, K. (1997) 'Społeczne, Ekonomiczne i Polityczne Uwarunkowania Emigracji z Polski w Latach 1945–1995', in J. E. Zamojski (ed.) *Migracje i Społeczeństwo* (Warszawa: Instytut Historii PAN), pp. 97–112.

Ihan, A. (2001) '(Ob)vladamo!' (We manage!), *Delo*, 10 February, p. 32.

Jessop, B. (2002) *The Future of the Capitalist State* (Cambridge: Polity Press).

Jessop, B. (2004) 'The European Union and Recent Transformations of Statehood', in S. Puntscher-Riekmann, M. Latzer and M. Mokre (eds) *The State of Europe: Transformations of Statehood from a European Perspective* (Frankfurt am Main: Campus), pp. 75–94.

Jessop, B. (2005) 'The Political Economy of Scale and European Governance', *Tijdschrift voor Economische en Sociale Geografie*, 96 (2), pp. 225–30.

Jessop, B. and K. Nielsen (2003) 'Institutions and Rules', Network Institutional Theory – Research Paper 11/03 (Roskilde: University of Roskilde).

Johnstone, B. (2001) 'Discourse Analysis and Narrative', in D. Schiffrin, D. Tannen and H. E. Hamilton (eds) *The Handbook of Discourse Analysis* (Oxford: Blackwell), pp. 635–49.

Jones, P. R. and M. Krzyżanowski (2008) 'Identity, Belonging and Migration: Beyond Constructing "Others" ', in G. Delanty, P. R. Jones and R. Wodak (eds) *Identity, Belonging and Migration* (Liverpool: Liverpool University Press), pp. 38–53.

Kaneff, D. (2002) 'The Shame and Pride of Market Activity', in R. Mandel and C. Humphrey (eds) *Markets and Moralities* (Oxford: Berg), pp. 33–52.

Karlsreiter, A. (2003) *Media in Multilingual Societies: Freedom and Responsibility* (Vienna: OSCE, Office of the Representative on Freedom of the Media).

Kelly-Holmes, H. (1999) 'United Consumers? Advertising Discourse and Constructions of German Identity', in P. Stevenson and J. Theobald (eds) *Relocating Germanness: Discursive Disunity in Unified Germany* (Basingstoke and London: Palgrave Macmillan) pp. 91–108.

Kennedy, M. D. (ed.) (1994) *Envisioning Eastern Europe. Postcommunist Cultural Studies* (Ann Arbor: University of Michigan Press).

Kennedy, M. D. (2002) *Cultural Formations of Postcommunism. Emancipation, Transition, Nation, and War* (Minneapolis: University of Minnesota Press).

Kienpointner, M. (1992) *Alltagslogik: Struktur und Funktion von Argumentationsmustern* (Stuttgart: Frommann-Holzboog).

Kirill, M. (2007) 'Molit'sia budem po-russki', *Belgorodskaia pravda*, 30 July.

Knox, Z. (2005) *Russian Society and the Orthodox Church: Religion in Russia after Communism* (London and New York: RoutledgeCurzon).

Koczanowicz, L. and D. Kołodziejska (1999) 'Nation, Identity, Transition', in J. Miklaszewska (ed.) *Democracy in Central Europe 1989–1999* (Kraków: Meritum).

Kołodko, G. (2001) 'Globalization and Catching-Up: From Recession to Growth in Transition Economies.' Paper Delivered at the Workshop on European Integration and Transnational Policy-Making, Carleton University, Ottawa, 7–8 May 2001.

Kołodko, G. and M. Piątkowski (eds) (2002) *Nowa Gospodarka i Stare Problemy. Perspektywy Szybkiego Wzrostu w Krajach Posocjalistycznych* (Warsaw: WSPiZ).

Kondrat'eva, O. N. (2002) 'Tserkovnoslavianskii Iazyk—Iazyk Kul'ta i Kul'tura', in G. N. Minenko (ed) *Pravoslavie, kul'tura, obrazovanie: sbornik statei po materialam mazhregional'noi nauchno-prakticheskoi konferentsii (g. Kemerovo, 24–25 noiabria 2000 goda)* (Kemerovo: Izd-vo Kuzbassvuzizdat), pp. 361–70.

Konopasek, Z. and M. Andrews (2000) 'A Cautious Ethnography of Socialism: Autobiographical Narrative in the Czech Republic', in M. Andrews, S. D. Sclater, C. Squire and A. Treacher (eds) *Lines of Narrative: Psychosocial Perspectives* (London: Routledge), pp. 92–103.

Kopperschmidt, J. (1989) *Methodik der Argumentationsanalyse* (Stuttgart: Frommann-Holzboog).

Koselleck, R. (1989) *Vergangene Zukunft* (Frankfurt am Main: Suhrkamp).

Kostecki, W., K. Żukrowska and B. Góralczyk (2000) *Transformations of Post-communist States* (Basingstoke: Macmillan Press, and New York: St Martin's Press).

Kovács, A. and R. Wodak (eds) (2003) *NATO, Neutrality and National Identity* (Vienna: Böhlau).

Kovács, J. M. (ed.) (1994) *Transition to Capitalism? The Communist Legacy in Eastern Europe* (New Brunswick: Transaction Publishers).

Kravetskii, A. G. and A. A. Pletneva (2001) *Istoriia Tserkovnoslavianskogo Iazyka v Rossii (konets XIX-XX v.)* (Moscow: Iazyki russkoi kul'tury).

Krzyżanowska, N. (2006) 'O Nierówności Płci w Sferze Publicznej na Przykładzie Wyborów do Parlamentu Europejskiego 2004', in M. G. Woźniak (ed.). *Nierówności Społeczne a Wzrost Gospodarczy. Część 1: Problemy Globalizacji i Regionalizacji* (Rzeszów: Uniwersytet Rzeszowski), pp. 391–411.

Krzyżanowski, M. (2003) '"My European Feelings Are Not Only Based on the Fact that I Live in Europe": On the New Mechanisms in European and National Identification Patterns Emerging under the Influence of EU Enlargement', *Journal of Language and Politics,* 2 (1), pp. 175–204.

Krzyżanowski, M. (2005a) '"European Identity Wanted!": On Discursive and Communicative Dimensions of the European Convention', in R. Wodak and P. Chilton (eds) *A New Research Agenda in CDA: Theory and Multidisciplinarity.* (Amsterdam and Philadelphia: John Benjamins), pp. 137–64.

Krzyżanowski, M. (2005b) *Identity Spaces In-Between: On Collective Identities in Europe at the Times of Major Socio-Political Change.* Unpublished PhD thesis, University of Vienna.

Krzyżanowski, M. (2008) 'Konstrukcja Tożsamosci Narodowych i Europejskich w Polskim Dyskursie Polityki po Roku 1989: Analiza Dyskursywno-Historyczna', in A. Duszak and N. Fairclough (eds) *Krytyczna Analiza Dyskursu. Interdyscyplinarne Podejście do Komunikacji Społecznej* (Krakow: Universitas), pp. 267–305.

Krzyżanowski, M. (forthcoming) *Becoming European: Discourses of Identity and Social Change in Polish Politics after 1989* (Amsterdam: John Benjamins).

Krzyżanowski, M. and F. Oberhuber (2007) *(Un)Doing Europe: Discourses and Practices of Negotiating the EU Constitution* (Brussels: PIE–Peter Lang).

Krzyżanowski, M. and R. Wodak (2007) 'Multiple/Collective Identities, Migration and Belonging', in C-R. Caldas-Coulthard and R. Iedema (eds) *Identity Trouble: Critical Discourse and Contested Identities* (Basingstoke: Palgrave Macmillan), pp. 95–119.

Kurczewska, J. (ed.) (1999) *Zmiana Społeczna* (Warsaw: IFiS PAN).

Kuzio, T. (2001) 'Identity and Nation-building in Ukraine: Defining the "Other"', *Ethnicities,* 1 (3), pp. 343–66.

Lakoff, G. (1981) *Metaphors We Live By* (Chicago: University of Chicago Press).

Langston, K. (1999) 'Linguistic Cleansing: Language Purism in Croatia after the Yugoslav Break-up', *International Politics*, 36, pp. 179–201.

Lassen, I., J. Strunck and T. Vestergaard (eds) (2006) *Mediating Ideology in Text and Image. Ten Critical Studies* (Amsterdam: John Benjamins).

Le Couteur, A. (2001) 'On Saying Sorry: Repertoires of Apologising to Australia's Stolen Generations', in A. McHoul and M. Rapley (eds) *How to Analyse Talk in Institutional Settings: A Casebook of Methods* (London: Continuum International), pp. 148–60.

Lee, J. (1984) 'Innocent Victims and Evil Doers', *Women's Studies International Forum*, 7 (1) pp. 69–73.

Lemke, J. (1995) *Textual Politics: Discourse and Social Dynamics* (London: Taylor and Francis).

Lepper, G. (2000) *Categories in Text and Talk: A Practical Introduction to Categorisation Analysis* (London: Sage).

Likhachev, D. S. (1999) 'Russkii Iazyk v Bogosluzhenii i Bogoslovskoi Mysli', in N. Tikhon and A. Kaverin (eds) *Bogosluzhebnyi Iazyk Russkoi Tserkvi* (Moscow: Izdanie Sretenskogo Monastyria), pp. 276–9.

Linde, C. (1993) *Life Stories: The Creation of Coherence* (Oxford: Oxford University Press).

Linklater, B. (1999) 'Narratives of the GDR: What Parents Will Tell Their Children', in P. Stevenson and J. Theobald (eds) *Relocating Germanness: Discursive Disunity in Unified Germany* (Basingstoke and London: Palgrave Macmillan) pp. 150–66.

Literaturnaia Rossiia (1994a) 'Po povodu sobytii vokrug moskovskogo Sretenskogo monastryia, shto na Bol'shoi Lubianke', unsigned article, vol. 9 (1621) (4 March).

Literaturnaia Rossiia (1994b) 'S' pros'boi opublikovat' ego Sviateishestvu, Patriarkhu Moskovskomu i Vseia Rusi Aleksiiu II', unsigned article 10 (1622), 11 March.

Livingston, E. (1995) *An Anthropology of Reading* (Bloomington: Indiana University Press).

Lovell, S. (2000) *The Russian Reading Revolution: Print Culture in the Soviet and Post-Soviet Eras* (New York: St. Martin's Press).

Luhmann, N. (1995) *Social Systems* (Stanford: Stanford University Press).

Luhmann, N. (1997) *Die Gesellschaft der Gesellschaft. Vol. 1–2* (Frankfurt am Main: Suhrkamp).

Lynch, M. (1999) 'Archives in Formation: Privileged Spaces, Popular Archives and Paper Trails', *History of the Human Sciences*, 12 (2) pp. 65–87.

Lynch, M. and D. Bogen (1996) *The Spectacle of History: Speech, Text, and Memory at the Iran-Contra Hearings* (Durham NC and London: Duke University Press).

Lyotard, J. F. (1984) *The Postmodern Condition: A Report on Knowledge* (Manchester: Manchester University Press).

Malmborg, M af, and B. Stråth (2002) 'Introduction: The National Meanings of Europe', in M. af Malmborg and B. Stråth (eds) *The Meaning of Europe* (Oxford: Berg), pp. 1–27.

Mandel, R. and C. Humphrey (eds) (2002) *Market and Moralities. Ethnographies of Postsocialism* (Oxford, New York: Berg).

Martin, J. R. and R. Wodak (eds) (2003) *Re/Reading the Past: Critical and Functional Perspectives on Time and Value* (Amsterdam: John Benjamins).

Mastnak, T. (1995) 'Zagovor nacionalizma' (Plea for Nationalism), in D. Strajn (ed.) *Meje Demokracije* (The Limits of Democracy) (Ljubljana: Liberalna Akademija), pp. 133–50.

Matras, Y. (1999) 'Writing Romani: the Pragmatics of Codification in a Stateless Language', *Applied Linguistics*, 20, pp. 481–502.

Mautner, G. (2000) *Der Britische Europa-Diskurs. Methodenreflexion und Fallstudien zur Berichterstattung in der Tagespresse* (Vienna: Passagen Verlag).

McBride, W. L. (1999) *Philosophical Reflections of the Changes in Eastern Europe* (Lanham: Rowman and Littlefield).

McLeish, E. (1998) 'Introduction: Processes of Educational Transition in Countries Moving from Authoritarian Rule to Democratic Government', in E. McLeish and D. Phillips (eds) *Processes of Transition in Education Systems*, Oxford Studies in Comparative Education (Oxford: Symposium), pp. 9–22.

McLeish, E. and Phillips, D. (eds) (1998) *Processes of Transition in Education Systems*, Oxford Studies in Comparative Education (Oxford: Symposium).

Mebrahtu, T., M. Crossley and D. Johnson (eds) (2000) *Globalisation, Educational Transformation and Societies in Transition*, Oxford Studies in Comparative Education (Oxford: Symposium).

Meinhof, U. H. and D. Galasiński (2005) *The Language of Belonging* (Basingstoke and New York: Palgrave Macmillan).

Mény, Y., P. Muller and J-L. Quermonne (eds) (1996) *Adjusting to Europe: The Impact of the European Union on National Institutions and Policies* (London: Routledge).

Merkel, W. (ed.) (1994) *Systemwechsel I: Theorien, Ansätze und Konzepte der Transformationsforschung* (Opladen: Leske und Budrich).

Merkel, W. (1999) *Systemtransformation: Eine Einführung in die Theorie und Empirie der Transformationsforschung* (Opladen: Leske und Budrich).

Meyendorff, P. (1994) 'Liturgicheskii Put' Pravoslavnoi Tserkvi v Amerike v XX v.', *Pravoslavnaia Obshchina*, 19 (1), pp. 105–15.

Meyer, C. O. (2005) 'The Europeanisation of Media Discourse: A Study of Quality Press Coverage of Economic Policy Co-ordination since Amsterdam', *Journal of Common Market Studies*, 43 (1), (2005), 121–48.

Mezzadra, S. (2004a) 'Drzavljanstvo v gibanju' (Citizenship in Movement) *Casopis za kritiko znanosti*, 22/217–218, pp. 59–66.

Mezzadra, S. (2004b) 'Evropa migrantov' (Europe of Migrants) *Casopis za kritiko znanosti*, 22/217–218, pp. 162–75.

Miller, B. (1999) *Narratives of Guilt and Compliance in Unified Germany: Stasi Informers and their Impact on Society* (London: Routledge).

Miller, B. (2003) 'Portrayals of Past and Present Selves in the Life Stories of Former Stasi Informers', in R. Humphrey, R. Miller and E. Zdravomyslova (eds) *Biographical Research in Eastern Europe: Altered Lives and Broken Biographies* (Aldershot: Ashgate), pp. 101–14.

Milohnic, A. (ed.) (2002) *The European Gate-keepers. Migration and Asylum Policies in Eastern Europe* (Ljubljana: Mirovni institut).

Ministry of Healthcare (2005) 'The Declaration of the Ministry of Healthcare Concerning the Intention of the Foundation STATIM to Establish "Babybox" for Anonymous Abandonment of Children on the Wall of Clinic for Gynecology and Obstetrics', 19 April. Available at www.mzcr.cz

Misztal, B. (2003) *Theories of Social Remembering* (Maidenhead, Philadelphia: Open University Press).

Morawska, E. (1989) 'Labour Migration of Poles in the Atlantic World Economy, 1880–1914', *Comparative Studies in Society and History*, 3 (2), 237–72.

Morawska, E. (2001) 'Structuring Migration: The Case of Polish Income-seeking Travellers to the West', *Theory and Society*, 30, pp. 47–80.

Morley, D. (2000) *Home Territories. Media, Mobility and Identity* (London: Routledge).

Moskovich, W. (1999) 'The Terminology of Modern Russian: Ultranationalism and Antisemitism', in J. A. Dunn (ed.) *Language and Society in Post-communist Europe*, pp. 86–101.

Mouzelis, N. (1995) *Sociological Theory: What Went Wrong?* (London: Routledge).

Mungiu-Pippidi, A. (2006) 'Europeanisation without Decommunisation: A Case of Elite Conversion'. CDDRL, Stanford University, Working Paper No 64, June.

Muntigl, P., G. Weiss and R. Wodak (2000) *European Union Discourses on Unemployment. An Interdisciplinary Approach to Employment Policy-Making and Organisational Change* (Amsterdam and Philadelphia: John Benjamins).

Neuhold, H., P. Havlik and A. Suppan (eds) (1995) *Political and Economic Transformation in East Central Europe* (Boulder: Westview Press).

Oberhuber, F. (2005) 'Deliberation or "Mainstreaming"? Empirically Researching the European Convention', in R. Wodak and P. Chilton (eds) *A New Research Agenda in CDA: Theory and Multidisciplinarity* (Amsterdam and Philadelphia: John Benjamins), pp. 165–89.

Oberhuber, F., C. Bärenreuter, M. Krzyżanowski, H. Schönbauer and R. Wodak (2005) 'Debating the European Constitution: On Representations of Europe/ the EU in the Press', *Journal of Language and Politics*, 4 (2), pp. 227–71.

Ochs, E. and L. Capps (2001) *Living Narrative: Creating Lives in Everyday Storytelling* (Cambridge MA: Harvard University Press).

OECD (Organisation for Economic Co-operation and Development) (2001a) *Reviews of National Education Policies. Estonia* (Paris: OECD Publications).

OECD (Organisation for Economic Co-operation and Development) (2001b) *Reviews of National Education Policies. Latvia* (Paris: OECD Publications).

OECD (Organisation for Economic Co-operation and Development) (2002) *Reviews of National Education Policies. Lithuania* (Paris: OECD Publications).

Okuka, M. (1998) *Eine Sprache, viele Erben. Sprachenpolitik als Nationalisierungsinstrument in Ex-Jugoslawien* (Klagenfurt: Wieser).

Oprea, M. (2002) *'Banalitatea Răului. O istorie a Securităţii în Documente* ('The Banality of Evil': A Documentary History of the Securitate') (Iaşi: Polirom).

Osborn, M. (2005) 'A World of Difference? The Social and Cultural Construction of the European Teacher and Learner'. Inaugural Lecture, University of Bristol (unpublished manuscript).

Osipovic, D. (2007) 'Household and Family Situation of Recent Polish Migrants in the UK. What it Reveals about the Dynamics of Settlement.' Paper presented to 'The New Europeans under Scrutiny' workshop on state-of-the-art research on Polish migration to the UK, 2 February, University of Wolverhampton.

Outhwaite, W. and L. Ray (2005) *Social Theory and Postcommunism* (Malden, Oxford, Carlton: Blackwell).

Pajnik, M., P. Lesjak-Tusek and M. Gregorcic (2001) *Immigrants, Who Are You? Research on Immigrants in Slovenia* (Ljubljana: Mirovni institut).

Pajnik, M. and S. Zavratnik Zimic (ed.) (2003) *Migration – Globalization – European Union* (Ljubljana: Mirovni institut).

Papkov, I. A. (2004) 'The Resurgence of Russian Orthodoxy and its Implications for Russian Democracy', in C. Marsh (ed.) *Burden or Blessing? Russian Orthodoxy and the Construction of Civil Society and Democracy* (Boston: Institute on Culture, Religion and World Affairs, Boston University), pp. 37–44.

Parsons, T. (1964) *The Social System* (Glencoe: Free Press).

Parsons, T. (1966) *Societies: Evolutionary and Comparative Perspectives* (Englewood Cliffs: Prentice Hall).

Parthé, K. F. (2004) *Russia's Dangerous Texts: Politics between the Lines* (New Haven: Yale University Press).

Passerini, L. (ed.) (2005) *Memory and Totalitarianism* (new edition) (New Brunswick: Transaction Publishers).

Phillips, D. and M. Kaser (eds) (1992) 'Education and Economic Change in Eastern Europe', *Oxford Studies in Comparative Education*, 2 (1).

Pickles, J. and A. Smith, (eds) (1998) *Theorising Transition: The Political Economy of Post-Communist Transformations* (London: Routledge).

Pine, F. (2002a) 'Dealing with Money: Zlotys, Dollars and Other Currencies in the Polish Highlands', in R. Mandel and C. Humphrey (eds) *Market and Moralities. Ethnographies of Postsocialism* (Oxford, New York: Berg), pp. 75–97.

Pine, F. (2002b) 'Retreat to the Household', in C. Hann (ed.) *Postsocialism* (London: Routledge), pp. 95–113.

Plummer, K. (2001) *Documents of Life 2: An Invitation to Critical Humanism* (London: Sage).

Polanyi, K. (1944) *The Great Transformation* (London: Beacon Press).

Pomerantz, A. (1986) 'Extreme Case Formulations: A Way of Legitimating Claims', *Human Studies*, 9, pp. 219–29.

Preece, J. (1996) 'Damaged Lives? (East) German Memoirs and Autobiographies, 1989–1994', in O. Durani, C. Good and K. Hilliard (eds) *The New Germany: Literature and Society after Unification* (Sheffield: University of Sheffield Press) pp. 349–64.

Preoteasa, I. (2002) 'Intellectuals and the Public Sphere in Post-Communist Romania: A Discourse Analytical Perspective', *Discourse & Society*, 13 (2), pp. 269–92.

Priedīte, A. (2005) 'Surveying Language Attitudes and Practices in Latvia', in 'Language and Social Processes in the Baltic Republics Surrounding EU Accession', *Journal of Multilingual and Multicultural Development*, 26 (5), Special Issue (G. Hogan-Brun, guest editor), pp. 409–24.

Priewe, J. and R. Hickel (1991) *Der Preis der Einheit – Bilanz und Perspektiven der deutschen Einigung* (Frankfurt am Main: Fischer Verlag).

Prior, L. (2004) 'Documents', in C. Seale, G. Gobo, J. F. Gubrium, and D. Silverman, (eds) *Qualitative Research Practice* (London: Sage), pp. 375–90.

Ramet, S. (1998) *Nihil Obstat: Religion, Politics, and Social Change in East-Central Europe and Russia* (Durham NC: Duke University Press).

Rancière, J. (1995) 'Politics, Identification and Subjectivization', in J. Rajchman (ed.) *The Identity in Question* (New York, London: Routledge), pp. 63–70.

Rancière, J. (2005) *Nerazumevanje* (*La mesentente*) (Ljubljana: Zalozba ZRC SAZU).
Rausing, S. (2002) 'Re-constructing the "Normal"', in R. Mandel and C. Humphrey (eds) *Markets and Moralities* (Oxford: Berg), pp. 127–42.
Reisigl, M. (2003) 'Voicing the "Other": Reading and Writing Indigenous Australians', in G. Weiss and R. Wodak (eds) *Critical Discourse Analysis. Theory and Interdisciplinarity* (Basingstoke: Palgrave Macmillan), pp. 199–219.
Reisigl, M. and R. Wodak (2001) *Discourse and Discrimination* (London: Routledge) (Revised ed., 2009).
Remneva, M. L. (1995) 'Tserkovnoslavianskii Iazyk na Rusi', in A. Ia. Esalnek (ed.) *Russkaia Dukhovnaia Kul'tura* (Moskva: Izd-vo MGU), pp. 71–81.
Riha, R. (1995) 'Demokracija za vsako rabo' ('Democracy for every use'), in D. Strajn (ed.) *Meje Demokracije* (*The Limits of Democracy*) (Ljubljana: Liberalna Akademija), pp. 173–208.
Riordan, J. and S. Bridger (eds) (1992) *Dear Comrade Editor: Readers' Letters to the Soviet Press under Perestroika* (Bloomington and Indianapolis: Indiana University Press).
Romaniszyn, K. and J. Nowak (2003) 'Poland: State, Nation Formation and Europe', in B. Stråth and A. Triandafyllidou (eds) *Representations of Europe and the Nation in Current and Prospective Member States: Media, Elites and Civil Society* (Brussels: European Commission), pp. 244–72.
Rosamond, B. (2000) 'Europeanisation and Discourses of Globalisation: Narratives of External Structural Context in the European Commission', CSGR, University of Warwick, Working Paper No. 51/00.
Rundell, J. (2004) 'Strangers, Citizens and Outsiders: Otherness, Multiculturalism and the Cosmopolitan Imaginary in Mobile Societies', *Thesis Eleven,* 78 (1), pp. 85–101.
Ryazanova-Clarke, L. and T. Wade (1999) *The Russian Language Today* (London and New York: Routledge).
Sachs, J. D. (1991) 'Poland's Big Bang after One Year', *Skandinaviska Enskilda Banken Quarterly Review,* 1–2, pp. 3–7.
Sachs, J. D. (1992) 'The Economic Transformation in Eastern Europe: The Case of Poland', *Economics of Planning,* 25, pp. 5–19.
Sachs, J. D. (1995) 'Old Myths About Poland's Reforms Die Hard', *Transition: The Newsletter About Reforming Economies,* 6 (11–12), pp. 11–12.
Sachs, J. D. and D. Lipton (1990) 'Poland's Economic Reform', *Foreign Affairs,* 69 (3), pp. 47–66.
Sacks, H. (1995) *Lectures on Conversation* (Oxford: Blackwell).
Sakwa, R. (1999) *Postcommunism* (Buckingham: Open University Press).
Salecl, R. (1994) *The Spoil of Freedom: Psychoanalysis and Feminism after the Fall of Socialism* (London and New York: Routledge).
Salecl, R. 'The Ideology of Mother Nation in Yugoslav Conflict', in M. D. Kennedy, (ed.) *Envisioning Eastern Europe* (Ann Arbor: University of Michigan Press), pp. 87–101.
Samuel, R. and Thompson, P. (eds) (1990) *The Myths We Live By* (London and New York: Routledge).
Schiffrin, D., D. Tannen, D. and H. Ehernberger Hamilton (eds) (2003) *Handbook of Discourse Analysis* (Malden: Blackwell Publishers).

Schneiberg, F. (2005a) 'The Attitude Towards the Establishment of Babybox in the Area of the General University Hospital Clinic for Gynecology and Obstetrics.' *Aktuality STATIM*, available at www.statim.cz/

Schneiberg, F. (2005b) 'Speech by MUDr František Schneiberg', quoted in T. Šimůnková, 'Mojžíšové z popelnic.' *Literární noviny*, 24, p. 1.

Schneider, P. (1990) *Extreme Mittellage – Eine Reise durch das deutsche Nationalgefühl* (Reinbek bei Hamburg: Rowohlt).

Schramm, W. (1964) *Mass Media and National Development* (Stanford: Stanford University Press).

Sebba, M. (2006) 'Ideology and Alphabets in the Former USSR', *Language Problems & Language Planning*, 30 (2), pp. 99–125.

Shütz, A. (1962) *Collected Papers. Vol. I.: The Problem of Social Reality* (The Hague: Martinus Nijhoff).

Shütz, A. (1967) *The Phenomenology of the Social World* (Evanston: Northwestern University Press).

Skopljanac Brunner, N., S. Gredelj, A. Hodižić and B. Krištofić (eds) (2000) *Media & War* (Zagreb and Belgrade: Centre for Transition and Civil Society Research, Agency Argument).

Šimůnková, T. (2005) 'Mojžíšové z popelnic' ('Moses from Dustbins'), *Literární noviny*, 24, p. 1.

Škiljan, D. (2001) 'Languages with(out) Frontiers', in N. Švob-Đokić (ed.) *Redefining Cultural Identities* (Zagreb: Institute for International Relations), pp. 87–101.

Škiljan, D. (2002) *Govor Nacije. Jezik, Nacija, Hrvati* (Zagreb: Golden Marketing).

Slany, K. (ed.) (1997) *Orientacje Emigracyjne Polaków* (Kraków: Uniwersytet Jagielloński, Instytut Socjologii).

Smith, D. (1990a) 'The Active Text: A Textual Analysis of the Social Relations of Public Textual Discourse', in D. Smith, *Texts, Facts and Femininity: Exploring the Relations of Ruling* (London: Routledge), pp. 120–58.

Smith, D. (1990b) 'Textually Mediated Social Organization', in D. Smith, *Texts, Facts and Femininity: Exploring the Relations of Ruling* (London: Routledge), pp. 209–24.

Sowiński, P. (2006) 'Turystyka Zagraniczna a Czarny Rynek w Polsce (1956–1989)', in S. Kott, M. Kula, and T. Linderberger (eds) *Socialism w Życiu Powszednim* (Warsaw, Potsdam: Wydawnictwo TRIO & Zentrum fur Zeithistorische Forschung), pp. 189–98.

Sparks, C. (2000) 'Media Theory after the Fall of European Communism: Why the Old Models from East and West Won't Do Any More', in J. Curran and P. Myung-Jin (eds) *De-Westernizing Media Studies* (London and New York: Routledge), pp. 35–50.

Stanley, L. (1993) 'On Auto/Biography in Sociology', *Sociology*, 27 (1), pp. 41–52.

Stark, D. and L. Bruszt (1998) *Postsocialist Pathways: Transforming Politics and Property in East Central Europe* (Cambridge: Cambridge University Press).

Statham, P. and E. Gray (2005) 'The Public Sphere and Debates about Europe in Britain. Internalized and Conflict-Driven?', *Innovation*, 18 (1), pp. 61–81.

STATIM (2005) 'Considerations of STATIM Concerning the Position of MUDr. František Schneiberg', *Aktuality STATIM* , available at www.statim.cz

Stola, D. (2001) 'Międzynarodowa Mobilność Zarobkowa w PRL', in E. Jaźwińska and M. Okólski (eds) *Ludzie na Huśtawce* (Warsaw: Scholar) pp. 62–100.

Sumic-Riha J. (2005) 'Aisthesis politike' ('Aisthesis of Politics'), in J. Rancière *Nerazumevanje* (*La mesentente*) (Ljubljana: Zalozba ZRC SAZU), pp. 177–97.

Suprun, V. I. (1997) 'Tserkovnoslavianskii Iazyk kak Chast' Russkoi Iazykovoi Kul'tury', in *Kirillo-Mefodievskie Chteniia* (Samara: Izd. Samarskoi Gumanitarnoi Akademii), pp. 39–46.

Svašek, M. (ed.) (2006) *Postsocialism: Politics of Emotions in Central and Eastern Europe* (Oxford: Berghahn).

Sword, K. (1996) *Identity in Flux. The Polish Community in Britain.* School of Slavonic and East European Studies Occasional Paper No 36, University of London.

Sztompka, P. (1991) *Society in Action: The Theory of Social Becoming* (Chicago: University of Chicago Press).

Sztompka, P. (1993) *The Sociology of Social Change* (Oxford: Blackwell).

Sztompka. P. (ed.) (1999) *Imponderabilia Wielkiej Zmiany* (Warsaw: Wydawnictwo Naukowe PWN).

Taguieff, P-A. (2001) *The Force of Prejudice. On Racism and Its Doubles* (Minneapolis: University of Minnesota Press).

Taylor, P. (1999) *Modernities. A Geohistorical Interpretation* (Cambridge: Polity Press).

Thomas, G. (1991) *Linguistic Purism* (London and New York: Longman).

Thompson, M. (1999) *Forging the War. The Media in Serbia, Croatia, Bosnia and Herzegovina* (London: University of Luton Press).

Thompson, M. (2000) *Slovenia, Croatia, Bosnia and Herzegovina, Macedonia (FYROM) and Kosovo. International Assistance to Media* (Vienna: OSCE, Office for the Representative on Freedom of the Media).

Thornborrow, J. and J. Coates (2005a) 'The Sociolinguistics of Narrative: Identity, Performance, Culture', in J. Thornborrow and J. Coates (eds) *The Sociolinguistics of Narrative* (Amsterdam and Philadelphia: John Benjamins) pp. 1–16.

Thornborrow, J. and J. Coates (eds) (2005b) *The Sociolinguistics of Narrative: Theory, Context and Culture in Oral Story-telling* (Amsterdam and Philadelphia: John Benjamins, 2005).

Tikhon, A. and Kaverin, N. (eds) (1999) *Bogosluzhebnyi Iazyk Russkoi Tserkvi: Istoriia, Popytki Reformatsii* (Moscow: Izdanie Sretenskogo Monastyria).

Tiryakian, E. A. (1991) 'Modernisation: Exhumetur in Pace (Rethinking Macrosociology in the 1990s)', *International Sociology*, 6 (2), pp. 165–80.

Tiryakian, E. A. (1995) 'Modernization in a Millenarian Decade: Lessons for and from Eastern Europe', in B. Grancelli (ed.) *Social Change and Modernisation* (Berlin: Walter de Gruyter), pp. 249–64.

Tiryakian, E. A. (1996) *Rethinking Modernization. Legacies of Parsons and Hilbert*, Wissenschaftszentrum Berlin, Discussion Paper FS-III 96–406.

Titscher, S., M. Meyer, R. Wodak and E. Vetter (2000) *Methods of Text and Discourse Analysis* (London: Sage).

Toolan, M. (2001) *Narrative: A Critical Linguistic Introduction* (London and New York: Routledge).

Treuhandgesetz (1990) *Gesetz zur Privatisierung und Reorganisation des volkseigenen Vermögens (Treuhandgesetz) vom 17. Juni 1990*, accessed at www.dhm.de/lemo/html/dokumente

Triandafyllidou, A. (ed.) (2006) *Contemporary Polish Migration in Europe. Complex Patterns of Movements and Settlement* (Lewinston, Queenston, Lempeter: The Edwin Mellen Press).

Triandafyllidou, A. and R. Wodak (2003) 'Conceptual and Methodological Questions in the Study of Collective Identities: An Introduction', *Journal of Language and Politics,* 2 (2), pp. 205–25.

Tzankoff, M. (2001) 'Die Deutsche Transformationsforschung nach 1989 – Ein Überblick', in B. Thomaß and M. Tzankoff (eds) *Medien und Transformation in Osteuropa* (Wiesbaden: Westdeutscher Verlag), pp. 3–39.

Ustinova, I. P. (2005) 'English in Russia', *World Englishes,* 24 (2), pp. 239–51.

van Dijk, T. A. (1984) *Prejudice in Discourse* (Amsterdam: John Benjamins).

van Dijk, T. A. (1985) 'Introduction: Discourse Analysis in (Mass) Communication Research', in T. A. van Dijk (ed.) *Discourse and Communication* (Berlin: Walter de Gruyter), pp. 1–9.

van Dijk, T. A. (1987) *Communicating Racism. Ethnic Prejudice in Thought and Talk* (Newbury Park: Sage).

van Dijk, T. A. (1991) *Racism and the Press* (London: Routledge).

van Dijk, T. A. (1993) *Elite Discourse and Racism* (Newbury Park: Sage).

van Dijk, T. A. (1998) *Ideology: A Multidisciplinary Approach* (London: Sage).

van Dijk, T. A. and R. Wodak (eds) (2000) *Racism at the Top* (Klagenfurt: Drava).

van Eemeren, F. H., R. Grootendorst and T. Kruiger (1987) *Handbook of Argumentation Theory* (Dordrecht: Foris Publications).

van Leeuwen, T. (1996) 'The Representation of Social Actors', in C. R. Caldas-Coulthard and M. Coulthard (eds) *Readings in Critical Discourse Analysis* (London: Routledge, 1996), pp. 33–70.

van Leeuwen, T. and R. Wodak (1999) 'Legitimizing Immigration Control: A Discourse-Historical Analysis', *Discourse Studies,* 1 (1), pp. 83–118.

Vasiliev, Y. (2000) 'Pastor from Lubianka', translated by Paul D. Steeves. Archived at www.stetson.edu/~psteeves/relnews/0009a.html

Verdery, K. (1996) *What Was Socialism and What Comes Next?* (Princeton: Princeton University Press).

Verschueren, J. (1999) *Understanding Pragmatics* (London: Arnold).

Vink, M. (2002) 'What is Europeanisation and Other Questions on a New Research Agenda.' Paper delivered at the Second YEN Research Meeting, Milan, 22 November.

Vodičková, M. (2006) 'Complaint and Application for the Criminal Persecution of Police Detective Alena Plšková.' *Aktuality STATIM,* 16 March, available at www.statim.cz

von Beyme, K. (1994) *Systemwechsel in Osteuropa* (Frankfurt am Main: Suhrkamp).

Wagner, I. and R. Wodak (2006) 'Performing Success: Identifying Strategies of Self-representation in Women's Biographical Narratives', *Discourse & Society,* 17 (3), pp. 385–411.

Walters, P. (2004) 'The Orthodox Church Seeks to Place Itself in Russian Society', in C. Marsh (ed.) *Burden or Blessing? Russian Orthodoxy and the Construction of Civil Society and Democracy* (Boston: Institute on Culture, Religion and World Affairs, Boston University), pp. 83–90.

Warhola, J. (2004) 'Religiosity, Politics, and the Formation of Civil Society in Multinational Russia', in C. Marsh (ed.) *Burden or Blessing? Russian Orthodoxy and the Construction of Civil Society and Democracy* (Boston: Institute on Culture, Religion and World Affairs, Boston University), pp. 91–8.

Watson, R. (1997) 'Ethnomethodology and Textual Analysis', in D. Silverman (ed.) *Qualitative Research: Theory, Method and Practice* (London: Sage), pp. 80–98.

Webber, S. L. and I. Liikanene (2001) *Education and Civic Culture in Post-communist Countries* (London and New York: Palgrave).

Wedel, J. (1998) *Collision and Collusion: The Strange Case of Western Aid to Eastern Europe* (London and New York: Palgrave).

Weinar, A. (2006) *Europeizacja Polskiej Polityki wobec Cudzoziemców* (Krakow: Scholar).

Weiss, G. (2002) 'Searching for Europe: The Problem of Legitimisation and Representation in Recent Political Speeches on Europe', *Journal of Language and Politics*, 1 (1), pp. 59–83.

Weiss, G. and R. Wodak (eds) (2003) *Critical Discourse Analysis. Theory and Interdisciplinarity* (Basingstoke: Palgrave Macmillan).

Wetherell, M. (2001) 'Themes in Discourse Research: The Case of Diana', in M. Wetherell, S. Taylor, and S. J. Yates, *Discourse Theory and Practice* (London: Sage, in association with The Open University), pp. 14–28.

White, H. (1996) 'The Value of Narrativity in the Representation of Reality', in S. Onega and J. Á. García Landa (eds) *Narratology* (Harlow: Longman), pp. 273–85.

White, S. (2000) *Russia's New Politics: the Management of a Postcommunist Society* (Cambridge and New York: Cambridge University Press).

Wilson, J. (1990) *Politically Speaking: The Pragmatic Analysis of Political Language* (Oxford: Blackwell).

Wodak, R. (1986) *Language Behaviour in Therapy Groups* (Los Angeles: University of California Press).

Wodak, R. (1996) *Disorders of Discourse* (London: Longman).

Wodak, R. (2001) 'The Discourse-Historical Approach', in R. Wodak and M. Meyer (eds) *Methods of Critical Discourse Analysis* (London: Sage), pp. 63–94.

Wodak, R. (2002) 'Introduction', *Journal of Language and Politics,* 1 (1), pp. 1–3.

Wodak, R. (2005) 'Editorial: Global and Local Patterns in Political Discourses – Glocalisation', *Journal of Language and Politics,* 4 (3), (2005), pp. 367–70.

Wodak, R. (2006) 'Mediation Between Discourse and Society: Assessing Cognitive Approaches in CDA', *Discourse Studies* 8 (1), pp. 179–90.

Wodak, R. (2008) 'Introduction: Discourse Studies – Important Concepts and Terms', in R. Wodak and M. Krzyżanowski (eds) *Qualitative Discourse Analysis in the Social Sciences* (Basingstoke: Palgrave Macmillan), pp. 1–29.

Wodak, R., R. de Cilia, M. Reisigl and K. Liebhart (1999) *The Discursive Construction of National Identity* (Edinburgh: Edinburgh University Press).

Wodak, R. and M. Krzyżanowski (eds) (2008) *Qualitative Discourse Analysis in the Social Sciences* (Basingstoke: Palgrave Macmillan).

Wodak, R., F. Menz, R. Mitten and F. Stern (1994) *Sprachen der Vergangenheiten* (Frankfurt am Main: Suhrkamp).

Wodak, R. and M. Meyer (2001) *Methods of Critical Discourse Analysis* (London: Sage).

Wodak, R., P. Nowak, J. Pelikan, H. Gruber, R. de Cilia and R. Mitten (1990) *Wir Sind Alle Unschuldige Tater: Diskurshistorische Studien zum Nachkrigsantisemitismus* (Frankfurt am Main: Suhrkamp).

Wodak, R. and G. Weiss (2004) 'Visions, Ideologies and Utopias in the Discursive Construction of European Identities: Organising, Representing and Legitimising Europe', in M. Pütz, J-A. Neff-van Aertselaer and T. A. van Dijk (eds) *Communicating Ideologies: Language, Discourse and Social Practice* (Frankfurt am Main: Peter Lang), pp. 225–52.

Wortham, S. (2001) *Narratives in Action* (New York: Teachers College Columbia Press).

Young, I. M. (1987) 'Impartiality and the Civic Public', in D. Cornell and S. Benhabib (eds) *Feminism as a Critique* (Cambridge: Polity Press), pp. 56–76.

Zapf, W. (ed.) (1990) *Die Modernisierung moderner Gesellschaften* (Frankfurt am Main: Campus).

Zapf, W. (1991) 'Der Untergang der DDR und die soziologische Theorie der Modernisierung', in B. Giesen and C. Leggewie (eds) *Experiment Vereinigung. Ein sozialer Grossversuch* (Berlin: Rotbuch), pp. 38–51.

Zapf, W. (1995) 'Modernisierungstheorien und Transformationsforuschung', *Politische Vierteljahresschrift*, 26, pp. 169–81.

Zepa, B. (2003) 'Citizenship, Official Language, Bilingual Education in Latvia: Public Policy in the Last 10 Years', in C. Giordano, A. Žvinklienė and D. Hensler (eds) *Baltic States. Looking at Small Societies on Europe's Margin* (Fribourg: University Press Fribourg), pp. 84–97.

Zhuravlev, V. K. (1994) *Tserkovnoslavianskii Iazyk v Sovremennoi Russkoi Natsional'noi Shkole* (Viatka: Sviato-Troitskii zhenskii monastyr).

Ziółkowski, M. (1999) 'O Imitacyjnej Modernizacji Społeczeństwa Polskiego', in P. Sztompka (ed.) *Imponderabilia Wielkiej Zmiany* (Warsaw: Wydawnictwo Naukowe PWN) pp. 38–65.

Žagar, I. Ž. (2003) 'How Refugees Became Illegal Migrants: Construction, Reconstruction, Deconstruction...', in J. Allwood and B. Dorriots (eds) *Intercultural Communication at Work.* Göteborg University, Papers in Anthropological Linguistics.

Index

CPI Antony Rowe
Eastbourne, UK
December 04, 2019